# FRANKFURT STADTBAHN ALBUM

**The Frankfurt Light Rail Network**

**Berlin**
**2008**

Robert Schwandl

# FRANKFURT STADTBAHN ALBUM

## The Frankfurt Light Rail Network

Nahverkehr in Deutschland - Band 12
Urban Transport in Germany - Vol. 12

Mein Dank für ihre Hilfe geht an | My sincere thanks are due to:
Alexander Piesenecker, Alexander Seefeldt, Andreas Behrndt, Felix Thoma, Fritz D. Kegel, Helmut Roggenkamp, Hildegard Schweitzer-Thoma, Klaus Piesenecker, Matthias Frey, Olaf Wenke, Thomas Lusmöller, Philipp Krammer und ganz besonders Stephan Kyrieleis

Wir danken der Verkehrsgesellschaft Frankfurt (VGF) und traffiQ für die freundliche Unterstützung.

Robert Schwandl Verlag
Hektorstraße 3
D-10711 Berlin

Tel. +49 (0) 30 - 3759 1284
Fax +49 (0) 30 - 3759 1285

www.robert-schwandl.de
books@robert-schwandl.de

**Hauptwache** – B-Ebene | *Mezzanin*

1. Auflage, 2008



English Translation by Robert Schwandl & Mark Davies

Druck: Ruksaldruck Berlin

ISBN 978-3-936573-21-3

## _ VORWORT

Vor genau 40 Jahren wurde die erste Tunnelstrecke der Frankfurter Stadtbahn zwischen Miquel-/Adickesallee und Hauptwache (A-Strecke) eröffnet, und seither sagen die Frankfurter zu ihrer Stadtbahn ‚U-Bahn'. Im Laufe der letzten 40 Jahre ist das Netz der U-Bahn auf ca. 60 km angewachsen. Auf drei Stammstrecken mit mehreren Ästen erreichen die Bahnen in der VGF-Hausfarbe ‚Subaru Vista Blue' fast alle Teile der Mainmetropole. Auch wenn es anfangs geplant war, so konnte die U-Bahn die traditionelle Straßenbahn doch nicht ganz verdrängen, ganz im Gegenteil – auch das Trambahn-Netz wächst wieder. In einem kurzen Kapitel stellt Stephan Kyrieleis dieses Verkehrsmittel vor. Kurz deshalb, weil der in Frankfurt lebende Autor die Geschichte und Fahrzeuge der Straßenbahn im Jahr 2009 in einem eigenen Band behandeln wird (Näheres erfahren Sie rechtzeitig auf unserer Website).

Neben der U-Bahn und der Straßenbahn spielt in und um Frankfurt auch die S-Bahn eine wichtige Rolle. Sie fährt sowohl durch die Frankfurter als auch durch die Offenbacher Innenstadt im Tunnel und bietet abschnittsweise Metro-ähnlichen Verkehr.

Ich lade Sie nun ein, mit mir eine Tour durch ‚Mainhattan' zu unternehmen. Ich werde Sie dabei mit allen Besonderheiten der Frankfurter U-Bahn und ihrer Bahnhöfe und Haltestellen vertraut machen.

Berlin, im September 2008

*Robert Schwandl*

Einer der ersten Wagen vom Typ ‚U5-25' an der Tunnelausfahrt Industriehof *(Foto Thomas Lusmöller, 06/2008)*
*– one of the first units of class 'U5-25' near the tunnel portal at Industriehof*

## _ FOREWORD

*The first underground section of the Frankfurt light rail system opened exactly 40 years ago between Miquel-/Adickesallee and Hauptwache (route A). Ever since, the people of Frankfurt have called their light rail system the 'U-Bahn'. During the past 40 years, the U-Bahn network has grown to almost 60 km; the trains painted in the VGF corporate colour 'subaru vista blue' now run on three trunk routes with several branches, and thus reach almost every part of the city. Although initially planned to, the U-Bahn did not succeed in replacing the conventional tram system, and instead, the tram lines are once again being extended, too. In a short chapter, Stephan Kyrieleis describes this means of urban rail transport – short because the Frankfurt-based author will dedicate an entire book to the history and the rolling stock of the Frankfurt tram system in 2009 (watch our website for updated details!).*

*Besides the U-Bahn and the tram systems, the S-Bahn plays an important role in the transport system in and around Frankfurt. It runs underground through the city centres of Frankfurt and Offenbach, and provides a metro-like service along many sections.*

*So let me be your guide on our ride through Frankfurt, and I will show you every fascinating detail of Frankfurt's U-Bahn and its stations.*

*Berlin, September 2008*

*Robert Schwandl*

S-Bahn – S2 Dietzenbach Mitte

### Inhalt *Contents*

Frankfurter Skyline von der Ignatz-Bubis-Brücke gesehen, rechts der Dom | *Frankfurt's skyline seen from the Ignatz Bubis Bridge, with the cathedral on the right*

## _ Stadt und Region

Frankfurt am Main ist mit 670.000 Einwohnern (03/2008; 248 km$^2$) nach Berlin, Hamburg, München und Köln die fünftgrößte Stadt in Deutschland. In der engeren Umgebung liegen die Städte Neu-Isenburg (35.000), Offenbach (117.000), Maintal (37.000), Bad Vilbel (32.000), Bad Homburg (52.000), Oberursel (43.000) sowie die kleineren Kommunen am Fuße des Taunus wie Steinbach (10.000), Kronberg (18.000), Eschborn (21.000), Schwalbach (14.500), Sulzbach (8000) und Liederbach (8000). Mainabwärts grenzen noch die Kommunen Kriftel (10.500), Hattersheim (25.000) und Kelsterbach (14.000) an das Stadtgebiet von Frankfurt, so dass die Gesamteinwohnerzahl der Stadt Frankfurt mit den umliegenden Städten und Gemeinden bei etwa 1,1 Mio liegt. In der von der S-Bahn Rhein-Main erschlossenen Region (siehe Plan Seite 142), leben etwa 2,5 Mio Menschen – darunter die Städte Hanau (89.000), die hessische Landeshauptstadt Wiesbaden (276.000), Darmstadt (141.000), sowie Mainz, die Landeshauptstadt von Rheinland-Pfalz (196.000).

Frankfurt und das Rhein-Main-Gebiet gehören zu den wirtschaftlich stärksten Regionen in Deutschland. Mit dem Sitz der Europäischen Zentralbank (EZB) und der Deutschen Bundesbank, mit der Frankfurter Wertpapierbörse sowie den Zentralen vieler Großbanken ist Frankfurt zweifellos die Finanzhauptstadt Deutschlands. Die Wolkenkratzer dieser Konzerne prägen auch die Skyline der Stadt, die eher an eine amerikanische als eine typisch deutsche Stadt erinnert und Frankfurt den Kosenamen ‚Mainhattan' eingebracht hat. In Frankfurt liegt außerdem der wichtigste Flughafen Deutschlands, und für das deutsche Bahnnetz gilt der Frankfurter Hauptbahnhof als bedeutende Drehscheibe.

## _ *The City and the Region*

*With 670,000 inhabitants (03/2008; 248 km$^2$), Frankfurt am Main is Germany's fifth largest city after Berlin, Hamburg, Munich and Cologne. The city is surrounded by the municipalities of Neu-Isenburg (35,000), Offenbach (117,000), Maintal (37,000), Bad Vilbel (32,000), Bad Homburg (52,000), Oberursel (43,000), as well as some smaller towns at the foot of the Taunus Mountains, like Steinbach (10,000), Kronberg (18,000), Eschborn (21,000), Schwalbach (14,500), Sulzbach (8,000) and Liederbach (8,000). Down the Main River, the municipalities of Kriftel (10,500), Hattersheim (25,000) and Kelsterbach (14,000) all border on Frankfurt, bringing the total population of Frankfurt plus its neighbouring municipalities to approximately 1.1 million. The area served by the 'S-Bahn Rhein-Main' (see map on page 142) is home to some 2.5 million people – an area including the cities of Hanau (89,000), Wiesbaden, capital of the state of Hesse (276,000), Darmstadt (141,000), as well as Mainz, capital of the state of Rhineland-Palatinate (196,000).*

*Frankfurt and the Rhine-Main area together form one of Germany's leading economic regions. The European Central Bank (ECB), the German Federal Bank, and all the major German banks have their headquarters in Frankfurt, and with the Frankfurt Stock Exchange, the city is without question the financial capital of Germany. Many skyscrapers dominate the city's skyline, which is more reminiscent of an American than of a typical German city, and the city well deserves its nickname 'Mainhattan'. Frankfurt also has Germany's busiest airport, and the city's central station is a major hub in the German and European railway networks.*

Das Stadtgebiet von Frankfurt erstreckt sich beiderseits des Mains, wobei die Altstadt rund um den Römer, das Bankenviertel im Bereich Hauptbahnhof/Taunusanlage sowie die Einkaufsmeile Zeil (zwischen Hauptwache und Konstablerwache) am Nordufer des Flusses liegen. Im Süden ist das Stadtgebiet durch den riesigen Frankfurter Stadtwald begrenzt, im Norden steigt das Gelände leicht an und geht in den Taunus, ein Mittelgebirge, über. Während das Stadtzentrum auf knapp 100 m über N.N. liegt, erreicht auch die höchste Erhebung im Osten des Stadtgebiets nur 212 m.

Bis 1866, als die Stadt von Preußen annektiert wurde, war Frankfurt eine Freie Stadt innerhalb des Deutschen Bundes, hier hatte bereits 1848/49 die *Frankfurter Nationalversammlung*, das erste frei gewählte Parlament aller deutschen Staaten, getagt. Bereits seit dem 16. Jahrhundert waren in Frankfurt sämtliche Kaiser des Heiligen Römischen Reichs gekrönt worden. Trotz dieser langen Tradition schaffte es Frankfurt nach der Teilung Deutschlands 1949 nicht, zur neuen Hauptstadt der Bundesrepublik Deutschland gewählt zu werden, und unterlag dem kleineren Bonn. Als Hauptstadt des Bundeslandes Hessen war 1945 Wiesbaden auserkoren worden.

*The city extends on both sides of the Main River, with the historical centre around the Römer, the banking district in the area of the Central Station and the Taunusanlage, as well as the city's main shopping artery, the Zeil, which lies between Hauptwache and Konstablerwache, all located north of the river. To the south, the city is limited by a huge forested area, the Frankfurter Stadtwald, while to the north, the terrain slowly climbs up to the Taunus Mountains. While the city centre is about 100 m above sea level, the highest point within the city boundaries is only 212 m, located in the east.*

*Until 1866, when the city was annexed by Prussia, Frankfurt was a free imperial city within the German Confederation, and in 1848/49 it hosted the Frankfurter Nationalversammlung, the first freely elected assembly uniting all the German states. Since the 16th century, every emperor of the Holy Roman Empire had been crowned in Frankfurt. Despite this long tradition, Frankfurt failed in its bid to become the new capital of the Federal Republic of Germany in 1949, being defeated by the smaller city of Bonn. Frankfurt had already seen Wiesbaden become the state capital of Hesse in 1945.*

## _ Das öffentliche Verkehrsnetz in und um Frankfurt

Aus dem dicht besiedelten Umland strömen täglich ca. 300.000 Pendler nach Frankfurt, was nur mit einem gut funktionierenden öffentlichen Nahverkehr zu bewältigen ist. Alle Verkehrsmittel (RE, RB, S-Bahn, U-Bahn, Straßenbahn und Busse) sind seit 1995 Teil des *Rhein-Main-Verkehrsverbunds* (RMV), der nicht nur die eigentliche Region Rhein-Main umfasst, sondern mehr als die Hälfte des Bundeslandes Hessen abdeckt und Städte wie Limburg, Marburg oder Fulda miteinschließt. Von 1974 bis 1995 existierte bereits der *Frankfurter Verkehrs- und Tarifverbund* (FVV). Im Gebiet des RMV (14.000 $km^2$) leben etwa 5 Mio Menschen. Das Tarifgebiet ist in Zonen eingeteilt, wobei die Stadt Frankfurt die Zone 50 darstellt – hier gilt die Preisstufe 3 (Einzelfahrt 2,20 €), zum Flughafen bezahlt man allerdings die Preisstufe 4 (3,60 €). Für Fahrten mit der S-Bahn ist von Frankfurt aus maximal die Preisstufe 5 (6,75 €) fällig. Für Besucher der Stadt bietet sich die Tageskarte für 5,60 € an, was preislich im bundesdeutschen Durchschnitt liegt. Zeitkarten (auch Tageskarten), die über die Stadtgrenzen hinwegen gelten, beziehen sich jeweils auf eine bestimmte Strecke und nicht wie in vielen anderen Großräumen auf Ringe rund um den Ausgangspunkt. Die Tageskarte der Preisstufe 7 (25,40 €) ist jedoch im gesamten Verbundbereich gültig. Ab zwei Personen reist man allerdings mit dem Hessen-Ticket für 30 € wesentlich günstiger. Der Preis für eine Monatskarte für das Stadtgebiet liegt derzeit (alle Preisangaben beziehen sich auf das Jahr 2008) bei 70,90 €, was Frankfurt im bundesdeutschen Durchschnitt eher teuer erscheinen lässt. Allerdings weist die Stadt Frankfurt und die Region Rhein-Main eines der dichtesten Schienennahverkehrsnetze in Deutschland auf. Die Straßenbahn verkehrt auf ihrem ca. 60 km langen Streckennetz ausschließlich im Stadtgebiet von Frankfurt, die U-Bahn hingegen fährt über die Stadtgrenzen hinweg auch in die Städte Bad Homburg (U2) und Oberursel (U3). Auf Frankfurter Gebiet liegen außerdem 26 S-Bahnhöfe, an denen mindestens alle 15 Minuten eine Bahn in jede Richtung fährt. Dazu kommen zahlreiche RE- und RB-Verbindungen, die weiter entfernt liegende Orte im Halbstunden- oder Stundentakt mit Frankfurt verbinden.

Für das Gebiet der Stadt Frankfurt ist seit 2001 die städtische *Lokale Nahverkehrsgesellschaft traffiQ* für die Vergabe und Kontrolle von Verkehrsleistungen zuständig. So wurden bereits mehrere Buslinien ausgeschrieben, während die U-Bahn- und Straßenbahnlinien bis mindestens 2011 von der *Verkehrsgesellschaft Frankfurt* (VGF) betrieben werden.

## _ *The Public Transport Network in and around Frankfurt*

*From the densely populated surrounding area about 300,000 commuters travel into Frankfurt every day, which is only possible with an efficient public transport system. Since 1995, all modes of transport (RE trains, RB trains, S-Bahn, U-Bahn, tramways and buses) have been integrated into the RMV fare system (Rhein-Main-Verkehrsverbund), which covers not only the Rhine-Main area, but half the state of Hesse, including towns like Limburg, Marburg and Fulda. Prior to the RMV, the 'Frankfurter Verkehrs- und Tarifverbund' (FVV) had existed between 1974 and 1995. The RMV area (14,000 $km^2$) is home to some 5 million people. The area is divided into fare zones, with the city of Frankfurt constituting zone 50, for which price category 3 has to be paid (2.20 € for a single ride), while a ride to the airport is charged at the price of category 4 (3.60 €). The maximum fare between Frankfurt and any station on the S-Bahn network is 6.75 €, which corresponds to price category 5. Visitors can acquire a flexible day pass for the city area for 5.60 €, which is about average compared to other German cities. All passes (including day passes) for travel beyond the city boundaries are valid for a certain route rather than for all the zones of the same fare category around the central zone, as is the case in many other cities. A day pass for price category 7 (25.40 €), however, is valid in the entire RMV area. When more than two people travel together though, a Hessen-Ticket at 30 € is a much cheaper option. The price for a monthly pass only valid in Frankfurt is 70.90 €, which for Germany is rather expensive (all prices refer to 2008). But Frankfurt and the Rhine-Main area also boast one of Germany's densest railway networks. While the 60 km tramway network lies completely within the Frankfurt city boundaries, the U-Bahn extends further out into Bad Homburg (U2) and Oberursel (U3). On Frankfurt territory, there are also 26 S-Bahn stations, with a train at least every 15 minutes in each direction. The rapid transit system is complemented by numerous RE and RB trains, which link Frankfurt with towns further away every hour or half-hour.*

*Since 2001, the local transport authority 'traffiQ' has been responsible for awarding transportation contracts and supervising service within Frankfurt. Many bus lines have since been transferred to private companies, while the U-Bahn and tramway lines will be operated by the VGF (Verkehrsgesellschaft Frankfurt) at least until 2011.*

**Festhalle/Messe** (U4) – eine richtige U-Bahn? | *A real metro?*

## _ Die U-Bahn

Das Frankfurter U-Bahn-Netz besteht aus drei Stammstrecken, auf denen jeweils 2-3 Linien verkehren. Die aus den Planungen stammenden Streckenbezeichnungen A (U1-U3), B (U4, U5) und C (U6, U7), die auch zur Gliederung dieses Buchs verwendet werden, haben seit einer Änderung der Linienbezeichnungen im Jahr 1978 für den Fahrgastverkehr keine Bedeutung mehr. Anders als etwa in Hannover, wo man einen ähnlichen Netzaufbau findet, sind die parallel verlaufenden Linien auf den Netzplänen nicht in derselben oder einer ähnlichen Farbe dargestellt, sondern haben jeweils eine eigene Linienfarbe. Das U-Bahn-Netz hat eine Gesamtstreckenlänge von 58,4 km – davon sind 20,7 km unterirdisch, 1,6 km oberirdisch, jedoch U-Bahn-mäßig trassiert, 1,4 km abmarkiert, 1,2 km straßenbündig, und die restlichen 33,5 km auf eigenem Gleiskörper. Nur 1,2 km (der nördlichste Abschnitt der U3) sind eingleisig.

Morgens fahren die ersten U-Bahn-Züge ab ca. 4:00 Uhr von den äußeren Endpunkten Richtung Stadtzentrum, stadtauswärts verkehren die letzten Züge zwischen 1:00 und 1:30 Uhr. Der Takt ist je nach Linie und Streckenabschnitt unterschiedlich und wird daher bei den einzelnen Stammstrecken erwähnt.

Die sieben U-Bahn-Linien werden wie die sieben Straßenbahnlinien von der **Verkehrsgesellschaft Frankfurt am Main** (VGF) im Auftrag der städtischen Nahverkehrsgesellschaft ***traffiQ*** betrieben. Die VGF ist Bestandteil der **Stadtwerke Frankfurt am Main Holding GmbH** und Partner in dem 1994 gegründeten **Rhein-Main Verkehrsverbund** (RMV). Der tägliche Verkehr wird in der zentralen Betriebsleitstelle in der Elefantengasse (unweit der Tunnelausfahrt der U5) überwacht.

## _ *The U-Bahn*

*The Frankfurt U-Bahn network comprises three trunk routes, each shared by two to three lines. The designations used during the planning stage, A (U1-U3), B (U4, U5) and C (U6, U7), which have also been used to divide this book into chapters, lost their relevance for the everyday passenger when the current line numbers were introduced in 1978. Unlike in Hanover, for example, where a similar network layout can be found, the lines running parallel are not shown in the same or a similar colour on network maps, but each has a totally different colour. The U-Bahn network has a total length 58.4 km - with 20.7 km underground, 1.6 km on the surface but totally grade-separated, 1.4 km on a reserved lane in the roadway, 1.2 km on-street shared with car traffic, and the remaining 33.5 km on a dedicated right-of-way with level crossings. Only 1.2 km (the northernmost section of line U3) is single-track.*

*In the morning, the first trains leave the outer termini at around 04:00, while the last trains leave the city centre between 01:00 and 01:30. As headways vary between different lines and sections, these are mentioned in the relevant chapters.*

*Like the seven tram lines, the seven U-Bahn lines are operated by the 'Verkehrsgesellschaft Frankfurt am Main' (VGF) on behalf of the local transport authority 'traffiQ'. The VGF is a part of the 'Stadtwerke Frankfurt am Main Holding GmbH' and a partner in the 'Rhein-Main Verkehrsverbund' (RMV) founded in 1994. The control centre for the entire transport system is located at Elefantengasse (near the U5 tunnel portal).*

### ‚U-Bahn' oder ‚Stadtbahn'

Kaum eine andere Frage taucht in deutschen Bahn-Internetforen häufiger auf als die Frage ‚Hat Frankfurt wirklich eine U-Bahn?'. Hält man sich an die allgemein anerkannte Definition, dass eine ‚U-Bahn' ein in sich abgeschlossenes Schienennahverkehrssystem ist, das völlig vom übrigen Verkehr (sowohl Autos als auch anderen Bahnen) getrennt verkehrt, dann hat Frankfurt keine U-Bahn, da es auf den oberirdischen Strecken sehr wohl Bahnübergänge gibt, die U5 sogar auf kurzen Abschnitten straßenbündig, also wie eine klassische Straßenbahn verkehrt. Deshalb ist es richtiger, von einer ‚Stadtbahn' zu sprechen, da das System Eigenheiten sowohl von U-Bahnen als auch von Straßenbahnen aufweist. Andererseits wird auch der Begriff ‚Stadtbahn' heute andernorts für Systeme verwendet, die überhaupt nichts U-Bahn-artiges aufweisen, sondern lediglich modernisierte Straßenbahnen sind (z.B. Erfurt, Braunschweig), die auch streckenweise auf eigenem Gleiskörper verlaufen, was aber bei Neubaustrecken mittlerweile ohnehin quasi Standard ist. Gleichzeitig wird der Begriff ‚Stadtbahn' z.B. in Karlsruhe auch für jene Bahnen verwendet, die sowohl auf Straßenbahn- als auch auf Eisenbahnstrecken verkehren, oder in Berlin für die bereits seit 1882 befahrene Ost-West-Strecke der S-Bahn.

Bereits seit Inbetriebnahme der ersten Tunnelstrecke im Jahr 1968 wird in Frankfurt für die Stadtbahn der Begriff ‚U-Bahn' verwendet, und ein durchschnittlicher Fahrgast kann mit dem Begriff ‚Stadtbahn' auch nichts anfangen. So kann es vorkommen, dass eine ‚U-Bahn-Haltestelle' aus nur einem Haltestellenschild besteht, was wiederum Besucher aus anderen U-Bahn-Städten sehr in Staunen versetzt. Es muss aber auch festgehalten werden, dass der Teil des Frankfurter Stadtbahnnetzes, der U-Bahn-mäßig ausgebaut ist, auch als eigenständiges Schnellbahnnetz sinnvoll nutzbar wäre, d.h. würde man diese Strecken von den *nur* stadtbahnmäßig ausgebauten trennen, so bliebe ein Netz bestehen, das sehr wohl die Klassifizierung als U-Bahn verdienen würde: drei Linien (knapp 18 km) mit insgesamt 30 U-Bahnhöfen, mit 100 m langen Bahnsteigen und 75 m bzw. 100 m langen Zügen bei einem 5-Minuten-Takt außerhalb der Hauptverkehrszeiten. Dazu kommt noch die voll U-Bahn-mäßig ausgebaute Strecke zwischen Heddernheimer Landstraße und Ginnheim. Die direkte Verknüpfung dieser voll ausgebauten U-Bahn-Strecken mit den oberirdischen Zulaufstrecken ist für die Fahrgäste natürlich vorteilhafter, weshalb insgesamt für Frankfurt das derzeitige System ‚Stadtbahn' (hier eben ‚U-Bahn' genannt) sinnvoller ist als eine echte U-Bahn. Langfristig wird auch in Frankfurt seit Langem keine echte U-Bahn mehr angestrebt, sondern Neubaustrecken wie derzeit auf den Riedberg werden als typische Stadtbahn geplant, also oberirdisch auf eigenem Gleiskörper, aber mit Bahnübergängen.

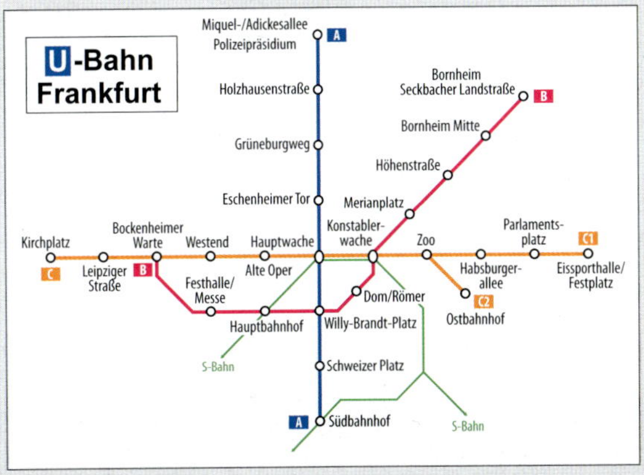

**Musterschule** (U5) – eher eine Straßenbahn? | *more like a tramway?*

### *'U-Bahn' or 'Stadtbahn'*

*One of the most frequently asked questions on German internet forums for metro enthusiats is 'Does Frankfurt really have an U-Bahn?'. If one follows the generally accepted definition that 'U-Bahn' is the German equivalent of 'Metro', and a metro is a completely independent system, i.e. it does not interfere with road traffic or any other type of railway, then Frankfurt cannot claim to have an 'U-Bahn'. Along the surface routes, there are many level crossings, and line U5 even operates like a conventional street tramway along short sections. The German term 'Stadtbahn' would therefore be more appropriate, as the system combines features typical of tramway systems with those of a real metro. On the other hand, some cities use the term 'Stadtbahn' for tramways which have no metro-like features at all (e.g. Erfurt and Brunswick), and although their tramways run on reserved tracks along some sections, this has now become the standard for all modern tramways. In Karlsruhe, the term 'Stadtbahn' is used for 'tram-trains', i.e. tramways that continue their journeys on mainline tracks; and in Berlin, the term 'Stadtbahn' has been identified with the east-west S-Bahn route ever since it opened as a steam railway back in 1882.*

*Since the first underground section opened in Frankfurt in 1968, the term 'U-Bahn' has been used, and the average passenger may not even understand what the term 'Stadtbahn' really means. On the other hand, an 'U-Bahn-Station' may consist of little more than a simple pole indicating a stop, which can be quite a culture shock for visitors from cities with real metro systems.*

*Those sections of the Frankfurt Stadtbahn network which actually have full metro standard would make a reasonable system that could be operated like a real metro, if these sections were separated from the surface Stadtbahn sections: three lines with a total length of 18 km and 30 metro stations, 100 m platforms with 75 or 100 m long trains, and a 5-minute headway during peak hours give the impression of a proper metro system. Besides the underground network in the central area, the section between Heddernheimer Landstraße and Ginnheim also has full metro standard. For passengers, however, a direct connection between these full metro routes and the surface light rail routes is without doubt more convenient, so for Frankfurt the present Stadtbahn system (which they may call an 'U-Bahn') is certainly a better option than a proper metro system. The long-term goal of a totally grade-separated system has long been given up in Frankfurt, and new routes, like the future Riedberg line, are typical Stadtbahn lines, i.e. on a dedicated surface right-of-way, but with level crossings.*

## _ Die Geschichte der Frankfurter Stadtbahn

Nach dem Zweiten Weltkrieg wurde in der stark zerstörten Stadt das Straßenbahnnetz schnell wieder instandgesetzt und anschließend noch erweitert. Trotzdem konnte das traditionsreiche Verkehrsmittel den steigenden Verkehr nicht mehr zufriedenstellend bewältigen, denn durch die Teilung Deutschlands war Frankfurt ins Zentrum Westdeutschlands gerückt und profitierte somit in besonderer Weise vom Wirtschaftsaufschwung der fünfziger Jahre. Innerhalb von 10 Jahren, von 1950 bis 1960, stieg die Einwohnerzahl von rund 532.000 auf 670.000 Einwohner. Im gleichen Zeitraum versechsfachte sich die Zahl der in Frankfurt zugelassenen Personenkraftwagen von 14.600 auf 89.320. Immer öfter standen die Straßenbahnen deshalb im Verkehrsstau. Angesichts der Wachstumsprognosen für die Stadt und der sich verschärfenden Verkehrssituation wurde seit Anfang der 1950er Jahre immer wieder die Forderung nach einer Trennung der Straßenbahn vom Autoverkehr laut. Da für eine echte U-Bahn keine Finanzierungsmöglichkeit gesehen wurde, sollte die ‚Trambahn' wenigstens an wichtigen Punkten in die ‚2. Ebene' verlegt werden.

Im Jahr 1958 stellte die Firma ALWEG-Forschung die von ihr entwickelte Einschienen-Hochbahn in Frankfurt vor und lud Vertreter der Stadt zu einer Besichtigung der Versuchsanlage in Köln-Fühlingen ein. Seit 1952 hatte ALWEG dort einen Zug im Maßstab 1:2,5 getestet und die Erfahrungen in einen Versuchszug im Maßstab 1:1 umgesetzt, der im Juli 1957 der Öffentlichkeit vorgestellt worden war. Der Besuch in Köln weckte nun bei vielen Teilnehmern aus Frankfurt das Interesse an dem neuen Verkehrssystem.

Im Herbst 1958 wurde die Beauftragung zweier Gutachten beschlossen, die anhand der exemplarischen Darstellung von Einzelprojekten die Möglichkeiten einer ALWEG-Bahn bzw. einer Schnellstraßenbahn mit Tunnelabschnitten aufzeigen sollte. 1959 lagen zwei Vorschläge zur Lösung der Verkehrsprobleme vor:

1) Die Firma ALWEG schlug ein 2-Linien-Netz als Einschienen-Hochbahn vor, das später mit Außenstrecken und unterirdischen Innenstadtabschnitten erweitert werden sollte.
2) Die Philipp Holzmann AG legte mehrere Varianten für ein U-Strab-Netz vor.

Die Resonanz auf die beiden Vorschläge war geteilt. Während sich beispielsweise die Direktion der Straßenbahnverwaltung aufgrund der höheren Kosten und der fehlenden Erfahrungen in der Praxis gegen die ALWEG-Bahn aussprach, wurde die aufgeständerte Bahn wegen der geringeren Bauzeit und den

**Oberursel Bahnhof** – ‚M'-Wagen 623 im August 1963 auf der heutigen Strecke der U3 nach Hohemark (*Foto Sammlung VDVA*)
– *'M' car 623 in August 1963 on today's U3 route to Hohemark*

## _ *The History of the Frankfurt Stadtbahn*

*Severely damaged in World War II, the tramway network was rapidly rebuilt and subsequently even expanded. But conventional trams were increasingly unable to cope with the rising demand. The division of Germany left Frankfurt in the centre of West Germany, and the city thus particularly profited from the country's economic boom of the 1950s. Within 10 years, from 1950 to 1960, the city's population rose from 532,000 to 670,000, and within the same period, the number of registered cars climbed from 14,600 to 89,320, i.e. a sixfold increase. With the population expected to rise still further, the separation of the tramway routes from car traffic had already been postulated as the ideal solution to solve traffic problems in the long run. If a full metro seemed unviable due to the high costs of implementation, the most important sections of the existing 'Trambahn' could at least be put on a separate level, i.e. elevated or underground.*

*In 1958, the company 'ALWEG-Forschung' proposed its elevated monorail system, inviting representatives of the city to visit the company's trial route at Fühlingen, in the north of Cologne. From 1952, ALWEG had been testing a 1:2.5 model train, and in July 1957, a 1:1 test train had been unveiled. The new technology aroused great interest among the visitors from Frankfurt.*

*In autumn 1958, two studies were commissioned to examine the feasibility of either an ALWEG monorail network or an upgraded tramway system with tunnel sections. As a result, two proposals were made in 1959:*

*1) ALWEG suggested a 2-line network with elevated monorail routes, which at a later stage were to be extended into the suburbs, and underground through the city centre.*
*2) The construction holding Philipp Holzmann AG presented various alternatives for an underground tramway network.*

*The reactions to the two proposals were not unanimous – while the tramway administration was against the ALWEG monorail because of its higher implementation costs and lack of experience, some politicians favoured it as the construction time was shorter, meaning less disruption of car traffic. With no decision yet on the definitive technology, the city council commissioned a general project for a 'Stadtbahn', which was to run underground in the central area. The study was carried out by Professor Dr. Leibbrand from the University of Zurich together with three construction companies based in Frankfurt (Philipp Holzmann AG, Wayss & Freitag KG and Hochtief AG), a workgroup later known as 'ARGE Stadtbahnplanung'. In late 1960, ALWEG-Forschungs GmbH was accepted into the workgroup.*

*The general project compared three different types of systems in terms of their costs and effects on the entire transport network - 1) ALWEG monorail; 2) U-Bahn (full metro); and 3) 'Tiefbahn' (tramway with underground routes through the city centre). Although the results revealed in June 1961 were not conclusive, the figures were clear enough. Despite the higher travel speeds of the ALWEG and U-Bahn trains, the 'Tiefbahn' got the best marks as it was able to provide 75% more direct connections, while the ALWEG monorail and the U-Bahn would have required feeder buses, and time would have been wasted transferring from system to system. Within the city centre, where the highest demand was expected, the underground trams were just as fast as the other two systems. The operating costs of the 'Tiefbahn', however, would be the lowest of the three systems by far. And because it was possible to link the 'Tiefbahn' to the existing tramway network, completed tunnel sections were able to be operated immediately, whereas for the ALWEG system or the U-Bahn, parallel tramway routes would have had to be maintained until those systems were*

damit geringeren Beeinträchtigungen des Autoverkehrs von einigen politischen Entscheidungsträgern favorisiert. Um den in der Verwaltung und den Parteien ausgebrochenen Streit um die Systeme zu objektivieren, beauftragte die Stadt im Juli 1960 eine Arbeitsgemeinschaft mit Prof. Dr. Leibbrand von der Universität Zürich und drei in Frankfurt ansässigen Baufirmen (Philipp Holzmann AG, Wayss & Freitag KG, Hochtief AG), die spätere „ARGE Stadtbahnplanung", mit der Erstellung einer planerischen Gesamtübersicht für eine Stadtbahn, die in der Innenstadt im Tunnel verlaufen sollte, unabhängig vom zu wählenden Bahnsystem. Ende 1960 wurde auch die ALWEG-Forschungs GmbH vertraglich in die Erarbeitung dieses Gutachtens einbezogen.

In der planerische Gesamtübersicht wurden Netze der Systeme ALWEG-Bahn, U-Bahn und ‚Tiefbahn' (Straßenbahn mit unterirdischer Führung in der Innenstadt) bezüglich ihrer Kosten und verkehrlichen Auswirkungen miteinander verglichen. Auch wenn das im Juni 1961 fertig gestellte Gutachten auftragsgemäß keine Empfehlung für oder gegen ein System gab, sprachen die Zahlen eine eindeutige Sprache. Trotz der höheren Geschwindigkeiten der ALWEG- und der U-Bahn schnitt die Tiefbahn aufgrund einer um 75% höheren Zahl umsteigefreier Verbindungen beim Verkehrswert am besten ab. Bei ihr ging weniger Reisezeit durch Umsteigen oder langsame Buszubringer verloren als bei der ALWEG- und U-Bahn. Zudem war sie bezüglich ihrer Reisegeschwindigkeit in der Innenstadt, wo das höchste Fahrgastaufkommen prognostiziert wurde, den anderen Systemen ebenbürtig. Gleichzeitig würden die Betriebskosten bei einer Tiefbahn im Vergleich zur ALWEG-Bahn bzw. U-Bahn wesentlich niedriger ausfallen. Für die Tiefbahn sprach zudem die Möglichkeit, fertig gestellte Teilstücke gleich ins Straßenbahnnetz einzubinden, während bei der ALWEG- oder U-Bahn bis zur Fertigstellung längerer Strecken parallele Straßenbahninfrastruktur vorgehalten werden müsste. Weil die ALWEG-Bahn teilweise auch im Tunnel verlaufen sollte, kamen ihre Vorteile bei den Baukosten nicht wirklich zum Zuge. Zudem wären bei der ALWEG-Bahn die Umsteigewege teilweise länger als bei der U-Bahn und Tiefbahn gewesen, da zur Vermeidung doppelstöckiger Kreuzungsbahnhöfe in Hochlage sich teilweise Strecken im Tunnel und in Hochlage kreuzen sollten. Gleichzeitig zur Abgabe des Gutachtens unternahmen im Juni 1961 Mitglieder des Magistrats und der Stadtverordnetenversammlung eine Studienfahrt nach Italien, wo eine Besichtigung der U-Bahn in Mailand und der während der Ausstellung „Italia'61" in Turin aufgebauten ALWEG-Strecke auf dem Programm stand. Die Fahrt in Turin dämpfte die Euphorie bei einigen ALWEG-Bahn-Befürwortern, denn diese hatte ihre Fahrgäste am Besuchstag der Delegation rumpelnd und mit unangenehmer Geräuschentwicklung befördert, was die ALWEG-Techniker auf ein defektes Verschleißteil zurückführten. Aufgrund der Zahlen der planerischen Gesamtübersicht und technischer sowie ästhetischer Bedenken gegen die ALWEG-Bahn fiel deshalb am 4. Juli 1961 die Entscheidung zugunsten einer ‚Stadtbahn', in Form einer ‚Tiefbahn', die aber zumindest in den Tunnelabschnitten das Erscheinungsbild einer Schnellbahn haben sollte und stufenweise zu einer solchen zu entwickeln sei. Mit dem Begriff ‚Stadtbahn' vermied man eine klare Festlegung auf ein System, verstand darunter aber eher die langfristige Entwicklung zu einer Voll-U-Bahn. So wurde der Gedanke an eine U-Strab (Unterpflasterstraßenbahn) in der weiteren Planungsphase schrittweise fallen gelassen und das Gleisbild immer mehr an U-Bahn-Parameter angepasst.

In den folgenden Jahren wurden verschiedene Netzvarianten diskutiert, beschlossen und wieder abgeändert, kurzzeitig gab es auch Gespräche mit der *Deutschen Bundesbahn* über einen Mischbetrieb auf gewissen Strecken. Anfang 1963 konnten die vorbereitenden Arbeiten am 1. Bauabschnitt Dornbusch – Gr. Gallusstraße in Angriff genommen werden, denn hier war die Verkehrsbelastung besonders stark und die Trassierung wurde nicht in Frage gestellt.

Einschienen-Hochbahnsystem von ALWEG | *ALWEG elevated monorail system* (Abb. Krupp, Archiv Christoph Groneck)

*fully completed. The fact that the ALWEG trains would also have had to run partly in tunnels offset the lower construction costs of the elevated sections. To avoid massive 2-level elevated stations, the ALWEG option included interchange stations with elevated and underground levels, but this would have implied long walks between lines.*
*With this comparative study in their hands, members of the Frankfurt city council went to Italy in June 1961 to visit both the Milan Metro and an ALWEG monorail, which was in passenger service during the Italia'61 exhibition in Turin. The monorail ride in Turin finally dampened the enthusiasm of the ALWEG supporters, as the trains made a bumpy and noisy performance, which according to the ALWEG engineers was the result of a defective component. With the numbers quoted in the comparative study, as well as technical and aesthetic doubts about the ALWEG system, the city council decided on 4 July 1961 to build a 'Stadtbahn' in the form of the proposed 'Tiefbahn', with metro-like specifications at least along the underground sections. The term 'Stadtbahn' (literally 'urban railway') was deliberately chosen to get around having to make a final decision on the system's technology, although it clearly implied that a real metro was to be developed in the long run. Gradually, the initial concept of an underground tramway system was lost, and the routes were designed more and more with metro parameters.*

*Over the following years, many network alternatives were discussed, approved and then modified. For a short time, there were also talks with the 'Deutsche Bundesbahn' to operate a joint service on some routes. In early 1963, preliminary works began on the Dornbusch – Große Gallusstraße section, where the traffic situation was particularly bad and the route alignment was not in question.*

*From 1964, the Stadtbahn project was promoted as the 'Frankfurt solution': fully grade-separated metro-like routes initially to be used by tramway vehicles, and later in mixed operation by both tramway and U-Bahn cars. Similar approaches, however, were being made at the same time in Cologne and Stuttgart.*

*On 23 October 1964, an agreement was signed between the city of Frankfurt and the 'Deutsche Bundesbahn' over the construction of an S-Bahn tunnel. A section of the S-Bahn tunnel was to be built together with the Stadtbahn tunnels to achieve a network of five trunk routes, rather like what we have today:*
*Route A: Dornbusch – Hauptwache – Schweizer Platz – Sachsenhäuser Berg/Mörfelder Landstraße*

**Miquel-/Adickesallee** – Prototyp-Wagen 1001 am Tag der offenen Tür 1966 (*Foto Walter Steinberger/Sammlung VDVA*)
*– prototype car 1001 on display on Open Day in 1966*

Ab 1964 wurde die Stadtbahnplanung als ‚Frankfurter Lösung' vorgestellt: voll ausgebaute U-Bahn-Strecken, die anfangs von Straßenbahnen, dann im Mischbetrieb mit U-Bahn-Fahrzeugen genutzt werden sollten. Ähnliche Planungsansätze gab es zu jener Zeit allerdings auch in Köln oder Stuttgart.

Am 23. Oktober 1964 wurde ein Vertrag zwischen der Stadt Frankfurt und der *Deutschen Bundesbahn* zum Bau eines S-Bahn-Tunnels, der streckenweise zusammen mit der Stadtbahn errichtet werden würde, unterzeichnet, nachdem sich allmählich das heute bekannte Netz der fünf Schnellbahn-Stammstrecken herauskristallisiert hatte:

A-Strecke: Dornbusch – Hauptwache – Schweizer Platz – Sachsenhäuser Berg/Mörfelder Landstraße
B-Strecke: Bornheim/Eckenheim – Konstablerwache – Hauptbahnhof – Mainzer Landstraße (mit Verbindung zwischen Ostbahnhof und Römer)
C-Strecke: Bockenheim – Westbahnhof – Hauptwache – Zoo – Bornheimer Hang (Eissporthalle)/Riederhöfe
D-Strecke: Nordweststadt – Bockenheimer Warte – Hauptbahnhof – Niederrad (der nördliche Abschnitt sollte anfangs - wie heute - Bestandteil der B-Strecke werden und tauchte erst ab Mitte der siebziger Jahre als eine eigenständige Linie auf)
S-Bahn-Strecke: Hauptbahnhof – Hauptwache – Konstablerwache – Südbahnhof/Mühlberg

Bis etwa 1980 sollten alle unterirdischen Strecken innerhalb des Anlagenrings errichtet werden. Langfristig sollte ein Stadtbahnnetz mit 130 km Streckenlänge entstehen, wovon etwa 30 km im Tunnel verlaufen sollten. Fertig gestellte Abschnitte sollten vorübergehend über Rampen an das bestehende Straßenbahnnetz angeschlossen werden. Die Regelbahnsteighöhe wurde anfangs mit 80 cm, ab 1967 mit 87 cm festgelegt (die Fußbodenhöhe der neuen ‚U2'-Wagen lag bei 97 cm über Schienenoberkante), die Länge der Bahnsteige sollte 100 m sein, bei einem Radius von minimal 700 m. Für die Tunnelstrecken wurde eine lichte Breite von 7,10 m und eine lichte Höhe von 4,80 m festgesetzt.

Nach den ersten Erfahrungen mit dem Mischbetrieb mit neuen Stadtbahn-Fahrzeugen und umgebauten Straßenbahnwagen auf der A-Strecke ab 1968 wurde ein solcher auf zukünftigen Strecken nicht mehr angestrebt, da der Fahrgastwechsel bei den älteren Fahrzeugen wesentlich länger dauerte und diese außerdem eventuelle durch den Straßenverkehr verursachte Verspätungen mit in den Schnellbahntunnel brachten,

*Route B: Bornheim/Eckenheim – Konstablerwache – Hauptbahnhof – Mainzer Landstraße (with a link between Ostbahnhof and Römer)*
*Route C: Bockenheim – Westbahnhof – Hauptwache – Zoo – Bornheimer Hang (Eissporthalle)/Riederhöfe*
*Route D: Nordweststadt – Bockenheimer Warte – Hauptbahnhof – Niederrad (as it is once again, the northern section was initially designed to be part of route B and only appeared as a separate trunk route during the mid-1970s)*
*S-Bahn Route: Hauptbahnhof – Hauptwache – Konstablerwache - Südbahnhof/Mühlberg*

*All the underground routes in the old town were to be completed by 1980, with the Stadtbahn network planned to eventually reach a total length of 130 km, including some 30 km in tunnels. Completed sections were to be linked to the tramway network via temporary ramps. The standard platform height was initially fixed at 80 cm, but changed to 87 cm in 1967 (the floor height of the new 'U2' cars was 97 cm above the rail top); the platforms were to be 100 m long, with a minimum radius of 700 m. For the tunnels, a width of 7.10 m and a height of 4.80 m was established as the standard specification.*

*From 1968, the route A tunnel was operated both with new Stadtbahn cars as well as modified tram vehicles. This early experience showed that this type of mixed service would be undesirable on the other routes, because alighting and boarding the older cars took so much longer and any delays resulting from on-street operation were carried down into the tunnels, making a regular service rather difficult. Consequently, several planned ramps, e.g. on Gutleutstraße west of Theaterplatz (now Willy-Brandt-Platz) for route B, were deleted from the plans. The fenced-off right-of-way along Eschersheimer Landstraße was perceived as a clear line of division, and was not to be repeated on any other routes either. The 'Frankfurt solution' was thus in fact dead, with the conventional tramway surviving for the time being. Passengers, however, would have to get used to more transfers.*

*All in all, route A was very successful and passenger figures rose significantly, so that the expansion of the system was not questioned. The construction of route B had already begun in 1966, although the first tunnel section did not open until 1974. It was initially operated with 2.35 m wide cars, but these were withdrawn from the underground section in 1980, when line U4 started operating as Frankfurt's first real*

**Niederursel** – Prototyp-Wagen 1002 im Mai 1967 (*Foto Maximilian Krafft/Sammlung VDVA*)
*– prototype car 1002 in May 1967*

weshalb ein regelmäßiger Betrieb schwierig erschien. Infolgedessen wurden weitere provisorische Rampen, z.B. in der Gutleutstraße westlich des Theaterplatzes (heute Willy-Brandt-Platz) auf der B-Strecke, aus den Planungen gestrichen. Außerdem wollte man die trennende Wirkung des eigenen abgezäunten Gleiskörpers entlang der Eschersheimer Landstraße auf anderen Strecken nicht wiederholen, womit die ‚Frankfurter Lösung' vorerst gestorben war und der Erhalt der Straßenbahn vorläufig gesichert schien, stattdessen mussten sich die Fahrgäste auf gebrochenen Verkehr, d. h. eventuelles Umsteigen einstellen.

Insgesamt waren die Erfahrungen auf der A-Strecke jedoch sehr positiv und die Fahrgastzahlen stiegen bedeutend an, so dass dem weiteren Ausbau des U-Bahn-Netzes nichts im Wege stand. Der Bau der B-Strecke hatte bereits 1966 begonnen, die Eröffnung des ersten Tunnelstücks fand allerdings erst 1974 statt. Dieses wurde anfangs im Vorlaufbetrieb mit 2,35 m breiten Wagen betrieben, bis 1980 mit der heutigen U4 die erste echte Frankfurter U-Bahn-Linie in Betrieb genommen werden konnte. Trotz der höheren finanziellen Zuwendungen ab 1971 aufgrund des GVFG (Gemeindeverkehrsfinanzierungsgesetz), welches Bundesmittel aus der Mineralölsteuer für den städtischen Nahverkehr bereitstellte, wurde auch in Frankfurt Mitte der siebziger Jahre allmählich klar, dass die Größe der Stadt nicht ausreichend für ein echtes U-Bahn-Netz sei, und man sich deshalb auf die Verwirklichung eines effizienten Mischsystems mit U-Bahn-mäßig ausgebauten Strecken in der Innenstadt und einer Trassierung auf weitgehend eigenem Gleiskörper, jedoch mit Bahnübergängen, auf den Außenstrecken konzentrieren sollte. Im Gesamtverkehrsplan von 1976 sprach man deshalb auch wieder von ‚Stadtbahn' statt von ‚U-Bahn', auch wenn der letztere Begriff bis heute im offiziellen Sprachgebrauch dem Kunden gegenüber beibehalten wurde. Wie bereits die sechziger Jahre waren auch die siebziger Jahre durch zahlreiche Umplanungen und Verschiebungen der Prioritäten gekennzeichnet. Die Auflistung sämtlicher Varianten würde den Rahmen dieses Buchs sprengen, verschiedene Planungsstadien seien exemplarisch anhand von mehreren Plänen dargestellt. Soweit sie für das heutige Netz relevant sind, werden diese bei den einzelnen Strecken näher beleuchtet.

Während man insgesamt also die Ziele etwas niedriger steckte, definierte man zu jener Zeit eine vierte Stammstrecke D, die von Niederrad (südlich des Mains) über Hauptbahnhof, Messe, Ginnheim, Nordweststadt über den Riedberg nach Bad Homburg verlaufen sollte. Der mittlere Abschnitt war vorher Teil der B-Strecke und wird, soweit gebaut, heute auch als Teil dieser betrieben, planerisch spricht man jedoch weiterhin von der D-Strecke (z.B. Abschnitt DI für Hauptbahnhof – Bockenheimer Warte), auch wenn die zweite Mainquerung derzeit nicht mehr verfolgt wird. Gleichzeitig regte sich Ende der siebziger Jahre in der Bevölkerung der erste Widerstand gegen den völligen Ersatz der Straßenbahn durch die Stadtbahn, vor allem was die verbliebenen Strecken durch die Innenstadt betraf.

Im 1983 beschlossenen Generalverkehrsplan war eine nördliche Tunnelverlängerung der A-Strecke bis Weißer Stein und im Süden bis zur Sachsenhäuser Warte vorgesehen. Der Tunnel der B-Strecke sollte vom Hauptbahnhof bis zur Mönchhofstraße, sowie von der Konstablerwache bis zum Hauptfriedhof (U5) verlängert werden; im Osten sollte die U4 von Bornheim

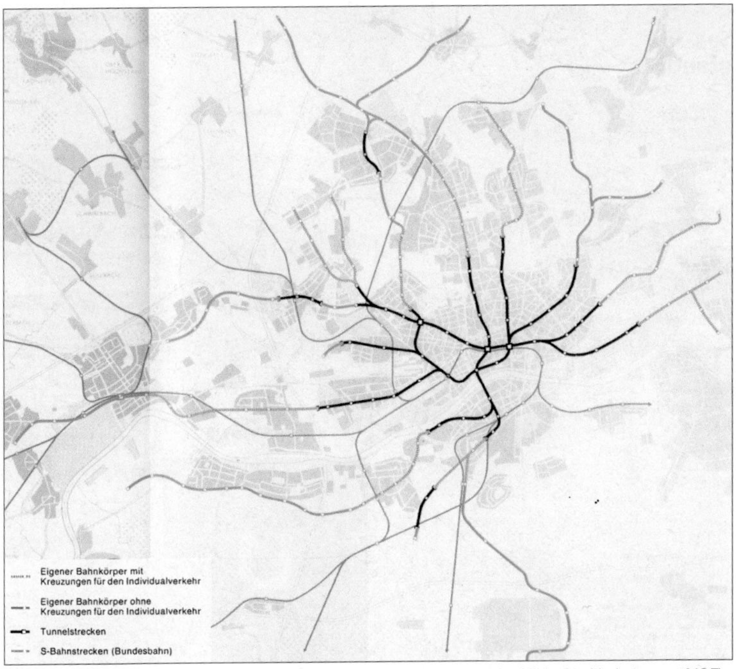


Planungsstand 1968 zum Zeitpunkt der Eröffnung der ersten Tunnelstrecke (*Abb. Stadtbahnbauamt/VGF*) – *Planning status in 1968, when the first tunnel section opened*

*metro line. Despite additional federal funds becoming available from 1971 through the 'Municipal Transport Financing Act' (GVFG), which distributed revenue from a special petrol tax, Frankfurt too had to realise in the mid-1970s that the city's size is actually too small for a proper U-Bahn system, and that a hybrid system, with metro-like sections in the city centre, and upgraded routes on outer sections, mostly on separate rights-of-way but with level crossings, would be a much better option. The 1976 master plan thus uses the term 'Stadtbahn' instead of 'U-Bahn', although the latter has remained the official term in customer publications. Like the 1960s, the 1970s were characterised by a series of project modifications and changes in priority. To list all the proposed and approved alternatives would be impossible, so a selection of the various stages is presented here. Alternative options relevant to today's network are mentioned in the respective chapters.*

*While the overall goals were downscaled, a fourth trunk route D was identified, running from Niederrad (on the south side of the Main River) via Hauptbahnhof, Messe, Ginnheim, Nordweststadt and Riedberg to Bad Homburg. The middle section was previously a branch of route B, and the part that has been built now operates jointly with route B. The corresponding sections are only designated as route D (e.g. DI for Hauptbahnhof – Bockenheimer Warte) in the plans, but the second Main crossing is no longer being pursued. Towards the end of the 1970s, the local population began to protest against plans to eventually replace the entire tramway system by the Stadtbahn, especially the routes through the city centre.*

*The 1983 master plan still included some ambitious tunnel projects: a route A extension north to Weißer Stein, and south to Sachsenhäuser Warte; a route B extension from Hauptbahnhof to Mönchhofstraße, and from Konstablerwache to Hauptfriedhof for line U5, as well as from Bornheim via Seckbach to Bergen for line U4. Route C, which was to surface on Adalbertstraße, i.e. west of Bockenheimer Warte sta-*

Nordwestzentrum – früher Nordweststadt, kurz vor Änderung der Linienbezeichnung A1 in U1 (*Foto Helmut Roggenkamp, 05/1978*)
*– formerly called Nordweststadt; photo taken shortly before the line designation was changed from A1 to U1.*

über Seckbach bis Bergen unterirdisch weiterfahren. Die C-Strecke, für die vorher eine Rampe in der Adalbertstraße, also westlich der Bockenheimer Warte vorgesehen war, sollte nun unterirdisch entlang der Leipziger Straße weitergeführt werden und erst am Industriehof an die Oberfläche kommen; im Osten sollte der Tunnel bis zur Eissporthalle (U7) bzw. bis zum Ratswegkreisel (U6 - östlich der Tramhaltestelle Riederhöfe) führen. Die D-Strecke sollte unterirdisch von Niederrad bis Ginnheim verlaufen. Wie ein Blick auf den derzeitigen Netzplan zeigt, wurden von diesen ehrgeizigen Projekten jedoch bislang nur die C-Strecke (außer Ostbahnhof – Ratswegkreisel) sowie der Abschnitt Hauptbahnhof – Bockenheimer Warte der D-Strecke (heute U4) verwirklicht.

*tion, was now to be extended underground all the way to Industriehof, while at the eastern end, the tunnels were to run to Eissporthalle (U7) and Ratswegkreisel (U6; east of today's Riederhöfe tram stop). Route D was to be built underground from Niederrad to Ginnheim. A look at today's network map shows that only route C (except Ostbahnhof – Ratswegkreisel) and the route D section Hauptbahnhof – Bockenheimer Warte (now U4) have come to fruition.*

Rampe Große Gallusstraße – bis 1978 in Betrieb
*– Ramp on Große Gallusstraße – in service until 1978*
(*Foto Helmut Roggenkamp, 03/1978*)

**Wiesenau** – Güterverkehr auf der Stadtbahntrasse bis in die achtziger Jahre
*– Freight traffic on the Stadtbahn route continued until the 1980s.*
(*Foto Stephan Kyrieleis, 1983*)

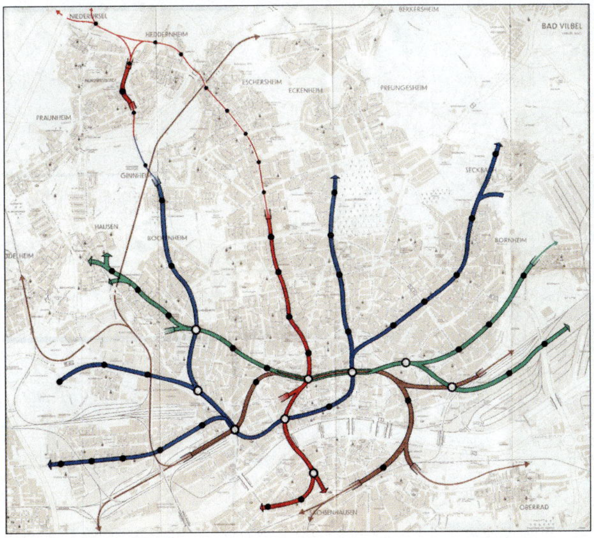


Planungsstand 1970 – nicht verwirklicht wurden bis heute diverse Äste der B-Strecke (blau dargestellt) sowie der Südost-Ast der C-Strecke (grün).

*– Planning status 1970 – some route B branches (shown in blue) as well as the southeastern branch of route C (green) have not been built.*

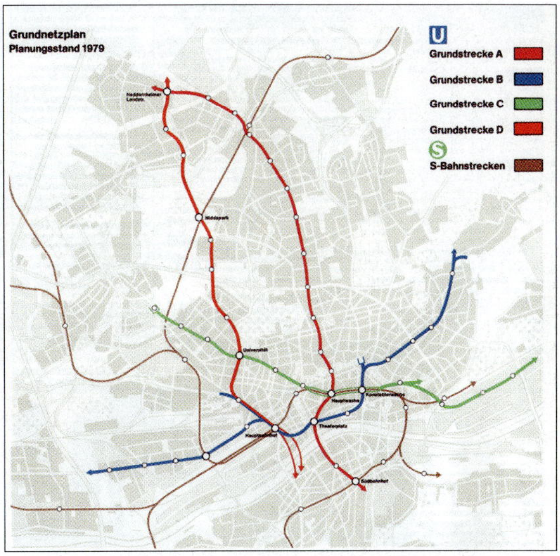


Planungsstand 1979 – während mehrere Äste der B-Strecke aus der Planung verschwunden waren, kam die neue D-Strecke (orange) hinzu; interessant auch zu sehen, dass der tatsächlich gebaute Ost-Ast der C-Strecke hier nicht enthalten ist, während der Ast entlang der Hanauer Landstraße heute am Ostbahnhof endet.

*– Planning status 1979 – while several of the previously planned route B branches had disappeared, a new route D (orange) was shown; it is also interesting to note that the actually realised eastern branch on route C is not included here, while the branch running along Hanauer Landstraße now terminates at Ostbahnhof.*

Planungsstand 1988 – erkennbar die Verlängerung der B-Strecke nach Bergen als Teil des Eingemeindungsvertrags von 1977, jedoch heute in ferne Zukunft gerückt.

*– Planning status 1988 – an extension of route B to Bergen was part of the 1977 annexation contract, although now this extension might only be built in the long-term future.*

(*Alle Abb. Stadtbahnbauamt/VGF*)

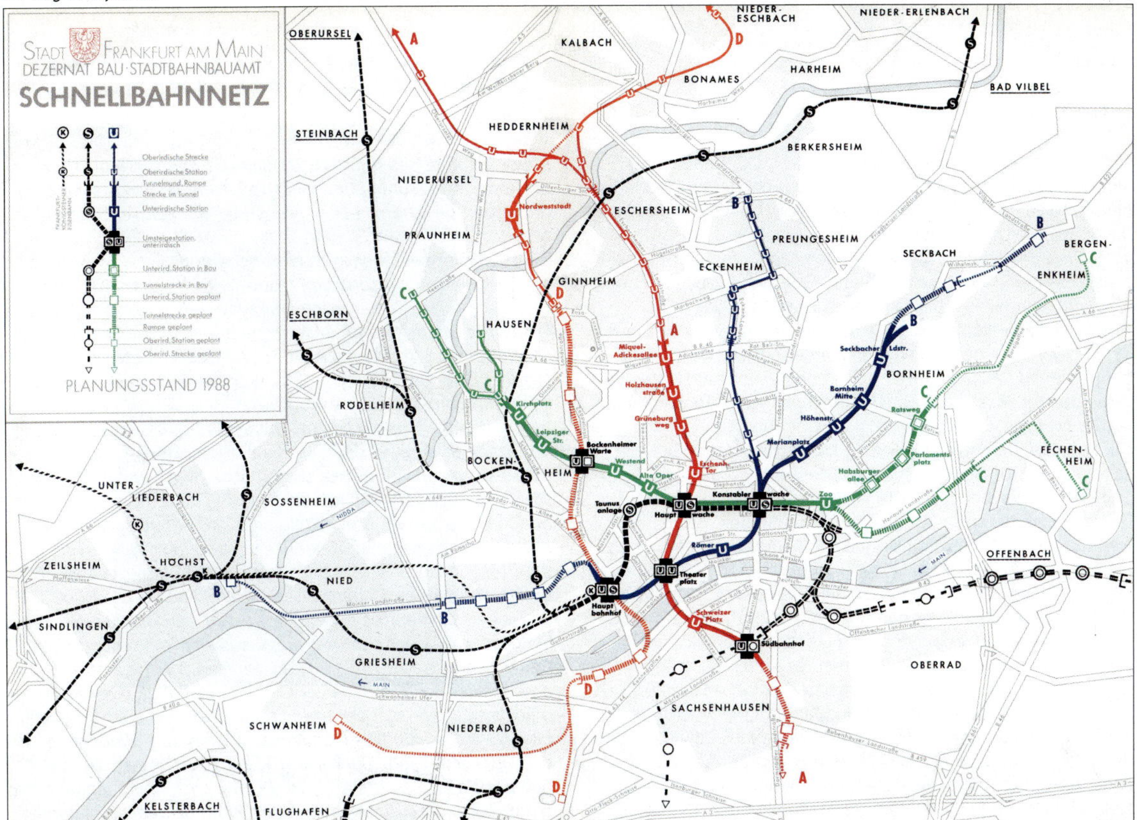

**Willy-Brandt-Platz** – ebener Einstieg von 80 cm hohen Bahnsteigen in einen Zug vom Typ ‚U4' unterwegs auf der Linie U2 nach Nieder-Eschbach
*– level access from 80 cm high platforms into a class 'U4' train, on its way to Nieder-Eschbach on line U2*

## _ A-Strecke

Auf der A-Strecke verkehren die Linien U1, U2 und U3. Der innerstädtische Abschnitt zwischen Südbahnhof und Heddernheim wird von allen drei Linien gemeinsam befahren, nördlich davon verzweigt sich die A-Strecke in drei Äste:

1) über das Nordwestzentrum nach Ginnheim (U1);
2) die ehemalige Lokalbahn nach Oberursel (U3);
3) die ehemalige Lokalbahn nach Bad Homburg (U2).

Während die beiden letzteren Äste den Charakter einer Überlandstraßenbahn behalten haben, ist der erstere weitgehend U-Bahn-mäßig ausgebaut. Er gehört planerisch zur D-Strecke, wird aber auf absehbare Zeit Bestandteil der A-Strecke bleiben.

Die U1 fährt wochentags ab 4:24 Uhr von Ginnheim zum Südbahnhof, früh morgens alle 15 Minuten, in der Hauptverkehrszeit (6:30-8:30; 15:00-18:30) alle 7/8 Minuten, tagsüber und abends bis 20:00 Uhr alle 10 Minuten und spät abends bis Betriebsschluss um ca. 1:00 Uhr alle 15 Minuten. Samstags wird früh morgens bis 6:00 Uhr alle 30 Minuten gefahren, dann bis 9:00 Uhr und ab 19:00 Uhr alle 15 Minuten, und tagsüber alle 10 Minuten. Sonntags fahren die Züge der U1 bis 9:00 Uhr im 30-Minuten-Takt, sonst durchgehend im 15-Minuten-Takt. Das Fahrplanangebot auf der Linie U2 ist sehr ähnlich, wobei allerdings außerhalb der Hauptverkehrszeiten jeder zweite Zug in Nieder-Eschbach endet. Weniger oft fahren die Züge der Linie U3. Sie verbinden den Südbahnhof mit Oberursel Hohemark durchgehend bis ca. 21:00 Uhr im 15-Minuten-Takt, dazu kommen während der Hauptverkehrszeiten Verstärkerzüge, die meist in Oberursel Bahnhof, manche auch in Heddernheim enden. Sonntags kann man mit der U3 nur alle 30 Minuten an den Fuß des Taunus gelangen. Mit drei Linien,

## _ *Route A*

*Route A comprises lines U1, U2 and U3. The section through the inner city from Südbahnhof to Heddernheim is shared by all three lines, before they branch out in different directions:*

*1) via Nordwestzentrum to Ginnheim (U1);*
*2) the former interurban tramway to Oberursel (U3);*
*3) the former interurban tramway to Bad Homburg (U2).*

*While the latter two preserve a certain interurban tramway character, the first is mostly a full-standard metro line, theoretically part of route D but for the foreseeable future remaining integrated into route A.*

*On line U1, the first train leaves Ginnheim for Südbahnhof at 04:24 on weekdays; in the early morning hours, trains operate every 15 minutes, during peak hours (06:30-08:30; 15:00-18:30) every 7/8 minutes, during daytime service and in the evenings until 20:00 every 10 minutes, and late evenings until the end of service at around 01:00 every 15 minutes. On Saturdays, trains run every 30 minutes before 06:00, then every 15 minutes until 09:00 and after 19:00; and every 10 minutes during the rest of daytime service. On Sundays, the 30-minute morning headway is extended until 09:00, while trains run every 15 minutes for the rest of the day. Service on line U2 is very similar, although during off-peak hours, every other train terminates at Nieder-Eschbach. Line U3 trains run less frequently, as they link Südbahnhof and Oberursel Hohemark every 15 minutes throughout the day until approximately 21:00. During peak hours, some extra trains terminate either at Heddernheim or Oberursel Bahnhof. The foot of the Taunus Mountains is only accessible every*

die in den Hauptverkehrszeiten jeweils alle 7/8 Minuten verkehren, gehört die A-Strecke zwischen Heddernheim und Südbahnhof zu den am stärksten belasteten Bahnstrecken in Deutschland. Während auf der U2 und zeitweise auch auf der U1 in den Hauptverkehrszeiten 100 m lange Züge eingesetzt werden, können auf der U3 aufgrund der beschränkten Bahnsteiglängen maximal 75 m lange Züge verkehren.

### _ Geschichte der A-Strecke

Die Bauarbeiten an der ersten Frankfurter Tunnelstrecke begannen offiziell am 28. Juni 1963 an der Kreuzung Miquelallee/Adickesallee. Der nördliche Abschnitt zwischen Dornbusch und Eschenheimer Tor wurde in offener Bauweise (‚Hamburger Bauweise') errichtet, indem alle zwei Meter Stahlträger zum Abstützen des Erdreichs in den Boden gerammt wurden. Im Innenstadtbereich entlang der Großen Eschenheimer Straße und an der Hauptwache wurde stattdessen eine schonendere Methode mit Bohrpfahlwänden bzw. Schlitzwänden angewandt. Außerdem wurden hier die Baugruben abgedeckt, um so den Verkehr an der Oberfläche so schnell wie möglich wieder fließen zu lassen, während im nördlichen Abschnitt auch die Straßenbahnen über Parallelstraßen umgeleitet werden mussten.

An der Hauptwache, mitten im Herzen der Stadt, entschied man sich Mitte 1965 vorausschauend für die ‚Große Lösung', d.h. die Bahnsteige für eine Ost-West-Stadtbahn sowie für die geplante S-Bahn wurden gemeinsam mit dem Bahnhof der A-Strecke errichtet. Gleichzeitig entstand ein großzügiges Zwischengeschoss mit zahlreichen Läden und sanitären Anlagen, die sog. ‚B-Ebene'. Zum Bau der dreigeschossigen Station musste das historische Gebäude der Hauptwache abgetragen werden, es wurde jedoch nach Fertigstellung des unterirdischen Bauwerks wieder aufgebaut.

Die Hauptwache war vorerst der südliche Endpunkt der neuen Stadtbahnstrecke, die jedoch auch von den Überland-Straßenbahnen aus Bad Homburg und Oberursel benutzt wer-

*30 minutes on Sundays. With three lines operating every 7/8 minutes during peak hours, the shared section between Heddernheim and Südbahnhof is one of the busiest railway lines in Germany. While 100 m trains are in service on line U2 during peak hours and some workings on line U1, the shorter platforms on line U3 allow a maximum train length of just 75 m.*

### *_ The History of Route A*

*The construction of Frankfurt's first tunnel section officially began at the intersection Miquelallee/Adickesallee on 28 June 1963. The northern segment between Dornbusch and Eschenheimer Tor was built by cut-and-cover (the so-called Hamburg method), with steel beams being rammed into the ground every two metres to shore up the soil. Closer to the city centre, along Große Eschenheimer Straße and at Hauptwache, a softer method was used, the side protection walls being built either with bored piles or diaphragm walls. The construction pits in this area were then covered so traffic could be re-established on the surface as soon as possible, while on the northern section even the trams had to be diverted through parallel streets.*

*The 'big solution' was chosen for Hauptwache, right in the heart of the city, in mid-1965, i.e. the station part for the future east-west Stadtbahn, as well as for the planned S-Bahn, was built together with the route A tunnels and a large mezzanine (the so-called 'level B') with toilets and numerous shops. The historic Hauptwache building had to be dismantled to excavate the 3-level station complex, and rebuilt after the completion of the station.*

*Hauptwache was the initial terminus for the new Stadtbahn route, which was shared by the interurban tramways from Bad Homburg and Oberursel. To allow these to*

31,1 km (ca. 5,6 km unterirdisch | *underground*), 40 Haltestellen | *stations*

*10-02-1908 Eschenheimer Tor – Eschersheim (Weißer Stein)**
*01-10-1909 Eschersheim – Heddernheim**
*04-05-1910 Heddernheim – Bad Homburg Markt**
*31-05-1910 Heddernheim – Oberursel Hohemark**

04-10-1968 Hauptwache – Miquel-/Adickesallee – Heddernheim – Nordwestzentrum
19-12-1971 Heddernheim – Bad Homburg Gonzenheim
04-11-1973 Hauptwache – Willy-Brandt-Platz
29-09-1974 Nordwestzentrum – Römerstadt
26-05-1978 Römerstadt – Ginnheim
27-05-1978 Zeilweg – Oberursel Hohemark
29-09-1984 Willy-Brandt-Platz – Südbahnhof
23-04-1989 + Niddapark
22-05-1997 + Rosengärtchen

Im Bau | *under construction*
~ 2010 Niederursel – Riedberg – Kalbach

** Frankfurter Lokalbahn:*
Beginn des elektrischen Betriebs | *Start of electric service*

**Lahnstraße** – eine 30 cm hohe Stufe muss beim Einstieg von 56 cm hohen Bahnsteigen in einen Zug vom Typ ‚U2' überwunden werden.
– *to access a class 'U2' train from a 56 cm high platform, a 30 cm high step has to be climbed.*

**Hauptwache** – ‚Mt'-Wagen 636 im Ursprungsanstrich (*Foto Helmut Roggenkamp, 05/1978*)
– *'Mt' car 636 in original livery*

den sollte. Um diese auch im Süden auf dem Straßenbahnnetz weiterfahren zu lassen, wurde unmittelbar hinter der Station Hauptwache in der Großen Gallusstraße eine Rampe errichtet.

Die Gestaltung der ersten U-Bahnhöfe folgte einem einheitlichen Schema nach einem Entwurf der Architekten Wolfgang Bader und Arthur Walter, wobei jeder Station eine Kennfarbe zugeordnet wurde, die bis auf den U-Bahnhof Grüneburgweg, der ursprünglich mit blauen Platten verkleidet war, und den später völlig umgestalteten weißen U-Bahnhof Nordwestzentrum noch weitgehend erhalten ist. Zur besseren Orientierung wurden am oberen Rand der Bahnsteigwände Farbstreifen angebracht, rot für die Linien Richtung Oberursel und Nordweststadt, und grün für die Linien Richtung Bad Homburg. Je kürzer diese Farbstreifen waren, desto weiter entfernt vom Ausgang befand sich der Fahrgast. Wie an der Hauptwache sollten in Zukunft an allen Umsteigebahnhöfen die Mittelstützen rot gestrichen werden. Außer Hauptwache liegen alle U-Bahnhöfe in eineinhalbfacher Tiefenlage, da das Zwischengeschoss gleichzeitig zur Unterquerung der Eschersheimer Landstraße dienen sollte. Während auf den Bahnsteigebenen durchweg Platten zur Wandverkleidung verwendet wurden, kamen in den Zwischenebenen teilweise auch Fliesen zum Einsatz.

Neben dem Tunnel in der Innenstadt entstand auch in der neuen Trabantenstadt Nordweststadt ein unterirdischer Bahnhof gemeinsam mit einem Einkaufszentrum und dem Stadtteilzentrum. Zur Erschließung des neuen Stadtteils plante man erst eine Straßenbahnverlängerung von Ginnheim aus, die jedoch sofort stadtbahnmäßig zusammen mit der Nordweststraße (heute Rosa-Luxemburg-Straße) trassiert werden und in Niederursel in die bestehende Strecke nach Oberursel münden sollte. Aus Kostengründen musste die Verbindung nach Ginnheim jedoch vorerst zurückgestellt werden, stattdessen wurde 1966 beschlossen, die neue Strecke provisorisch (bis heute) im Bereich der Heddernheimer Landstraße an die Überlandstraßenbahn nach Oberursel anzuschließen.

Bevor die Tunnelarbeiten vollendet werden konnten, musste auch die oberirdische Strecke entlang der Eschersheimer Landstraße ausgebaut werden. Auf diesem Abschnitt liegen bereits seit 1888 Gleise, die anfangs von Pferdebahnen, aber wenige Monate später schon von Dampfbahnen befahren wurden. Ab 1908 fuhren die elektrischen Straßenbahnen bis Eschersheim, ein Jahr später bis Heddernheim, bis schließlich 1910 der Überlandverkehr nach Oberursel und Bad Homburg aufgenommen werden konnte (siehe Kasten nächste Seite).

*continue further south on urban tramway tracks, a ramp was built immediately beyond Hauptwache station on Große Gallusstraße.*

*The design of the early underground stations followed the standard created by the architects Wolfgang Bader and Arthur Walter, with a particular colour being assigned to each station. These colours are still visible today, except at Grüneburgweg, which was initially clad with blue panels, and Nordwestzentrum, originally white, but later completely refurbished. For better orientation, colour stripes were added along the top end of the platform walls, with red for trains towards Oberursel and Nordweststadt, and green for trains towards Bad Homburg. The closer the stripes are to the exit, the longer they get. Like at Hauptwache, all interchange stations were to have red central pillars. All the platforms except those at Hauptwache are on level -2, which allowed the construction of a mezzanine which also functions as an underpass for pedestrians to cross Eschersheimer Landstraße. Unlike the platform level, which is clad with panels, the mezzanine walls were partly tiled.*

*Besides the tunnel through the city centre, an underground station was also built in the new district of Nordweststadt, together with a shopping mall and civic centre. Initially, the new area was to be served by a tramway from Ginnheim, which was to be built on a separate right-of-way together with the Nordweststraße dual carriageway (now Rosa-Luxemburg-Straße), and was then to connect with the Oberursel line at Niederursel. Due to financial reasons, the link from Ginnheim had to be deferred, and in 1966, a temporary link (still working today) from the Oberursel line at Heddernheimer Landstraße was decided upon instead.*

*Before tunnel construction was completed, the surface route along Eschersheimer Landstraße also had to be upgraded. This route had been served by rail transport since 1888, initially by horsetrams, and a few months later by a steam railway. In 1908, the electric tramway was extended to Eschersheim, and a year later to Heddernheim, with through service on the interurban routes to Oberursel and Bad Homburg starting in 1910 (see box next page). For Stadtbahn operation, the tracks were laid on a fenced-off right-of-way, while the road lanes were widened, which*

**Miquel-/Adickesallee** – ‚U2'-Wagen mit ursprünglich vor die Scheinwerfer gesetzter Glasscheibe (*Foto Stadtbahnbauamt/VGF*)
– *'U2' car 306 with original glass-covered headlights*

## _ Die Frankfurter Lokalbahn

Ab 1888 fuhren die Dampfzüge der *Frankfurter Lokalbahn AG* (FLAG) zwischen Frankfurt (Eschenheimer Tor) und Eschersheim (seit 1910 ein Stadtteil von Frankfurt).

1899 errichtete die FLAG eine 4,5 km lange Dampfbahnstrecke, die sog. ‚Gebirgsbahn', zwischen dem 1860 eröffneten Bahnhof Oberursel und Hohemark, da sich entlang des Urselbachs zahlreiche Industriebetriebe angesiedelt hatten. Neben dem wichtigen Güterverkehr herrschte auf der Strecke, die bereits damals auf eigenem Gleiskörper lag, besonders an Wochenenden reger Ausflugsverkehr in den nahegelegenen Taunus. Die Züge mussten dabei einen Höhenunterschied von etwas mehr als 100 m überwinden. Von Anfang an war geplant, die Strecke bis Frankfurt weiterzubauen, was jedoch noch einige Jahre auf sich warten ließ.

1901 ging die ‚Eschersheimer Lokalbahn' in das Eigentum der Stadt Frankfurt über, eine Teilstrecke wurde bald auch von den städtischen elektrischen Straßenbahnen mitbenutzt. Erst 1908 wurde die gesamte Strecke elektrifiziert und 1909 bis Heddernheim verlängert.

In der Nachbarstadt (seit 1912 ‚Bad') Homburg vor der Höhe gab es seit 1899 ein kleines elektrisches Straßenbahnnetz, die Bahnen erreichten ab 1900 (jedoch nur bis 1935) unter anderem das Römerkastell Saalburg.

Die FLAG konnte schließlich im Jahr 1910 auf den beiden Überlandstrecken den Personenverkehr aufnehmen, am 4. Mai nach Bad Homburg (Linie 25) und am 31. Mai nach Oberursel (Linie 24), womit sowohl das Netz in Bad Homburg als auch die FLAG-Strecke in Oberursel mit dem Frankfurter Straßenbahnnetz verbunden waren. Die beiden Linien, die jeweils im 30-Minuten-Takt verkehrten, endeten in Frankfurt am Schauspielhaus (heute Willy-Brandt-Platz), ab 1954 unweit der Hauptwache am Goetheplatz. Die Oberurseler Strecke war anfangs eingleisig, doch der zweigleisige Ausbau einzelner Abschnitte folgte bald nach der Inbetriebnahme. In Bad Homburg fuhr die Linie 25 auf den städtischen Straßenbahngleisen bis zum Markt (ab 1962 nur noch bis zum heutigen Rathaus) durch, wo sie an einem Gleisdreieck wendete.

Ab dem 1. Januar 1955 gehörten die FLAG-Linien als ‚Taunusbahnen' vollständig zum Netz der städtischen Frankfurter Straßenbahn. Sie waren noch bis 1959 als Kleinbahnen eingestuft, seither werden sie nach BOStrab betrieben.

Mit Inbetriebnahme der ersten Tunnelstrecke entlang der Eschersheimer Landstraße wurden die Linien 24 und 25 im Vorlaufbetrieb in das Stadtbahnnetz integriert. Die Linie 23 nach Bonames war 1963 eingerichtet worden. Ab 1971, nach Einstellung des Güterverkehrs, wurde die Strecke nach Bad Homburg mit Stadtbahnfahrzeugen als Linie A2 bedient, jedoch nur bis Gonzenheim, da die Innenstadtstrecken nicht stadtbahntauglich waren. Aus der Linie 23 wurde gleichzeitig die A4, und statt der Linie 24 sprach man nun von der A3. Diese beiden Linien wurden aber bis 1978 mit Straßenbahnwagen betrieben, die südlich der Station Hauptwache über eine Rampe an der Oberfläche weiterfuhren. Auf der oberen Oberurseler Strecke fuhren noch bis 1983 vereinzelt Güterzüge.

## _ *The 'Frankfurter Lokalbahn'*

*From 1888, the steam trains of the 'Frankfurter Lokalbahn AG' (FLAG) operated between Frankfurt (Eschenheimer Tor) and Eschersheim (since 1910 a part of Frankfurt).*

*In 1899, the FLAG built the so-called 'Gebirgsbahn' [mountain railway], a 4.5 km steam railway between Oberursel railway station, opened in 1860, and Hohemark, which was to serve the new industrial area growing along the Urselbach River. Besides the significant amount of freight traffic, the line was especially busy during weekends, when many people went from the city to the nearby Taunus Mountains. The steam trains had to negotiate a change in altitude of 100 m. From the start, there were plans to build a direct route to Frankfurt, which took several years to complete.*

*In 1901, the 'Eschersheimer Lokalbahn' was taken over by the city of Frankfurt, with some sections soon being shared by the electric urban tramways. By 1908, the entire route had been electrified, and in 1909 it was extended to Heddernheim.*

*In the neighbouring town of Homburg vor der Höhe (since 1912 with the 'Bad' prefix) a small electric tramway network had operated since 1899; among other destinations, from 1900 (but only until 1935) the trams reached Saalburg, a Roman castle.*

*The FLAG finally started passenger service on its interurban routes in 1910, on 4 May to Bad Homburg (line 25) and on 31 May to Oberursel (line 24), thus connecting the Bad Homburg network, as well as the FLAG route in Oberursel, with the Frankfurt tramway network. Both lines ran every 30 minutes, originally terminating in Frankfurt at Schauspielhaus (now Willy-Brandt-Platz), and from 1954, near the Hauptwache at Goetheplatz. The Oberursel route was initially single-track, although it was doubled along some sections soon after its inauguration. In Bad Homburg, line 25 continued on urban tramway tracks to terminate at Markt (cut back in 1962 to the present site of the town hall), where it reversed on a track triangle.*

*On 1 January 1955, the FLAG lines were fully integrated into the Frankfurt tramway network. Until 1959, they were classified as secondary railway lines, but they have been operated as tramways ever since.*

*When the Stadtbahn tunnel along Eschersheimer Landstraße opened, lines 24 and 25 became part of the new system. Line 23 to Bonames had first been introduced in 1963. In 1971, after freight traffic had been discontinued, the route to Bad Homburg was converted to Stadtbahn operation with a new line A2, but the line was curtailed at Gonzenheim as the Bad Homburg urban route was unsuitable for Stadtbahn trains. Line 23 was then renamed line A4, and line 24 became line A3. These two lines kept operating with tramway vehicles, which until 1978, emerged from the tunnel south of Hauptwache station to continue on the surface. Until 1983, a few goods trains still shared the tracks on the upper section in Oberursel.*

Wagen 400 der ‚Taunusbahn' im Verkehrsmuseum Frankfurt in Schwanheim
– *'Taunusbahn' car 400 in the tram museum at Schwanheim*

**Eschenheimer Tor** – ‚Mt'-Wagen 641 im neueren Anstrich (*Foto Helmut Roggenkamp, 10/1977*)
– *'Mt' car 641 in a later livery*

*required the removal of many trees. With an average station dwelling time of 20 seconds, the Stadtbahn trains were to reach Weißer Stein on a 'green wave'. The surface stations were made of prefabricated elements, and most of them were only accessible via underpasses. Crossing Eschersheimer Landstraße was now only possible through these underpasses, and the Stadtbahn route was therefore perceived as a barrier right from the start. Despite the large number of underground structures along the surface route, no proper provisions were made for a later extension of the Stadtbahn tunnel.*

*Due to the mixed service of both conventional tramway vehicles and Stadtbahn cars, the 100 m platforms on route A were only 56 cm high (in the underground stations this was achieved by adding extra ballast to the trackbed). The new 2.65 m wide and 23 m long vehicles of class 'U2' were therefore unable to provide level access either.*

*The first underground section was opened in Frankfurt on 4 October 1968. This tunnel was then used by Stadtbahn line A1, which ran between Nordweststadt and Hauptwache, but also by the tramway lines 23 (Bonames – Neu-Isenburg), 24 (Oberursel Hohemark – Hauptbahnhof) as well as 25 (Bad Homburg – Hauptbahnhof – Heilbronner Straße). These interurban lines were operated with vehicles of class 'Mt' and trailers of class 'mt', which were narrower than the Stadtbahn cars and had to be fitted with side bulges to bridge the gap between trains and platforms. To stop at low platforms along the outer sections, they were equipped with folding steps.*

*From 19 December 1971, the new cars of class 'U2' were also used on the former tramway route to Bad Homburg, which was now renamed the A2 and (temporarily) terminated at Gonzenheim; the upgrading of the route into the Bad Homburg town centre to Stadtbahn standard was not possible, and instead a new route was planned along the Dornbach River to terminate at Marienbader Platz adjacent to the railway station – although announced time and again, this extension is yet to be built after 37 years! At present, an extension along the S-Bahn route is being discussed in*

Für den Stadtbahnbetrieb wurden die Gleise durchgehend auf einen eigenen abgezäunten Gleiskörper gelegt. Gleichzeitig wurde die Straße verbreitert, wofür zahlreiche Bäume entfernt werden mussten. Bei einem durchschnittlichen Stationsaufenthalt von 20 Sekunden sollten die Stadtbahnzüge auf einer grünen Welle bis Weißer Stein gelangen. Die Haltestellen, die meist nur über Unterführungen zu erreichen waren, entstanden aus Fertigteilen. Das Überqueren der Eschersheimer Landstraße war fast nur bei diesen Unterführungen möglich, weshalb die Stadtbahnstrecke im Stadtteil Eschersheim von Anfang an als Barriere wahrgenommen wurde. Trotz der zahlreichen Tunnelbauten entlang der oberirdischen Strecke wurden keinerlei Vorleistungen für eine spätere Tunnelstrecke vorgenommen.

Wegen des Mischbetriebs mit herkömmlichen Straßenbahnfahrzeugen konnten die 100 m langen Bahnsteige auf der A-Strecke vorerst nur 56 cm hoch gebaut werden (was in den Tunnelstationen durch Aufschottern des Gleisbetts erfolgte), weshalb auch die neuen 2,65 m breiten und 23 m langen U-Bahn-Fahrzeuge des Typs ‚U2' keinen ebenen Einstieg bieten konnten.

Die erste Frankfurter Tunnelstrecke wurde am 4. Oktober 1968 eröffnet. Auf ihr fuhr einerseits die erste Stadtbahnlinie A1 von Nordweststadt bis Hauptwache, andererseits auch die Straßenbahnlinien 23 (Bonames – Neu Isenburg), 24 (Oberursel Hohemark – Hauptbahnhof) und 25 (Bad Homburg – Hauptbahnhof – Heilbronner Straße). Auf diesen Überlandlinien wurden Wagen des Typs ‚Mt' mit Beiwagen ‚mt' eingesetzt, die wegen der breiteren U-Bahn-Wagen seitliche Ausgleichswülste erhielten, um den Spalt zwischen Bahnsteig und Fahrzeug zu schließen. Sie hatten für die nicht schnellbahngerecht ausgebauten Haltestellen auf den Außenstrecken Klapptrittstufen.

Ab dem 19. Dezember 1971 fuhren die Fahrzeuge des Typs ‚U2' auch auf der ehemaligen Straßenbahnstrecke als Linie A2 nach Bad Homburg, allerdings (vorerst) nur bis Gonzenheim, da der Ausbau der Straßenbahnstrecke ins Homburger Stadtzentrum für den Einsatz der neuen Wagen nicht möglich war. Stattdessen sollte eine neue Trasse entlang des Dornbachs zum Marienbader Platz (Bahnhofsvorplatz) gebaut werden, was aber auch 37 Jahre später noch nicht geschehen ist, auch wenn es in regelmäßigen Abständen immer wieder als ‚geplant' auftaucht. Derzeit ist im Rahmen einer 2-System-Regionalstadtbahn (Regionaltangente-West) eine Verlängerung entlang der S-Bahn-Trasse im Gespräch.

**Oberursel-Hohemark** – ‚Mt'-Wagen 618 an der ehemaligen Ausstiegstelle, die sich an der Stelle der heutigen Station befand (▶ S. 49)
(*Foto Helmut Roggenkamp, 04/1978*)
– *'Mt' car 618 stopping at the former alighting point, which was located on the site of the present station (▶ p. 49)*

**Grüneburgweg** – Ursprungszustand mit blauer Wandverkleidung *(Foto Alexander Piesenecker, 02/1990)* – *original station with blue wall cladding*

Am 19. Dezember 1971 wurden auch die beiden anderen weiterhin mit Straßenbahnwagen durch den Innenstadttunnel verkehrenden Linien umbenannt, aus der Linie 24 wurde die A3 (Hauptbahnhof – Hohemark), und aus der Linie 23 die A4 (Hauptbahnhof – Bonames).

Für den Stadtbahnbetrieb mit einer Höchstgeschwindigkeit von 80 km/h mussten auf der ehemaligen Lokalbahnstrecke in Richtung Bad Homburg nach Einstellung des Güterverkehrs im Dezember 1970 die Gleise und die Stromversorgung bei laufendem Betrieb grundlegend erneuert werden, die Bahnübergänge wurden mit Halbschranken gesichert und bei den Ortsdurchfahrten wurde die Trasse abgezäunt. Die 80 m langen Seitenbahnsteige konnten wegen der Stufe in den ‚U2'-Wagen auch nur 56 cm hoch gebaut werden. Die Brücke über die Autobahn A661 wurde im Juni 1972 fertig gestellt.

Am 4. November 1973 wurden die A-Linien um wenige hundert Meter von der Hauptwache zum Theaterplatz (seit 1993 Willy-Brandt-Platz) verlängert. Da die südlich des U-Bahnhofs Hauptwache angeordnete Weichenanlage bis 1971 bis zum Kaiserplatz erweitert worden war, war der noch zu bauende Abschnitt sehr kurz und reichte nun bis zum Untermainkai, wo wiederum eine provisorische Wendeanlage eingerichtet wurde.

1974 wurde der Tunnel unter der Nordweststadt wie ursprünglich geplant um etwa 200 m nach Süden verlängert und die neue Endstation Römerstadt in Betrieb genommen. Hier sollte die Linie A1 fortan auch enden, die Verbindungsstrecke nach Ginnheim sollte hingegen von der Straßenbahnlinie 8, die sämtliche Universitätsstandorte erschließen sollte, bedient werden. Um den Mischbetrieb durch die Nordweststadt jedoch zu vermeiden und da der Bau des Uni-Campus auf dem Riedberg ohnehin noch nicht gesichert war, entschied man schließlich, die Linie A1 bis Ginnheim zu führen, wo eine fünfgleisige Umsteigeanlage für Stadtbahn und Straßenbahn entstand. Die teilweise auf einem Viadukt über dem Niddapark verlaufende Trasse war bereits mit der Nordweststraße rohbaumäßig errichtet worden.

Auf der Oberurseler Strecke bedeutete der Umbau der alten Lokalbahn den vollständigen zweigleisigen Ausbau der beste-

**Oberursel-Hohemark** – seit 1978 fahren die ‚U2'-Züge bis an den Fuß des Taunus; anfangs benutzten sie die ehemalige Wendeschleife. *(Foto Fritz D. Kegel, 1979)*
– *since 1978, 'U2' trains have been running to the foot of the Taunus Mountains; initially they made use of the long-gone terminal loop there.*

*conjunction with the 'Regionaltangente West' project, which would be operated with dual-system vehicles.*

*On 19 December 1971, the two remaining tram lines which shared the city tunnel were also renamed: line 24 became line A3 (Hauptbahnhof – Hohemark), and line 23 was now line A4 (Hauptbahnhof – Bonames).*

*For Stadtbahn operation at a maximum speed of 80 km/h, the tracks and power supply system along the former interurban tram route to Bad Homburg had to be replaced without interrupting the service on the line, and only after goods trains had stopped running on the line in December 1970; level crossings were safeguarded with half barriers, and through built-up areas the alignment was fenced off. Due to the existing step inside the 'U2' cars, the 80 m side platforms were only built 56 cm high. The bridge across the motorway A661 was completed in June 1972.*

*On 4 November 1973, the A lines were extended several hundred metres from Hauptwache to Theaterplatz (Willy-Brandt-Platz since 1993). As the tunnel beyond Hauptwache had already been built as far as Kaiserplatz in 1971 to improve reversing manoeuvres, the new section was rather short and ended right by the river bank, so temporary sidings for reversing were able to be laid south of the new terminus.*

*In 1974, the tunnel passing under the Nordweststadt was extended by 200 m as originally planned to reach Römerstadt station. This was then meant to become the permanent terminus for line A1, while tramway line 8 was supposed to be extended from Ginnheim to serve all University areas. To avoid mixed tram and Stadtbahn service on the route through Nordweststadt, and because the future of the University campus on Riedberg was not yet completely clear, in the end line A1 was to run on the section to Ginnheim, where a 5-track interchange was established for the Stadtbahn and the tram. Through the Niddapark this section lies on a viaduct, part of which had previously been built together with a dual carriageway.*

*For the route to Oberursel, the upgrade from interurban tramway to Stadtbahn implied the complete doubling of the line up to Kupferhammer (e.g. along the underpass to cross the mainline railway), once an underground route in Oberursel had been discarded, in particular in the area of the railway station. Most stations (except Wiesenau, Niederursel and Bommersheim) were initially rebuilt with platforms only 55 m long, long enough for 2-car units; as the line was*

**Kupferhammer** – wegen des Güterverkehrs nach Oberursel wurden die Bahnsteige ursprünglich nur 32 cm hoch gebaut. (*Foto Fritz D. Kegel, 1979*)
*– due to the freight traffic which shared the line to Oberursel, the platforms were only built 32 cm high.*

henden Strecke bis Kupferhammer (z.B. im Bereich der Eisenbahnunterführung), nachdem in Oberursel ernsthaft diskutierte Tunnellösungen, vor allem zur Unterfahrung des Bahnhofs, ausgeschieden waren. Die meisten Stationen (außer Wiesenau, Niederursel und Bommersheim) bekamen anfangs nur 55 m lange Bahnsteige für Doppeltraktionen, und da auf dieser Strecke weiterhin Güterverkehr stattfinden sollte, konnten diese nur 32 cm hoch sein. Anfang 1975 begannen die Arbeiten an der Grunderneuerung der Strecke nach Oberursel, so dass der Betrieb mit ‚U2'-Fahrzeugen im Mai 1978, wenn auch teilweise nur an provisorischen Bahnsteigen, beginnen konnte. Gleichzeitig wurde die Rampe in der Großen Gallusstraße, auf der seit 1968 die U-Straßenbahnen an die Oberfläche gelangen konnten, geschlossen. Seit dem 27. Mai 1978 werden die ehemaligen Linien A1, A2 und A3 als U1, U2 und U3 bezeichnet, die Linie A4 wurde in die U2 integriert.

Im Bereich Weißkirchen konnte der Umbau wegen eines ungeklärten Schnellstraßenprojekts erst 1983 abgeschlossen werden. Auch auf dem Abschnitt ab Oberursel Bahnhof gab es wegen genehmigungsrechtlicher Probleme erhebliche Zeitverzögerungen, so dass der zweigleisige Ausbau bis Portstraße bis März 1982 andauerte. Der anschließende Abschnitt verzögerte sich sogar so sehr, dass mittlerweile der Gütertransport aufgegeben worden war und somit im November 1987 ab Lahnstraße einige Stationen mit 56 cm hohen Bahnsteigen in Betrieb genommen werden konnten. Der Abschnitt ab Kupferhammer ist bis heute eingleisig geblieben.

Eine Verlängerung der A-Strecke ans Südufer des Mains war von Anfang an vorgesehen, allerdings war zunächst die Trassierung ab dem Schweizer Platz unklar. Als Anschlussstrecken boten sich die weitgehend unabhängig trassierten Straßenbahnstrecken nach Neu-Isenburg und nach Schwanheim an, außerdem sollte das Universitätsklinikum angeschlos-

*still used by freight trains, the platform height was limited to 32 cm. The upgrading of the route began in early 1975, and the 'U2' cars started running to Oberursel in May 1978, with only provisional platforms available at some stations. At the same time, the ramp on Große Gallusstraße, which had been used by the interurban trams to emerge from the tunnel since 1968, was abandoned. Since 27 May 1978, the former lines A1, A2 and A3 have been known as U1, U2 and U3, respectively, while line A4 has been fully integrated into the U2 timetable.*

*In the Weißkirchen area, the upgrading of the line was postponed until 1983 by an uncertain road scheme. The section beyond Oberursel Bahnhof was also delayed due to problems getting local planning permission, and the doubling of the line up to Portstraße took until March 1982. The following section had lagged so much behind schedule that in the meantime, freight train service had been discontinued, and some stations from Lahnstraße to Hohemark were therefore able to be re-opened with 56 cm high platforms in November 1987. The section between Kupferhammer and Hohemark has remained single-track.*

*The extension of route A towards the south bank of the Main River had been planned from the very beginning, although the alignment beyond Schweizer Platz had not yet been clearly defined. The existing and largely segregated tramway routes to Schwanheim and Neu-Isenburg were obvious options, but the university hospital also had to be linked. Once an additional trunk route, route D, had been added to the master plan, route A was able to be extended to Südbahnhof [south railway station], where an important interchange was created. South of Südbahnhof, a new route to Neu-Isenburg with a possible branch towards Oberrad was possible. The construction of the 1.6 km section to Südbahn-*

sen werden. Mit Ergänzung des Grundnetzes durch eine D-Strecke, die den Hauptbahnhof mit Niederrad verbinden sollte, konnte die A-Strecke zum Südbahnhof geführt werden, wo ein wichtiger Umsteigepunkt des Gesamtnetzes entstand. Südlich davon sollte eine Neubaustrecke nach Neu-Isenburg mit einem eventuellen Abzweig Richtung Oberrad gebaut werden. Mit dem Bau des 1,6 km langen Abschnitts bis zum Südbahnhof wurde im Mai 1976 begonnen. Dieser stellte die U-Bahn-Bauer vor bisher unbekannte Herausforderungen. Zur Unterquerung des Mains westlich der Untermainbrücke wurden zwei eingleisige Röhren per NÖT (Neue Österreichische Tunnelbauweise oder Spritzbetonbauweise) hergestellt, nachdem vorher der Boden unter dem Fluss vereist worden war, um etwaigen Wassereinbrüchen vorzubeugen. Am Südufer wurde pro Tunnelröhre je ein Fluttor eingebaut, am Nordufer eins für beide Gleise im offen gebauten Anfahrschacht. Südlich des Mains liegt die U-Bahn-Trasse mit dem U-Bahnhof Schweizer Platz unter der Bebauung, weshalb auch hier die NÖT zur Anwendung kam. Im Bahnhofsbereich wurden erst wie bei den Streckentunneln Röhren mit einem Durchmesser von 6,7 m aufgefahren, die dann zu 10,5 m Bahnsteigröhren aufgeweitet wurden. Anschließend wurde dazwischen das Mittelschiff ausgebrochen. Zur Stabilisierung des Bodens wurde teilweise die chemische Vereisung angewandt. Südlich des U-Bahnhofs Schweizer Platz führen ebenso eingleisige Röhren unter der Diesterwegstraße teilweise unter der Bebauung bis zur Kaulbachstraße, ab wo bis zum Südbahnhof wieder offen gebaut werden konnte. Vor Einfahrt in den U-Bahnhof Südbahnhof gibt es einen doppelten Gleiswechsel, so dass beide Bahnsteigseiten angefahren werden können. Für den Bau des U-Bahnhofs wurde der mittlere Teil des Empfangsgebäudes sowie die klassische Bahnsteighalle des Südbahnhofs von 1913 abgerissen. Während das Empfangsgebäude nach Fertigstellung des U-Bahn-Tunnels wieder aufgebaut wurde, verschwand die Bahnsteighalle endgültig. Anschließend wurden nach und nach die DB-Gleise auf neue Brücken über die Baugrube gelegt und schließlich der dreigeschossige U-Bahnhof darunter errichtet. Dahinter schließt eine in offener Bauweise hergestellte Weichenanlage an, die die Zufahrt zu den beiden äußeren Streckentunneln und zum mittleren Wendegleistunnel ermöglicht, die jeweils bergmännisch errichtet wurden und bis zum Grethenweg reichen. Während die Neubaustrecke zum Südbahnhof früher als geplant am 29. September 1984 in Betrieb genommen werden konnte, dauerten die Arbeiten an der Wendeanlage wegen verschiedener Probleme noch bis Mai 1988.

*hof began in May 1976, which faced the engineers with as yet unknown challenges. To cross under the Main River, two single-track tunnels were built west of the Untermainbrücke using the NATM (New Austrian Tunnelling Method), with the soil under the river having been frozen to prevent any sudden inrush of water. At the southern ends of the tunnels, an individual flood gate was built in for each tunnel, whereas at the northern end, a single gate was installed for both tunnels in a chamber built by cut-and-cover and previously used to start tunnel excavation. On the south bank of the Main River, the tunnel, including Schweizer Platz station, continues below the buildings, and therefore the NATM had to be used here too. First built with a diameter of 6.7 m like the adjacent running tunnels, the sections through the station were later widened to 10.5 m before a centre nave was excavated between the two to create a wide island platform. To stabilise the soil, chemical freezing was applied at some points. South of Schweizer Platz station, the single-track NATM tubes continue to Kaulbachstraße; from there to Südbahnhof, the tunnel was built by cut-and-cover. Before arriving at Südbahnhof, there is a scissors crossover which enables both sides of the island platform to be directly accessed by the trains. To allow for the construction of the underground station, the central part of the railway station building as well as the 1913 overall roof spanning over the platforms had to be demolished. Whereas the station building was reconstructed after the completion of the underground station, the iron roof had gone forever. One by one, the DB mainline tracks were relocated onto new bridges across the construction pit, and subsequently a 3-level underground station was excavated. Beyond the station, cut-and-cover was used to build a big box, which accommodates several crossovers that allow the trains to access three NATM tunnel stubs – the outer two were designed to accommodate the future running tracks, whereas the centre one is for reversing. The three stubs end below Grethenweg. While the section to Südbahnhof was brought into service on 29 September 1984, the adjacent sidings were not completed until May 1988 after a series of problems.*

*At the end of the 1980s, a southern extension from Südbahnhof seemed very likely. From the outer tunnel stubs, the NATM tubes were to continue all the way to Sachsenhäuser Warte, with an intermediate station at Mailänder Straße to be built at great depth like Schweizer Platz station. After passing under the southern cemetery, a temporary terminus*

**Südbahnhof** – auch die beiden Stationen südlich des Mains hatten anfangs nur 56 cm hohe Bahnsteige (man beachte die Stufe im ‚U2'-Wagen). (*Foto Hans-Ulrich Riedel*)
*– even the newer stations on the south bank of the Main River were initially built with only 56 cm high platforms (note the step inside the 'U2' vehicle).*

**Schweizer Platz** – inzwischen sind die Bahnsteige zwar auf 80 cm erhöht worden, aber auch 2008 waren noch ‚U2'-Wagen im früheren Anstrich zu sehen.
*– in the meantime the platforms have been raised to 80 cm, but even in 2008 some 'U2' cars were still running in the former livery.*

**Kalbach** > **Riedwiese** – Überlandstrecke auf der Linie U2 (*Foto Stephan Kyrieleis, 06/1990*)
*– interurban section on line U2*

*was to be established at Sachsenhäuser Warte (or Sachsenhäuser Berg), located under Babenhäuser Landstraße. A large park-and-ride facility was to be established there, plus an interchange with buses serving the southern region. There was also an option for a future surface extension along road B3 through the city forest to end at the present tramway terminus at the northern edge of Neu-Isenburg. In 1989, a design contest was held for the two stations, which were to serve an area that is home to some 10,000 people. Due to funding problems, however, this project was eventually shelved. Now that the S-Bahn links the southern region directly, the number of buses arriving in Frankfurt from this area has significantly decreased.*

*So while no southern extension can be expected in the foreseeable future, the existing sections of route A are currently being upgraded to the definitive standard. All platforms need to be raised from 56 cm to 80 cm (unlike the 87 cm on other routes) to provide level access into the newer vehicles. The older vehicles of class 'U2' will maintain a small step inside the car (see rolling stock section on p. 98). In most of the underground stations, the platform height was achieved by removing ballast from the trackbed, which had been planned when the tunnel was built. Paradoxically, this had not been done in the newest stations Schweizer Platz und Südbahnhof, where the platforms therefore had to be raised. All the stations will gradually be made fully accessible, with lifts being retrofitted in all underground stations.*

*At the time of writing, the construction of a surface route across Riedberg is about to start. The Riedberg area is home to a new University campus, as well as the site of a large new residential area. This area was to be served by line U4, which was to be extended from Bockenheimer Warte to Ginnheim, and from there on the existing U1 route to Heddernheimer Landstraße, where during the most optimistic years of U-Bahn planning, an interchange station on the line to Oberursel was planned. Newer plans included a track triangle, with line U4 running on U3 tracks to Niederursel, and from there, on a new*

Die weitere Verlängerung der A-Strecke Richtung Süden schien Ende der achtziger Jahre ziemlich sicher. Die für die Wendeanlage errichteten äußeren Tunnelröhren sollten bergmännisch bis zur Sachsenhäuser Warte weitergebaut werden. An der Mailänder Straße sollte in großer Tiefe ähnlich wie am Schweizer Platz ein Zwischenbahnhof unter Tage entstehen. Von dort würden die Streckentunnel unter dem Südfriedhof weiterführen und in die vorläufige Endstation Sachsenhäuser Warte bzw. Sachsenhäuser Berg münden, die unter der Babenhäuser Landstraße liegen würde. Hier sollte eine große Park&Ride-Anlage sowie eine Umsteigemöglichkeit zu den Bussen ins südliche Umland geschaffen werden. Eine mögliche oberirdische Weiterführung entlang der Bundesstraße 3 durch den Stadtwald bis zur derzeitigen Endstelle der Straßenbahn am Nordrand der Stadt Neu-Isenburg war dabei stets berücksichtigt worden. Bereits 1989 wurde für die beiden Stationen, in deren Einzugsgebiet etwa 10.000 Menschen lebten, bundesweit ein Gestaltungswettbewerb ausgeschrieben. Doch dann gab es Schwierigkeiten bei der Finanzierung dieses Abschnitts und die Planungen verschwanden in den Schubladen. Seit Inbetriebnahme der südlichen S-Bahn-Strecken ist auch die Anzahl der aus dem Umland nach Frankfurt führenden Buslinien stark zurückgegangen.

Während also eine Verlängerung der A-Strecke nach Süden in absehbarer Zeit nicht zu erwarten ist, werden die bestehenden Abschnitte seit einigen Jahren auf den endgültigen Standard gebracht. Dazu müssen sämtliche Bahnsteige von 56 cm auf nunmehr 80 cm (statt wie bei den anderen Strecken auf 87 cm) gebracht werden, um einen ebenen Einstieg in die neueren Fahrzeuge zu ermöglichen. Bei den älteren Wagen des Typs ‚U2' bleibt auch weiterhin eine Stufe im Wageninnern (siehe Fahrzeuge Seite 98). Die Bahnsteigangleichung erfolgte in den unterirdischen Stationen in der Regel durch Absenken des Schotterbetts, was beim Bau bereits so vorgesehen war, paradoxerweise jedoch nicht bei den beiden neueren Stationen in Sachsenhausen, nämlich Schweizer Platz und Südbahnhof, wo die Bahnsteige erhöht werden mussten. Nach und nach werden alle Stationen behindertengerecht ausgebaut, wozu die unterirdischen Bahnhöfe mit Aufzügen nachgerüstet werden müssen.

In Bauvorbereitung befindet sich derzeit die oberirdische Strecke über den Riedberg, wo neben dem neuen Universitätsgelände ein großes Wohngebiet im Entstehen ist. Ursprünglich

**Zeilweg** – Haltestelle im Wandel der Zeit: im September 1984 mit 32 cm hohen Bahnsteigen und ‚U2'-Wagen im originalen roten Anstrich
*– the evolution of a station: in September 1984 with 32 cm platforms and a 'U2' car in original red livery* (*Foto Stephan Kyrieleis*)

sollte dieses Gebiet über eine Verlängerung der D- bzw. B-Strecke angeschlossen werden, indem die Linie U4 in einem neuen Tunnel von der Bockenheimer Warte nach Ginnheim und von dort auf der bestehenden Trasse bis zur Heddernheimer Landstraße weiterfahren sollte. Zu Zeiten der optimistischen Planungen einer echten U-Bahn sollte hier ein Kreuzungsbahnhof mit der Strecke nach Oberursel entstehen, neuere Stadtbahnplanungen sahen ein Gleisdreieck vor, so dass die U4 auf der U3-Strecke bis Niederursel fahren könnte, nach dieser Station nach Norden abzweigen und so auf den Riedberg kommen würde. Nach Halt an den Haltestellen Uni-Campus Riedberg (Am Forum) und Riedberg kommt die neue Trasse vor der Station Kalbach auf die bestehende U2-Strecke zurück. Nachdem die derzeitige Stadtregierung diese baureifen Planungen Mitte 2006 auf Eis gelegt hat, wurden neue Möglichkeiten untersucht. Schließlich entschied man, die Riedberg-Neubaustrecke an die bestehende A-Strecke anzuschließen, wobei ab 2010 eine Linie U8 alle 15 Minuten vom Riedberg auf der Fahrplantrasse der U3-Verstärkerzüge, die derzeit in Oberursel oder Heddernheim enden, zum Südbahnhof fahren sollen, und eine Tangentiallinie U9 alle 15 Minuten zwischen Nieder-Eschbach und Ginnheim über den Riedberg pendeln soll. Nördlich der Haltestelle Riedberg wird für die U8 ein mittiges Kehrgleis gebaut. Die gesamte 3,8 km lange Strecke wird stadtbahnmäßig errichtet, d.h. vollkommen auf eigenem Gleiskörper, teils mit Rasengleis, teils mit Schottergleis, jedoch mit Straßenkreuzungen. Sollte die Kapazitätsgrenze auf der A-Strecke erreicht werden, kann das alte Projekt einer durchgehenden Stadtbahnstrecke zwischen Bockenheim und Ginnheim wieder aus den Schubladen geholt werden (▶ S. 56).

**Dornbusch** – Standardhaltestelle in der Eschersheimer Landstraße vor dem Umbau (▶ S. 32) (Foto Stephan Kyrieleis, 2002)
*– standard surface station on Eschersheimer Landstraße before the upgrading (▶ p.32)*

*route up to Riedberg. After serving the stations Uni-Campus Riedberg (Am Forum) and Riedberg, line U4 would have joined the present U2 route at Kalbach. In mid-2006, a newly elected city government surprisingly shelved this project, the construction of which had been about to start. Other options were then examined. The present plan is to connect the new Riedberg section to the existing route A. From 2010, a new line U8 is to operate every 15 minutes between Riedberg and Südbahnhof, replacing the present U3 extra trains which terminate at Oberursel or Heddernheim; in addition, the tangential line U9 is to shuttle between Nieder-Eschbach and Ginnheim via Riedberg. To the north of Riedberg station, a centre siding will be laid to allow line U8 to reverse. The entire 3.8 km route will be built to Stadtbahn standard, i.e. completely on a dedicated right-of-way, partly with grass-covered tracks, partly on ballast trackbed, but with some level crossings. Should route A then reach the limit of its capacity, the former project, with a through route between Bockenheim and Ginnheim, can still be revived (▶ p. 56).*

**Zeilweg** – im Juni 1999 mit neuen Fahrtzielanzeigern und ‚U2'-Wagen in neuem Anstrich, aber weiterhin mit niedrigen Bahnsteigen
*– in June 1999, with new destination signs and a 'U2' car in new livery, but still with low platforms* (Foto Stephan Kyrieleis)

**Zeilweg** – seit Herbst 1999 nun mit 80 cm hohen Bahnsteigen, dem neuen Standard auf der A-Strecke
*– since autumn 1999 with 80 cm high platforms, the new standard on route A*

①

②

**_ Südbahnhof**

Der mehrgeschossige U-Bahnhof, der vom Architekten Willy Orth gestaltet wurde, liegt rechtwinkelig unter den Gleisen des DB-Bahnhofs Frankfurt Süd (▶ S. 132). Direkt unter den Bahnbrücken verläuft eine Zwischenebene, die als Fußgängertunnel die Nord- und Südseite der Bahnanlagen verbindet und als Zugang zu allen vier Bahnsteigen an der Oberfläche dient. Vom Nordende des U-Bahn-Bahnsteigs führen Rolltreppen direkt ins alte Empfangsgebäude, während der mittlere ② und südliche Aufgang in ein Zwischengeschoss ① münden, wo man Siebdrucke mit dem Henninger Turm und dem Goetheturm sehen kann. Die Ausgänge an der Südseite der Mörfelder Landstraße konnten erst im November 1986 geöffnet werden. Seit Anheben der Bahnsteige 2005 führt eine leichte Rampe zu den Aufgängen und Rolltreppen hinunter ②. In allen Bereichen des U-Bahnhofs dominieren Sechseck-Formen. An den Außenwänden sind Motive aus Alt-Sachsenhausen zu sehen ⑤.

③

*The multi-storey underground station Südbahnhof was designed by Willy Orth, and lies perpendicular to the tracks of the DB station Frankfurt Süd [South Station ▶ p. 132] – right below the railway bridges, there is a mezzanine which functions as a pedestrian tunnel between the northern and southern sides of the station, and provides access to the four surface platforms. Direct escalators lead to the old station building from the northern end of the underground platform, while the centre and southern exits connect with another mezzanine ①, which is decorated with images showing the Henninger Turm and the Goetheturm, two towers in the district of Sachsenhausen. The exits on the south side of Mörfelder Straße were only opened in November 1986. With the platforms having been raised in 2005, gentle ramps ② now lead down to the stairs and escalators. Every part of the station is dominated by hexagonal shapes. The side walls are decorated with historic photographs of Sachsenhausen ⑤.*

④

⑤

①

②

**_ Schweizer Platz**

Der dreischiffige U-Bahnhof liegt im Herzen des Stadtteils Sachsenhausen. Er wurde bergmännisch unter der Bebauung errichtet, nur das südliche Verteilergeschoss unter dem gleichnamigen Platz konnte in offener Bauweise ausgeführt werden; dieser Raum ist mit zwei Siebdruckmotiven verziert – das Mainufer und der für Sachsenhausen typische *Ebbelwei* (Apfelwein) ②.

Der Architekt Willy Orth zog bei der Gestaltung der Bahnsteigebene das Tunnelgewölbe bewusst mit ein und betonte den unterirdischen Charakter durch Verwendung rotbrauner Emailplatten. An den gerundeten Außenwänden findet man Hinweise zu den nahe gelegenen Museen am Mainufer ①. Ein Hell-Dunkel-Effekt entsteht durch eine Mischung direkter und indirekter Beleuchtung. Wie am Südbahnhof wurde der Bahnsteig im Sommer 2005 auf 80 m angehoben, da hier die Gleise nicht abgesenkt werden konnten, weshalb nun leichte Rampen zu den ursprünglichen Fest- und Fahrtreppen führen. Das nördliche Zwischengeschoss liegt ebenfalls unter der Bebauung, es zeigt Wandbilder der nahen Museen ④.

③

*This 3-nave station is located in the centre of the district of Sachsenhausen. Except for the southern mezzanine, which was built by cut-and-cover and is decorated with two themes, the Main riverbank and the typical apple wine ②, the station was excavated using the NATM as it lies below several buildings.*

*The architect Willy Orth incorporated the vaulted ceilings into the overall design of the station, using brownish panels to stress its underground character. The curved walls are decorated with information panels concerning the nearby museums ①. The mixture of direct and indirect lighting creates some peculiar visual effects. Like at Südbahnhof, the platforms were raised from 56 to 80 cm in summer 2005, which required the construction of ramps between the platform and the original stairs and escalators. Like the platform area, the northern mezzanine is also located below buildings; it is decorated with images ④ showing the museums lined up along the Main River.*

④

⑤

_ **Willy-Brandt-Platz** [bis | *until* 01-07-1993 ‚Theaterplatz'] Hier war ursprünglich ein Verzweigungsbahnhof unter der Kaiserstraße geplant, der verschiedene Linienführungen auf der A- bzw. B-Strecke (▶ S. 61) erlauben sollte. Man entschied sich schließlich für einen Turmbahnhof mit reinem Linienbetrieb, wobei die Abgänge zur B-Strecke am südlichen Ende der Bahnsteige der A-Strecke liegen. Von dort führt auch eine großzügige Fahrtreppenanlage ② zum Willy-Brandt-Platz, dem Platz zwischen Europäischer Zentralbank und den Städtischen Bühnen. In diesem Bereich liegt neben den beiden U-Bahn-Tunneln auch noch ein Ost-West-Straßentunnel. Die nördlichen Ausgänge führen zum Kaiserplatz ⑤. Am Theaterplatz war von 1973 bis 1984 die südliche Endstation der A-Strecke. Seit Herbst 2002 kann man hier an 80 cm hohen Bahnsteigen einsteigen.

*Initially, a 4-track station was planned below Kaiserstraße, allowing various line alternatives for routes A and B (▶ p. 61). However, in the end a separate station was built for each route, with the stairs that lead down to route B being located at the southern end of the route A platforms. From the same end, several escalators ② carry passengers up to Willy-Brandt-Platz, the square between the theatre complex and the European Central Bank. Besides the two Stadtbahn tunnels, an east-west road tunnel also passes beneath the square. The northern exits of the station are located on Kaiserplatz ⑤.*
*'Theaterplatz' was the terminus for the A lines from 1973 until 1984. 80 cm platforms have been available since autumn 2002.*

①

②

**_ Hauptwache**
Die Bahnsteige der A-Strecke liegen auf der untersten Ebene (-3), direkte Treppen führen zur S-Bahn (▶ S. 119) und C-Strecke (▶ S. 87 – beide auf Ebene -2) ④. Vom Südende der Bahnsteige führen Aufgänge ⑤ direkt zum Zwischengeschoss. Im November 2002 wurden die Gleise abgesenkt, um einen ebenen Einstieg in die Fahrzeuge zu ermöglichen.
Das Gebäude der Hauptwache ② wurde während der Bauarbeiten abgetragen und anschließend wieder mit historischer Dachform aufgebaut.
Im Stil der sechziger Jahre war die Verteilerebene, die sog. ‚B-Ebene', ursprünglich in reinem Sichtbeton gehalten und entwickelte sich immer mehr zu einem sozialen Brennpunkt, weshalb 1980/81 eine Neugestaltung nach einer Idee des Darmstädter Architektenteams Trojan, Trojan und Laske mit grünen und blauen Kacheln und Paneelen ① vorgenommen wurde (▶ S. 2).

③

*The route A platforms are located on the lowest level (-3), with direct stairs leading to the S-Bahn (▶ p. 119) as well as the route C platforms (▶ p. 87 – both on level -2) ④. From the southern end of the side platforms ⑤, stairs connect route A directly to the mezzanine. In November 2002, the tracks were lowered to provide level access into the vehicles.*

*At the start of construction, the Hauptwache building ② had to be dismantled; it was later rebuilt with its historical roof.*
*In typical 1960s style, the mezzanine was initially left in bare concrete. It was modernised in 1980/81 with a design of green and blue tiles and panels ① created by the architects Trojan, Trojan & Laske from Darmstadt (▶ p. 2).*

④

⑤

## _ Eschenheimer Tor

Weitgehend im ursprünglichen Zustand befindet sich der U-Bahnhof Eschenheimer Tor. Das großzügige Zwischengeschoss ②, das sich über die gesamte Station erstreckt und den Fußgängern das Überqueren der Straßenkreuzung nur unterirdisch erlauben sollte, bleibt heute jedoch ungenutzt, während sich hier früher einige Läden befanden. Anders als bei den drei folgenden Stationen sind die Bahnsteige etwas breiter, und die Treppen und Rolltreppen an beiden Bahnsteigenden schweben quasi im Raum, d.h. der Bereich dahinter ist nicht verbaut ③. Die Absenkung der Gleise im Bahnhofsbereich fand im Frühjahr 2004 statt. Der Eschenheimer Turm ① musste beim Bau des U-Bahnhofs durch eine Bohrpfahlwand geschützt werden. Nördlich der Station befindet sich mittig ein Abstellgleis, das nur vom Süden her anfahrbar ist.

*Eschenheimer Tor station has mostly been preserved in its original style, although the large mezzanine ②, which extends above the entire station and was once meant to be the only way for pedestrians to cross the road intersection, is now almost abandoned, with all the former shops having gone. Unlike the following three stations, the platforms here are somewhat wider, and the stairs and escalators located at each end of the platforms kind of float, i.e. the area behind them is not covered up ③. The tracks were lowered in spring 2004 to provide level access.*
*During the construction of the underground station, the Eschenheimer Turm ① had to be protected by means of a bored pile retaining wall. The centre siding to the north of the station is only accessible from the southern side.*

_ **Grüneburgweg**

Während die übrigen unterirdischen Stationen der A-Strecke (außer Nordwestzentrum) weitgehend ihr ursprüngliches Aussehen bewahrt haben, wurde der U-Bahnhof Grüneburgweg in den neunziger Jahren in Anlehnung an den Namen der Station mit grünen Kacheln verkleidet, nachdem die ursprünglich blauen Emailplatten (▶ S. 19) entfernt worden waren.
Die Anpassung der Bahnsteighöhe erfolgte wie am benachbarten U-Bahnhof Holzhausenstraße Ende 2001/Anfang 2002 durch Absenkung des Gleisbetts, was, wie von Anfang an geplant, durch Entnahme von Schotter erreicht wurde. Das mittig angeordnete Zwischengeschoss dient auch als Unterführung unter der Eschersheimer Landstraße. Je zwei Fest- und eine Fahrtreppe führen von den engen Seitenbahnsteigen zur ‚B-Ebene' ①. Die Station wird derzeit mit Aufzügen nachgerüstet.

*Whereas the rest of the underground stations on route A (except Nordwestzentrum) have hardly been modified since they first opened, Grüneburgweg station was refurbished during the 1990s with green tiles (obviously inspired by the station's name), replacing the original blue panels (▶ p. 19).*
*The platform height was adjusted in late 2001/early 2002 by removing ballast from the trackbed, a method taken into consideration when route A was built. The mezzanine is located in the middle and also functions as a pedestrian underpass to cross Eschersheimer Landstraße. Two sets of stairs and one escalator lead from each of the narrow side platforms to the mezzanine level ①. The station is currently being retrofitted with lifts.*

①

②

③

**_ Holzhausenstraße**

Statt der sonst einfachen Alu-Paneeldecken wurde der U-Bahnhof Holzhausenstraße mit einer besonderen Lichtdecke ② (*Foto Helmut Roggenkamp, 05/1978*) ausgestattet. Der Rest des Stationsaufbaus entspricht dem benachbarten U-Bahnhof Grüneburgweg, allerdings wurden hier im Zuge der Modernisierung in den neunziger Jahren nur Teilflächen des Zwischengeschosses mit Farbfliesen ergänzt ③. Nachdem das Gleisbett 2001 abgeschottert worden war, wurde der Bahnhof 2008 durch Einbau von zwei Aufzügen behindertengerecht ausgebaut ①. Während der Aufzug von der Oberfläche direkt zum stadtauswärtigen Bahnsteig führt, muss Richtung Innenstadt im Zwischengeschoss in den zweiten Fahrstuhl umgestiegen werden. Die Renovierungsarbeiten auf der Bahnsteigebene waren im Sommer 2008 noch nicht abgeschlossen, jedoch war in einigen Abschnitten bereits die neue Gitterdecke ④ sichtbar, die im Brandfall den Rauch höher aufsteigen lässt, womit den Fahrgästen einige Sekunden mehr zur Flucht zur Verfügung stehen würden.

④

*Instead of the simple aluminium panels used in the other stations, a specially illuminated ceiling ② was used in the underground station Holzhausenstraße. The rest of the station layout corresponds to the neighbouring Grüneburgweg station, although during modernisation here in the 1990s, only some areas of the mezzanine were clad in coloured tiles ③. With the trackbed having been lowered in 2001, the station was made fully accessible in 2008 ①. From the surface, a lift goes directly to the outbound platform, but for the inbound direction passengers have to transfer to a second lift in the mezzanine. By summer 2008, the refurbishment of the station had not yet been finished, although the new metal grid suspended from the ceiling was already visible ④. In the case of fire it would allow the smoke to rise, and thus provide some extra seconds for passengers to escape.*

①

②

**_ Miquel-/Adickesallee**
[seit 2005 mit Zusatz ‚Polizeipräsidium']
Der letzte unterirdische Bahnhof der Innenstadtstrecke liegt an der Kreuzung der Eschersheimer Landstraße mit dem stark befahrenen Alleenring, der eine Verbindung zwischen dem westlichen und dem östlichen Teil der Autobahn A66 darstellt, weshalb bereits beim Bau des U-Bahn-Tunnels im Bereich dieser Kreuzung auch die Tieferlegung des Straßenverkehrs in die Ebene -1 vorgesehen war. Kreuzende Buslinien sollten unterirdisch direkt neben den Abgängen zur U-Bahn halten. Ein provisorischer Gang ① verbindet heute die beiden Zwischenebenen, die beide eine interessante Lichtdecke ③ aufweisen.
Zur Anpassung der Bahnsteighöhe wurden die Gleise 2004 abgesenkt. An diesem Bahnhof begannen 1963 die Bauarbeiten der Frankfurter Stadtbahn. Er wurde damals mit nur 95 m langen Bahnsteigen errichtet, was zu kurz für 4-Wagen-Züge des Typs ‚U4' ist, so dass bei diesen dann die letzte Tür geschlossen bleiben muss.
Nördlich der Station befindet sich vor Erreichen der Rampe ein doppelter Gleiswechsel.

③

*Since 2005, this station has carried the appendage 'Polizeipräsidium'. Being the last underground station on the city centre section of route A, it is located at the point where Eschersheimer Landstraße intersects with the Alleenring, a busy ring road which links the eastern and the western parts of motorway A66. When the Stadtbahn tunnel was built, an east-west road tunnel was planned to run on level -1. Intersecting bus lines were to stop underground next to the U-Bahn entrances. A temporary walkway ① has since existed between the two vestibules, both of which boast an interesting ceiling ③.*
*The tracks in Miquel-/Adickesallee station were lowered in 2004 to provide level access into the trains. In 1963, the construction of the Stadtbahn had begun at this station, which was then built with only 95 m long platforms. These are now too short for a 4-car train of class 'U4', so when they are used, the last door has to remain locked.*
*North of the station, there is a scissors cross-over before the ramp.*

④

①

②

## _ Dornbusch

Die provisorische Rampe Humser Straße ① liegt genau zwischen dem U-Bahnhof Miquel-/Adickesallee und der Haltestelle Dornbusch. Die ehemalige Straßenbahnhaltestelle Humser Straße entfiel beim Umbau der Strecke zur Stadtbahn.
Das nördliche Ende der Bahnsteige der Haltestelle Dornbusch liegt etwa 120 m südlich der Kreuzung mit dem Marbachweg, der gesamte Bereich wurde großzügig untertunnelt. Die anfangs etwas trostlose unterirdische Anlage wurde in den achtziger Jahren nach einer Idee von Prof. Pininski umgestaltet und präsentiert sich heute farbenfroh mit interessanten Details ③, wirkt aber dennoch etwas verlassen, da es anders als an der Hügelstraße keinerlei Läden gibt.
Die Station Dornbusch (▶ S. 23) wurde im Frühjahr 2002 umgebaut und mit 80 cm hohen Bahnsteigen ausgestattet. Seither dürfen die Gleise am Südende, wo zuvor nur Zugänge von den jeweiligen Straßenseiten vorhanden waren, ebenerdig überquert werden. Erst kürzlich wurde wieder vorgeschlagen, den Tunnel komplett zu sperren und auch am Nordende oberirdische Zugänge mit Rampen zu schaffen.

*The temporary ramp at Humser Straße ① is located right between Miquel-/Adickesallee and Dornbusch stations. The former tram stop Humser Straße was abandoned when the line was converted into a Stadtbahn route.*
*The northern ends of the platforms at Dornbusch lie some 120 m from the Eschersheimer Landstraße/Marbachweg road intersection, with a long tunnel leading from there to the station. Before being redesigned by Professor Pininski in the 1980s, this underground corridor used to look rather dreary, but now it is very colourful with many surprising details ③. The lack of shops still makes it look rather deserted, though.*
*Dornbusch station (▶ p. 23) was rebuilt with 80 cm platforms in spring 2002, and the tracks may now be crossed at the station's southern end. Each platform had previously only been accessible from the corresponding side of the road. Only recently, the closure of the tunnel has been proposed, and instead a surface access with ramps should be built at the northern side of the station, too.*

③

①

②

## _ Fritz-Tarnow-Straße

Diese Haltestelle ②, die zu Straßenbahnzeiten Roseggerstraße hieß, war früher am Südende über einen engen Tunnel erreichbar. Dieser ist heute zwar noch vorhanden, die Aufgänge zu den Bahnsteigen sind jedoch zugemauert, denn die Bahnsteige sind seit Sommer 2002 an beiden Enden ebenerdig zugänglich ①.

*The stop at Fritz-Tarnow-Straße ②, called Roseggerstraße during the tramway period, was previously accessible via an underpass located at its southern end. This underpass still exists, but it is no longer connected to the platforms as these have been accessible at grade since summer 2002 ①.*

## _ Hügelstraße

Die versetzt angeordneten Bahnsteige liegen jeweils vor der verkehrsreichen Kreuzung Eschersheimer Landstraße/Hügelstraße. Unter dem Kreuzungsbereich befindet sich ein großzügiges Untergeschoss mit Zugängen von allen Ecken. Ähnlich wie an der Station Dornbusch wurde diese Anlage Ende der achtziger Jahre mit Malereien etwas aufgefrischt ③. Im Frühjahr 2003 wurden auch hier die Bahnsteige auf 80 cm erhöht. Seither gibt es auch am nördlichen Ende des stadteinwärtigen Bahnsteigs ⑤ einen Zugang mitsamt Bahnübergang.

*The staggered platforms are located before the busy Eschersheimer Landstraße/ Hügelstraße road intersection. A spacious 'mezzanine' with entrances from all street corners lies below the intersection. Like at Dornbusch, the underground distribution area ③ was redecorated during the 1980s. The platforms were raised to 80 cm in spring 2003; the inbound platform ⑤ is now also accessible via a level crossing at its northern end.*

③

④

⑤

①

## _ Lindenbaum

Ähnlich wie an der benachbarten Station Weißer Stein wurde der Fußgängertunnel, der sich am Nordende der Station unter der Straße Am Lindenbaum befindet, 1987 gefliest. Im Zuge der Anpassung der Bahnsteige Mitte 2002 wurden die Aufgänge von diesem Tunnel zu den Bahnsteigen jedoch geschlossen, dieser ist nun nur noch als Straßenunterführung ② erhalten. Die Station ist heute am nördlichen Ende über Rampen zugänglich, am südlichen weiterhin über Treppen ①.

*Like at the neighbouring stop Weißer Stein, the underpass, located at the northern end of the station at the intersection with Am Lindenbaum road, was tiled in 1987. When the platform height was adjusted in mid-2002, the platforms were cut off from this tunnel, though; it is now only available to cross the street ②. The station is accessible via ramps from the northern side, and steps from the southern ①.*

②

## _ Weißer Stein

Im Bereich dieser Station endete 1888 die ‚Eschersheimer Lokalbahn', der erste Vorläufer der heutigen Stadtbahnstrecke.
Die im mittleren Bereich der Bahnsteige liegenden Treppen zum Fußgängertunnel ③-⑤, der 1987 gelblich gefliest worden war, blieben beim Umbau im Frühjahr 2003 vor allem zur Sicherheit der hier ein- und aussteigenden Schüler erhalten. Die Bahnsteige sind aber auch an beiden Enden ebenerdig über Rampen zugänglich.

*In 1888, the 'Escherheimer Lokalbahn', the early predecessor of the present Stadtbahn, started terminating in the area of the Weißer Stein stop.*
*The stairs located in the middle of the platforms lead to a pedestrian tunnel ③-⑤, which was clad in yellowish tiles in 1987. At this stop, the underpass remained connected to the platforms when they were raised in spring 2003, mainly for the safety of the many students who board and alight here. The platforms are also accessible via ramps located at both ends.*

③

④

⑤

①

②

Nördlich der Station Weißer Stein ① überquert die Stadtbahn die Main-Weser-Bahn (S6) ② und anschließend den Fluss Nidda. In etwa 200 m Laufabstand zum Stadtbahnhalt befindet sich die S-Bahn-Station Eschersheim (▶ S. 127).

*North of Weißer Stein ①, the Stadtbahn crosses first the Main-Weser-Bahn (S6) ② and then the Nidda River. An S-Bahn station called Eschersheim (▶ p. 127) is located some 200 m from the Stadtbahn stop.*

③

### _ Heddernheim

Diese Station liegt südlich des Betriebshofs Heddernheim ③⑤ und hatte anfangs Seitenbahnsteige mit einer Fußgängerunterführung. 1986/87 wurde der östliche Bahnsteig zu einem Mittelbahnsteig erweitert und der Fußgängertunnel bis zu einem östlichen Ausgang verlängert. In der zweiten Hälfte des Jahres 2004 wurde die gesamte Station umgebaut, dabei entstand am Südende der Bahnsteige ein ebenerdiger Übergang, der somit einen behindertenfreundlichen Zugang ermöglicht. Zwei Buslinien halten neben dem stadteinwärtigen Bahnsteig. Die neue Dachkonstruktion wurde mit einem Lichtspiel versehen ④ *(Foto Alexander Piesenecker)*, das von ein- und ausfahrenden Zügen ausgelöst wird, eine Idee der Schoyerer Architekten.

*Heddernheim station lies to the south of the Stadtbahn depot ③⑤. Originally it had side platforms connected via an underpass. In 1986/87, the eastern side platform was converted into an island platform with an additional track; the underpass was extended and an eastern exit was built. The station was rebuilt in the second half of 2004, with a level crossing being added at the southern end to provide full accessibility. Two connecting bus lines stop at level with the inbound platform.*
*The new roof structure incorporates special light effects ④ triggered by arriving trains, an idea by Schoyerer Architekten.*

④

⑤

①

②

## _ Zeilweg

Während die Linie U2 am Betriebshof Heddernheim nach Norden abzweigt, wird diese Haltestelle ①② noch von den Linien U1 und U3 gemeinsam bedient. Wegen des lang andauernden Güterverkehrs (breiteres Profil) von und nach Oberursel konnten hier anfangs nur 32 cm hohe Bahnsteige errichtet werden. 1989 wurden diese auf 56 cm erhöht. Im Herbst 1999 brachte man sie schließlich auf die endgültige Höhe von 80 cm und verlängerte sie auf 100 m (▶ S. 22/23). Die Haltestelle Sandelmühle an der U2 liegt nur knapp 300 m entfernt.

*Whereas line U2 diverges towards the north at the Heddernheim depot, lines U1 and U3 continue on the same tracks up to the next stop called Zeilweg ①②. As freight traffic (wider profile trains) to and from Oberursel was also handled on these tracks for a long time, the platforms were initially only 32 cm high. They were raised to 56 cm in 1989. In autumn 1999 they were again rebuilt, this time to the standard height of 80 cm, and at the same time extended to 100 m (▶ p. 22/23). Sandelmühle stop on line U2 is only about 300 m away.*

## _ Heddernheimer Landstraße

Diese Station ③ liegt direkt am nördlichen Ende des Tunnels unter der Nordweststadt. Hier gab es anfangs nur 75 m lange Bahnsteige, da nördlich davon eine Straßenkreuzung war. Der Bahnübergang wurde 1989 für Fahrzeuge geschlossen und die Bahnsteige verlängert. Die bislang nur 56 cm hohen Bahnsteige werden wohl im Zuge des Baus der Riedberg-Strecke auf 80 cm erhöht werden.

*The Heddernheimer Landstraße stop ③ is located right at the northern end of the tunnel which runs below the Nordweststadt. The platforms were initially only 75 m long because of a road intersection at the northern side. This level crossing was closed for motorised traffic in 1989 and the platforms were extended. Currently 56 cm high, they will be rebuilt in the near future together with the new route via Riedberg.*

③

①

②

**_ Nordwestzentrum**
[bis | *until* 1990 ‚Nordweststadt']

③

Der unterirdische Bahnhof Nordwestzentrum wurde gemeinsam mit dem gleichnamigen Einkaufs- und Stadtteilzentrum errichtet. Beim Bau stieß man auf Funde der Römerstadt Nida. Die Bahnsteigebene war ursprünglich wie die Station Miquel-/Adickesallee mit weißen Stahlblechplatten verkleidet (▶ S. 12). Hier war von 1968 bis 1974 Endstation, die Abfahrt erfolgte von beiden Seitenbahnsteigen, weshalb im Zwischengeschoss eine entsprechende Anzeigetafel notwendig war. Eine mit Glas geschützte Öffnung ② erlaubt einen Blick von der Verteilerebene, die auch als Zugang zum Parkdeck dient, auf die Bahnsteigebene. Ende der achtziger Jahre wurde die Station gestalterisch an das Einkaufszentrum ① angepasst und umbenannt. Im Herbst 2004 wurden die Gleise abgesenkt, um einen ebenen Einstieg zu ermöglichen.

*The underground station Nordwestzentrum was built together with the shopping mall of the same name and the district's civic centre. During construction, the remains of the Roman settlement of Nida were discovered. Like at Miquel-/Adickesallee, the platform level was initially clad in white panels (▶ p. 12). Between 1968 and 1974, the Stadtbahn terminated here, with trains departing from either platform; a platform indicator was therefore necessary in the mezzanine. A glass-protected opening ② provides a view from the mezzanine down to the platforms; on the mezzanine level there is a large car park. In the late 1980s, the station was refurbished to match the shopping mall ①, and renamed. In autumn 2004, the tracks were lowered to provide level access into the vehicles.*

④

**_ Römerstadt**

Dieser bis auf die bislang nur 56 cm hohen Bahnsteige voll nach U-Bahn-Kriterien ausgebaute oberirdische Bahnhof liegt wenige Meter nach dem südlichen Tunnelmund ①. Die Bahnsteige sind durchgehend mit einer Beton-Faltwerk-Decke überdacht. Während die Wände auf dem Bahnsteig Richtung Ginnheim in verschiedenen Grüntönen gestrichen sind ③, wurden sie auf der gegenüberliegenden Seite zum Schutz vor Vandalismus gefliest. Am Nordende führen eingehauste Treppen zu den Bushaltestellen auf einer Straßenbrücke hinauf, am Südende jedoch nach unten ②. Südlich der Station liegen auf der Nidda-Brücke zwei Abstellgleise. Bis kurz vor Ginnheim fährt die U1 als Hochbahn weiter.

*Römerstadt station was built to full metro standard, although the platforms are still only 56 cm high. It is located a few metres south of the southern portal ① of the Nordweststadt tunnel. The full length of each platform is covered by a concrete awning. While the wall along the platform towards Ginnheim is painted in various greenish tones ③, the opposite side was tiled to prevent vandalism. At the northern ends, encased stairs lead up to the bus stops on a road bridge, whereas at the southern ends, they go down to a road underpass ②.*
*South of the station, there are two sidings on the bridge across the Nidda River. Line U1 continues on an elevated structure to a point just before the Ginnheim terminus.*

④⑤ Niddapark

## _ Niddapark

Dieser Hochbahnhof ① wurde ursprünglich für die BUGA 1969 als ‚Ginnheimer Wäldchen' geplant, dann 1978 rohbaumäßig errichtet, und schließlich erst am 23.4.1989 für die BUGA 89 eröffnet. Seither wird er eher schlecht genutzt und befindet sich in einem desolaten Zustand (S. 38 ④⑤). Im Zuge des Ausbaus der S-Bahn nach Bad Vilbel ist hier eine Umsteigemöglichkeit zur S6 geplant.

*The elevated station Niddapark ① was first planned for a garden show held in 1969; it was then partly built in 1978, before eventually opening on 23 April 1989 for the German Garden Show (BUGA 89). It has always been badly frequented and is now in a pathetic state of abandonment (p. 38 ④⑤). Once the S-Bahn route to Bad Vilbel (S6) has been upgraded, Niddapark will become an interchange station.*

①

## _ Ginnheim

Die Stadtbahn erreichte Ginnheim am 26. Mai 1978 vom Norden her, die hier endende Linie trägt seit diesem Tag die Bezeichnung U1. Unmittelbar nördlich der Endstation fädelt die Strecke aus der Mittellage der Schnellstraße aus ③. In Ginnheim besteht bis auf Weiteres eine Umsteigemöglichkeit ②④ zur Straßenbahnlinie 16 Richtung Hauptbahnhof, nachdem 2006 der lang geplante und kurz bevorstehende Bau des fehlenden Abschnitts Bockenheimer Warte – Ginnheim wieder gestrichen wurde. Anstatt der heutigen Anlage, die nun wohl doch auch bald 80 cm hohe Bahnsteige erhalten wird, sollte die Stadtbahn (Linie U4) unterirdisch unter der Ginnheimer Landstraße halten.

*On 26 May 1978, the Stadtbahn reached Ginnheim from the northern side. Since that day, the line terminating here has been designated U1. Just to the north of the station, the Stadtbahn leaves the central alignment between the lanes of a dual carriageway ③. For the time being, Ginnheim will be the transfer point ②④ between the Stadtbahn and tram line 16 towards the central railway station, after the long-planned and seemingly imminent extension from Bockenheimer Warte to Ginnheim having been shelved by the current city government in 2006. The present station, which will probably soon be rebuilt with 80 cm platforms, was to be replaced by an underground station below Ginnheimer Landstraße for the extended line U4.*

②

③

④

①

②

③

## _ Sandelmühle

Diese Haltestelle ①② wurde erst im Herbst 2007 umgebaut und weist wesentlich zeitgemäßere Unterstände auf als die wenige Jahre zuvor umgestalteten Haltestellen entlang der Eschersheimer Landstraße. Diese werden von einer Partnerfirma für Außenwerbung gestellt und haben eine Standardtiefe von 1,75 m.
Die Strecke führt anschließend in östlicher Parallellage zur Olof-Palme-Straße ③ weiter, wobei das Gebiet östlich davon unbebaut ist.

*Sandelmühle station ①② was only rebuilt in autumn 2007, but with more modern shelters than those erected along Eschersheimer Landstraße a few years earlier. The shelters are provided by an advertising company and have a standard depth of 1.75 m.*
*From Sandelmühle, the route continues along the eastern side of Olof-Palme-Straße ③, with undeveloped land to the east of it.*

## _ Riedwiese/Mertonviertel

Zwischen den beiden ehemaligen Lokalbahnstrecken lag früher ein wichtiges Metallwerk, das in den letzten Jahren zu einem neuen Wohngebiet umgewandelt wurde – das Mertonviertel, das seit 2005 als Namenszusatz für die Haltestelle Riedwiese ④⑤ auch auf den Netzplänen aufscheint. Analog zu Sandelmühle wird wohl auch diese Station in naher Zukunft umgebaut.

*There used to be an important industrial estate between the two routes of the former Lokalbahn, but in recent years it was converted into a residential area called 'Mertonviertel'. This name was added to the station name Riedwiese ④⑤ in 2005. The station will be rebuilt in the near future to match its neighbour Sandelmühle.*

④

⑤

①

②

## _ Kalbach

Dieser Halt hieß vor dem Stadtbahn-Zeitalter Kalbacher Weg und liegt eigentlich im Stadtteil Bonames. Die Ortschaft Kalbach wurde erst 1972 nach Frankfurt eingemeindet, während Bonames schon seit 1910 Teil der Großstadt ist. Der Kalbacher Ortskern befindet sich ca. 1,7 km von der Stadtbahnstation entfernt.
Die Bahnsteige der Station Kalbach ①② wurden im Herbst 2007 umgebaut, wobei während der Bauzeit Behelfsbahnsteige errichtet wurden. Da es sich hier um einen wichtigen Umsteigepunkt zu mehreren Buslinien handelt, wurden die Unterstände mit 2,50 m Tiefe großzügiger ausgeführt als etwa an der Haltestelle Sandelmühle. An der Nordseite befindet sich ein großer Parkplatz.

*Before Stadtbahn operation, the present Kalbach station used to be called Kalbacher Weg; it is actually located in the district of Bonames. Kalbach was only annexed by Frankfurt in 1972, whereas Bonames has been part of the city since 1910. The Kalbach town centre lies some 1.7 km from the Stadtbahn station.*
*The platforms at Kalbach station ①② were rebuilt in autumn 2007, with temporary platforms being erected during reconstruction. As this is an important transfer point for several bus lines, the shelters were built 2.50 m deep. North of the station, there is a large parking facility.*

## _ Bonames Mitte

Die zweite Haltestelle in Bonames, nur etwa 500 m von der Station Kalbach entfernt, ist noch weitgehend im Zustand der siebziger Jahre zu sehen ③. Der Zusatz ‚Mitte' verweist einerseits auf seine zentralere Lage, diente andererseits aber auch zur Unterscheidung vom heutigen S-Bahnhof Frankfurter Berg, der bis Mitte der achtziger Jahre Bonames hieß.

*The second stop in Bonames, only about 500 m from Kalbach station, is mostly preserved in its 1970s style ③. The appendage 'Mitte' not only refers to the station's central location, but originally also helped to distinguish it from the S-Bahn station today called Frankfurter Berg, which until the mid-1980s used to be called Bonames.*

③

**_ Nieder-Eschbach**

Bis 1972 war Nieder-Eschbach eine eigenständige Gemeinde, jetzt befindet sich hier die letzte Station auf Frankfurter Stadtgebiet. Außerhalb der Hauptverkehrszeiten endet jeder zweite Zug der U2 in Nieder-Eschbach, weshalb hinter der Station mittig zwei Wendegleise ④ angeordnet sind.

Seit November 2007 präsentiert sich die Station mit 80 cm hohen Bahnsteigen ②, stadteinwärts wie in Kalbach mit 2,50 m tiefem Unterstand, stadtauswärts reicht die Standardausführung von 1,75 m ③. Die Bahnsteige sind nur am südlichen Ende zugänglich. Während des Umbaus wurden Behelfsbahnsteige eingerichtet. Der Zustand vor dem Umbau mit breiteren Bahnsteigdächern ist in Bild ① zu sehen.

*Until 1972, Nieder-Eschbach was an independent municipality, but the station of the same name is today the last station within the Frankfurt city boundaries. During off-peak hours it is the terminus for every other train on line U2, and two sidings are therefore located beyond the station for reversing ④.*

*Since November 2007, the station has been equipped with 80 cm platforms ②; on the inbound platform, there is a 2.50 m deep shelter, while on the outbound side, a standard 1.75 m shelter was considered sufficient ③. The platforms are only accessible from the southern end of the station. During reconstruction, temporary platforms were erected. The station's appearance before reconstruction, when it still had wider shelters, can be seen in photo ①.*

**_ Ober-Eschbach**

Zwischen den Haltestellen Nieder-Eschbach und Ober-Eschbach liegt eine Entfernung von 2,4 km, sowie die Stadtgrenze zwischen Frankfurt und Bad Homburg. Seit 1972 gehört Ober-Eschbach zu Bad Homburg. Die Haltestelle hinterlässt derzeit leider einen sehr traurigen Eindruck ①②, eine Sanierung steht im Zuge des behindertenfreundlichen Ausbaus der Gesamtstrecke wohl bald auf dem Programm. Bislang sind die Bahnsteige nur von einem Bahnübergang am Südende der Station zugänglich.

**_ Gonzenheim**

Da ein Weiterbau zum Bad Homburger Bahnhofsvorplatz fest geplant war, errichtete man hier 1971 eine provisorische Endstelle mit nur 50 m langen und 32 cm hohen Bahnsteigen. 1975 wurde der Halt dann zur vorläufig endgültigen Endstation für 3-Wagen-Züge ausgebaut und dabei leicht nach Süden verschoben. Die Bahnsteige wurden schließlich 2004 auf 80 cm angehoben und auf 100 m verlängert ③. Zur Weiterfahrt ins Stadtzentrum von Bad Homburg muss man auf den Bus umsteigen. Immer wieder wurde eine Verlängerung vorgeschlagen, und leider auch immer wieder verhindert.

*Between the stations Nieder-Eschbach and Ober-Eschbach there is a distance of 2.4 km, the two towns being separated by the border between Frankfurt and Bad Homburg. Ober-Eschbach has been a part of Bad Homburg since 1972. The station currently leaves a sad impression ①②, and hopefully its modernisation will soon be carried out along with the upgrading of the entire line to provide full accessibility. At present, the platforms are only accessible from a level crossing located at the southern side.*

*As an extension to the Bad Homburg railway station was imminent when Stadtbahn operation began in 1971, only a temporary terminus was erected at Gonzenheim. It was only 50 m long and had 32 cm high platforms. In 1975, it was rebuilt for the use of 3-car trains and at the same time relocated slightly further south. In 2004, the platforms were finally raised to 80 cm and extended to 100 m ③. To continue into the city centre, passengers have to transfer to buses. An extension has been proposed time and again, but there has always been some reason to shelve it.*

### _ Wiesenau

Die Haltestelle wurde für die Stadtbahn leicht aus der Kurve heraus verschoben und hatte von Anfang an 100 m Bahnsteige ①. Da auf der Linie U3 ohnehin keine 4-Wagen-Züge eingesetzt werden (im Normalfall fahren nur 2-Wagen-Züge) wurde das nordwestliche Ende ② beim Umbau 1987 nicht auf 56 cm angehoben. Wenige Jahre vorher verkehrten hier noch regelmäßig Güterzüge mit breiterem Profil (▶ S. 12), weshalb die Bahnsteige nicht eher angepasst werden konnten. In den nächsten Jahren wird wohl im Zusammenhang mit dem Neubau der Strecke über den Riedberg auch diese Station modernisiert und mit 80 cm hohen Bahnsteigen ausgestattet werden.

*For Stadtbahn operation, Wiesenau station was moved slightly west away from a curve; it had 100 m platforms ① right from the start. As no 4-car trains are used on line U3 anyway (normally only 2-car trains can be seen), the northwestern ends of the platforms were fenced off ② when the rest was raised to 56 cm in 1987. Some years earlier, the route was still being shared by regular freight trains with wider carriages (▶ p. 12), so the platforms were not yet able to be raised. In the near future, the station will be rebuilt with 80 cm platforms together with the new route to Riedberg.*

### _ Niederursel

Auch hier standen der Stadtbahn von Anfang an 100 m-Bahnsteige zur Verfügung. Diese wurden 1985 renoviert und 2000 auf 80 cm erhöht ③. Unmittelbar nordwestlich der Station soll ab 2010 die Neubaustrecke zum Riedberg abzweigen. Niederursel ist letzte Station innerhalb der Frankfurter Stadtgrenzen, hier endet auch das geschlossen bebaute Gebiet.

*Niederursel station also had 100 m platforms from the start. They were refurbished in 1985 and raised to 80 cm in 2000 ③. From 2010, the new route to Riedberg will diverge immediately northwest of the station. Niederursel is the last station within the Frankfurt city boundaries, and also the last within the continuously built-up area.*

**_ Weißkirchen Ost**

Dieser Halt liegt 2,4 km von Niederursel entfernt am östlichen Rand des Oberurseler Ortsteils Weißkirchen. Zur Unterscheidung der 1,8 km weiter südwestlich gelegenen S-Bahn-Station, die heute Weißkirchen/Steinbach heißt, trägt die Stadtbahn-Station seit den siebziger Jahren den Zusatz ‚Ost'. Seit November 1986 gibt es hier 75 m lange und 56 cm hohe Bahnsteige ①. Die Stadtbahntrasse verläuft bis Bommersheim in östlicher Parallellage zur Frankfurter Landstraße, das Gebiet östlich davon wird von Getreidefeldern geprägt.

*Weißkirchen Ost station lies on the eastern edge of the Oberursel district of Weißkirchen, and some 2.4 km from Niederursel. To distinguish it from the S-Bahn station now called Weißkirchen/Steinbach, located some 1.8 km further southwest, the Stadtbahn received the appendage 'Ost' in the 1970s. In November 1986, the platforms were extended to 75 m and raised to 56 cm ①. All the way to Bommersheim the Stadtbahn continues along the eastern side of Frankfurter Landstraße, with crop fields covering the area east of the Stadtbahn alignment.*

①

**_ Bommersheim**

Während die Lokalbahn früher versetzt beiderseits der Frankfurter Landstraße hielt, wurde für die Stadtbahn weiter südöstlich am Rand der Bebauung eine neue Haltestelle eingerichtet, deren Bahnsteige ② bislang nur auf einer Länge von 50 m eine Höhe von 56 cm aufweisen. Etwa 300 m weiter nördlich befindet sich ein kleiner Betriebshof aus FLAG-Zeiten, wo nachts mehrere Züge abgestellt werden können. Nach einem Bahnübergang am Gattenhöfer Weg ③ unterquert die Stadtbahn die DB-Gleise ④, auf denen die Linie S5 nach Friedrichsdorf verkehrt.

*Whereas the former Lokalbahn at Bommersheim had staggered stops on either side of Frankfurter Landstraße, the new Stadtbahn station was built further southeast on the edge of the built-up area. The length of the 56 cm high section is limited to 50 m ②.*
*A small depot about 300 m further north, which dates from the FLAG period, is used to stable some of the trains during night-time hours. After a level crossing at Gattenhöfer Weg ③, the Stadtbahn burrows under the DB tracks ④ used by S-Bahn line S5 to Friedrichsdorf.*

②

③

④

①

## _ Oberursel Bahnhof

Die Stadtbahnhaltestelle ① liegt an der Nordseite des Bahnhofs Oberursel. Das schmucke Haltestellenhäuschen, das 1987 gelb gestrichen wurde, steht noch auf der ursprünglichen Höhe der Bahnsteige von 32 cm. Nordöstlich der Station liegen parallel zu den DB-Gleisen mehrere Abstellgleise (ehem. Güterbahnhof der Lokalbahn), außerdem besteht hier noch eine Gleisverbindung zum DB-Netz.
Am Bahnhof Oberursel beginnt der älteste von Bahnen befahrene Abschnitt der heutigen Stadtbahn, die 1899 eröffnete sog. ‚Gebirgsbahn' der Frankfurter Lokalbahn.

*The Stadtbahn station ① is located on the northern side of Oberursel railway station. The neat station pavilion, painted yellow in 1987, sits on the inbound platform with the original height of only 32 cm. Northeast of the station, there are several sidings (formerly the Lokalbahn freight station) aligned parallel to the DB tracks, including a track link to the DB network.*
*In 1899, Oberursel railway station became the departure point for the so-called 'Gebirgsbahn', the oldest railway line now incorporated into the Stadtbahn system.*

## _ Oberursel Stadtmitte

Bis 1998 hieß dieser Halt ‚Liebfrauenstraße', danach stand auf den Netzplänen nur ‚Stadtmitte', was wohl zu manchen Verwirrungen geführt hat. Seit 2000 heißt die Station nun ‚Oberursel Stadtmitte', allerdings umfährt die Stadtbahn über die Berliner Straße den eigentlichen Stadtkern.
Die Haltestelle wurde im Herbst 2005 im neuen Standarddesign umgebaut und auf 75 m verlängert ②. Entlang der Berliner Straße und anschließend entlang der Hohemarkstraße verläuft die Trasse auf eigenem Gleiskörper in westlicher Randlage bis kurz hinter Kupferhammer.

*Before 1998, this station was called 'Liebfrauenstraße'. It was then renamed 'Stadtmitte' [city centre], but in 2000, 'Oberursel' was added, although the line actually bypasses Oberursel's town centre on Berliner Straße. In autumn 2005, the station was rebuilt to the present standard and extended to 75 m ②. Along Berliner Straße and Hohemarkstraße, the Stadtbahn operates on a separate right-of-way alongside the western edge of the road up to a point just beyond Kupferhammer station.*

②

①

## _ Portstraße

Von dieser Haltestelle ② ist der alte Stadtkern von Oberursel fußläufig erreichbar. Die Unterstände wurden 1987 beige/braun gestrichen, die ganze Anlage soll demnächst umgebaut und eventuell in ‚Oberursel Altstadt' umbenannt werden.

*From Portstraße station ②, the old Oberursel town centre is just a short walk away. The shelters on the platforms were repainted in a brownish tone in 1987. The entire station is expected to be rebuilt in the near future. It will possibly be renamed 'Oberursel Altstadt'.*

## _ Lahnstraße

Diese Haltestelle ① ersetzte im Juni 1987 die früheren Haltestellen Oberstedter Straße und Motorenfabrik. Da mittlerweile der Gütertransport eingestellt worden war, konnten hier sofort 56 cm hohe und 75 m lange Bahnsteige gebaut werden.

*In June 1987, Lahnstraße station ① replaced the former stops Oberstedter Straße and Motorenfabrik. As freight traffic had already ceased by that time, the platforms were able to be built 56 cm high and 75 m long.*

## _ Glöcknerwiese

Dieser Halt ③ wurde entlang der ehemaligen Lokalbahnstrecke erst 1957 eingerichtet, nachdem in der Umgebung zahlreiche Wohnungen entstanden waren. 1987 wurde die Station nach dem Modell von Lahnstraße umgebaut.

*Glöcknerwiese station ③ was only added to the former Lokalbahn route in 1957, by which time many new homes had been built in the area. In 1987, the station was rebuilt to the standard of the neighbouring Lahnstraße station.*

②

③

①

## _ Kupferhammer

2004 wurden die früher nur 50 m langen Seitenbahnsteige (▶ S. 20) abgerissen, die Gleise auseinandergezogen und dazwischen ein Mittelbahnsteig mit einer endgültigen Höhe von 80 cm errichtet ①. Direkt westlich der Station laufen die beiden Gleise zusammen. 250 m weiter wechselt die U3 von südlicher in nördliche Seitenlage und fährt eingleisig bis zum Endpunkt. Auf dem Oberurseler Abschnitt liegen mehrere Bahnübergänge, die nur als Zufahrten zu Wohnhäusern oder Betrieben dienen, wie hier ② direkt an der Haltestelle Kupferhammer.

*In 2004, the 50 m short side platforms (▶ p. 29) were demolished, the gap between the tracks was widened, and an island platform with a definitive height of 80 cm was constructed ①. Just to the west of the station, the two tracks converge into a single-track line. Some 250 m further west, line U3 changes from its southern alignment to the northern side of the road. The single-track route continues all the way to the terminus. Some of the level crossings along the Oberursel section, like this one ② adjacent to Kupferhammer station, are only used by residents or those travelling to one of the industrial estates.*

## _ Rosengärtchen

Aufgrund der regen Bautätigkeit im oberen Bereich von Oberursel wurde am 22. Mai 1997 entlang des eingleisigen Abschnitts der Halt Rosengärtchen eingerichtet, allerdings noch mit einem nur 56 cm hohen Bahnsteig ③.

*As a result of the rapid expansion of the residential areas of upper Oberursel, the stop at Rosengärtchen was added along the single-track section on 22 May 1997. Surprisingly, it was then only built with a 56 cm high platform ③.*

②

③

## _ Waldlust

Gleich einer Überlandstraßenbahn ② verkehrt auch die Stadtbahn von Rosengärtchen bis Waldlust. Dieser Halt verfügt wie die östliche Nachbarstation über nur eine Bahnsteigkante, die sich seit 2004 jedoch bereits auf der endgültigen Höhe von 80 cm befindet ①.

*The Stadtbahn runs like an interurban tramway line ② between Rosengärtchen and Waldlust. Like its eastern neighbour, the latter stop has only one platform edge, but here it was already brought to its final height of 80 cm in 2004 ①.*

## _ Hohemark

1986 wurde die Wendeschleife (▶ S. 18/19) der ehemaligen Lokalbahnlinie 24 (ab 1978 Linie A3) zu einer Stumpfendstelle umgebaut. Im Jahr 2004 wurde die Stumpfendstelle dann nach Osten in einen Einschnitt verschoben – Bild ③ (*Foto Stephan Kyrieleis*) zeigt den provisorischen und Bild ④ den heutigen Zustand.
Anfang der siebziger Jahre gab es Vorschläge für eine Verlängerung zur Talstation einer geplanten Seilbahn auf den Großen Feldberg; heute besteht hier stündlich Busanschluss in den Taunus.

*In 1986, the terminal loop of the former Lokalbahn line 24 (since 1978 line A3) was rebuilt into a stub terminus, which was relocated further east into a cutting in 2004 – photo ③ illustrates the temporary and photo ④ the permanent station.*
*In the early 1970s, there were proposals for an extension of the line to the bottom station of a once-planned cable car to the Großer Feldberg, which can now be reached hourly by a bus service.*

**Konstablerwache** – zur B-Strecke gehören mit der Linie U4 die U-Bahn-ähnlichsten Abschnitte des Stadtbahnnetzes.
*– Line U4, the closest thing to a real metro on the Frankfurt Stadtbahn system, is part of route B.*

## _ B-Strecke

Zur B-Strecke der Frankfurter Stadtbahn gehören die Linien U4 und U5, die sich wesentlich voneinander unterscheiden. Während die U4 lange Zeit vollkommen unterirdisch mit 75 m langen und 2,65 m breiten Fahrzeugen quasi als richtige U-Bahn verkehrte, ähnelt die U5 bis heute eher einer Straßenbahn, die den U-Bahn-Tunnel mitbenutzt. Sie wird mit nur 2,35 m breiten Wagen maximal in Doppeltraktion (50 m) betrieben. Direkt nördlich der Tunnelausfahrt zwischen Konstablerwache und Musterschule schließt ein straßenbündiger Abschnitt an, der mit kurzen Unterbrechungen bis zur Kreuzung Marbachweg/Eckenheimer Landstraße reicht. Ab hier steht auch der U5 ein eigener Gleiskörper, jedoch keine Hochbahnsteige zur Verfügung.

Der Takt auf der U4 zwischen Bockenheimer Warte und Seckbacher Landstraße ist je nach Tageszeit sehr unterschiedlich: Montag bis Freitag von 4:00 bis 5:30 Uhr und von 23:00 bis 1:00 Uhr alle 20 Minuten, von 5:30 bis 6:30 Uhr und von 19:30 bis 20:30 Uhr alle 10 Minuten, in den Hauptverkehrszeiten zwischen 7:00 und 9:30 Uhr sowie zwischen 15:45 und 19:30 Uhr alle fünf Minuten und dazwischen alle 7/8 Minuten. Samstags fahren die Bahnen der U4 tagsüber im 7/8-Minuten-Takt, sonntags ab 8 Uhr alle 10 Minuten. Das Zugangebot auf der U5 ist dem der U4 ähnlich, so dass in den Hauptverkehrzeiten auf dem Abschnitt Hauptbahnhof – Konstablerwache alle 2½ Minuten eine Bahn verkehrt. Seit dem Fahrplanwechsel am 15. Juni 2008 fahren manche Züge der U4 über die Gleise des Betriebshofs Ost bis zur Haltestelle Schäfflestraße an der Strecke der U7 im Stadtteil Riederwald, und zwar tagsüber alle 15 Minuten und in den Tagesrandzeiten alle 20 Minuten. Dabei handelt es sich um einen Probebetrieb, der vorerst ein halbes Jahr dauern soll.

## _ *Route B*

*Route B of the Frankfurt Stadtbahn comprises lines U4 and U5, which are quite different from each other: while for a long time line U4 operated like a real metro line, completely underground and with 75 m long and 2.65 m wide trains, line U5 resembles a tramway line which shares the U4 tunnel. Its trains are just 2.35 m wide, and can only run with a maximum of two vehicles coupled. Just north of the tunnel portal, which lies between Konstablerwache and Musterschule, the alignment changes to on-street running, which, with some interruptions, continues all the way to the intersection at Marbachweg/Eckenheimer Landstraße. From there to the terminus, a Stadtbahn-like right-of-way is available, although without high-level platforms.*

*The headways on line U4 between Bockenheimer Warte and Seckbacher Landstraße depend on the time of the day: Monday to Friday from 04:00 to 05:30 and from 23:00 to 01:00 every 20 minutes; from 05:30 to 06:30 and from 19:30 to 20:30 every 10 minutes; during peak hours between 07:00 and 09:30 as well as between 15:45 and 19:30 every five minutes; and every 7/8 minutes at other times. On Saturdays,*

12,2 km (ca. 6,9 km unterirdisch | *underground*), 22 Haltestellen | *stations* *

| | |
|---|---|
| 26-05-1974 | Gießener Straße – Konstablerwache – Willy-Brandt-Platz |
| 06-03-1977 | Gießener Straße – Preungesheim |
| 28-05-1978 | Willy-Brandt-Platz – Hauptbahnhof |
| 31-05-1980 | Konstablerwache – Bornheim/Seckbacher Landstraße |
| 10-02-2001 | Hauptbahnhof – Bockenheimer Warte |
| 15-06-2008 | Seckbacher Landstraße – Riederwald/Schäfflestraße (prov. \| *temp.*) |

* ohne Verlängerung bis Riederwald | *without Riederwald extension*

**Glauburgstraße** > **Deutsche Nationalbibliothek** – zur B-Strecke gehören mit der Linie U5 auch die straßenbahnähnlichsten Abschnitte des U-Bahn-Netzes.
*– With line U5, route B also includes the most tram-like sections of the U-Bahn system.*

## _ Geschichte der B-Strecke

Der Baubeginn an Frankfurts zweiter Stammstrecke war im Juni 1966, also mehr als zwei Jahre vor Inbetriebnahme des ersten Stadtbahntunnels entlang der A-Strecke. Wenige Monate später kam es aus finanziellen Gründen jedoch bereits zu einem mehrmonatigen Baustopp.

Nachdem die verschiedenen Trassenvarianten durch die Innenstadt gegeneinander abgewogen worden waren, wählte man statt der offensichtlicheren entlang der breiten Berliner Straße eine südlichere, die teilweise unter der Bebauung rund um den Römerberg verlief. Deshalb musste zwischen der Station Dom/Römer und der Kurt-Schumacher-Straße für den Bau von eingleisigen Röhren der teilmechanisierte Schildvortrieb angewandt werden, was wegen der stark wechselnden Bodenschichten eine besondere Herausforderung darstellte. Der Dom musste mit Hilfe einer Bohrpfahlwand abgesichert werden. Noch vor Baubeginn war im Januar 1966 die Entscheidung gefallen, den von Anfang an vorgesehenen Abzweig vom Römer Richtung Ostbahnhof aus Kostengründen zu streichen. Zum selben Zeitpunkt wurde auch die Konzeption des Umsteigepunkts am Theaterplatz (heute Willy-Brandt-Platz) verändert. Hier sollte ursprünglich ein 4-gleisiger Bahnhof auf zwei Ebenen gebaut werden, die von den Zügen der A- und B-Strecke im Richtungsbetrieb angefahren werden sollten, wodurch auch verschiedene Linienführungen zwischen den beiden Stammstrecken möglich gewesen wären. Nun entschied man sich aber zugunsten eines Kreuzungsbahnhofs im Linienbetrieb, die A-Strecke oben und die B-Strecke eine Ebene tiefer. An der Konstablerwache wurde, anders als einige Jahre zuvor beim Bau der A-Strecke an der Hauptwache, der Stationsteil für die C-Strecke bzw. die S-Bahn nur im Bereich des Bahnsteigs der B-Strecke miterrichtet. Dieser U-Bahnhof entstand gemeinsam mit einem Häuserdurchbruch zur Schaffung des heutigen breiten Straßenzugs Kurt-Schumacher-Straße/Konrad-Adenauer-Straße. Im Stationsbereich sowie beim nördlich anschließenden Streckentunnel konnte deshalb die offene Bauweise angewandt werden.

Aufgrund der Schwierigkeiten beim Schildvortrieb zwischen Römer und Konstablerwache wählte man schließlich für den Abschnitt westlich der Station Dom/Römer die NÖT (Neue Österreichische Tunnelbauweise bzw. Spritzbetonbauweise) für die ebenso eingleisigen Streckentunnel. Diese Methode bewährte sich im Frankfurter Boden und wurde fortan die Standardbauweise, wenn berg-

*line U4 operates every 7/8 minutes during daytime hours, and on Sundays after 08:00, every 10 minutes. The U5 timetable is quite similar to that of line U4, so that during peak hours there is a train every 2½ minutes between Hauptbahnhof and Konstablerwache. Since 15 June 2008, some U4 trains have been extended from Seckbacher Landstraße to Schäfflestraße on line U7 by taking advantage of the access tracks to the eastern depot (Betriebshof Ost). During the daytime, this extension is served every 15 minutes, and in the mornings and evenings, every 20 minutes. This trial service is initially planned to last six months.*

## _ *The History of Route B*

*The construction of Frankfurt's second trunk route started in June 1966, i.e. two years before route A was brought into service. A few months later, however, construction activities came to a halt for several months due to funding problems.*

*For the alignment through the city centre, several alternatives had been examined, and in the end it was not the most obvious route along the wide Berliner Straße that was chosen, but a more southerly alignment running partly below buildings in the area of the historical centre at Römerberg. The section between Dom/Römer station and Kurt-Schumacher-Straße was therefore built as single tube tunnels with a partly-mechanised shield, the ever-changing layers of earth making this a complicated task. The cathedral [Dom] had to be supported by means of bored pile walls. Even before construction started, a decision had been taken in January 1966 not to build the branch initially planned from Römer to Ostbahnhof. At the same time, the interchange layout at Theaterplatz (now Willy-Brandt-Platz) was modified. The original plan was to create a two-level station, with routes A and B sharing the same island platform, but stopping on opposite sides to allow cross-platform interchange. The new layout included a separate station for each route on different levels, with route A on the upper and route B on the lower level.*

*Unlike at Hauptwache a few years earlier, at Konstablerwache only those parts were built for the future route C and the S-Bahn which lie directly below the U4/U5 station. Konstablerwache station, as well as the adjacent tunnel north of it, was built by cut-and-cover in conjunction with a major new thoroughfare along Kurt-Schumacher-Straße and Konrad-Adenauer-Straße.*

*After the complications encountered on the section between Römer and Konstablerwache, the single-track tunnels west of Dom/Römer were excavated using the NATM (New Austrian Tunnelling Method or shotcrete method). This method was ideal for Frankfurt's ground conditions, and became the standard construction method for subterranean excavations (the stations would still be built by cut-and-cover where possible).*

*With the experience gained in daily service on route A, the plans for route B were once again modified. Instead of a mixed service with conventional tram vehicles and modern Stadtbahn cars, the new route was initially only meant to be*

männisch gebaut werden sollte (im Bereich der Bahnhöfe war auch weiterhin die offene Bauweise die Regel).

Nach den ersten Erfahrungen im Alltagsbetrieb auf der im Oktober 1968 eröffneten A-Strecke wurden die Planungen für die B-Strecke abermals abgeändert. Statt eines Mischbetriebs von Stadtbahn- und herkömmlichen Straßenbahnfahrzeugen sollte in einer ersten Phase reiner Vorlaufbetrieb mit den schmaleren Straßenbahnfahrzeugen stattfinden, der dann nach Vollendung der Tunnelstrecke nach Bornheim von einem reinen U-Bahn-Betrieb abgelöst werden sollte. Aus diesem Grund wurde auch auf die zweite Rampe nördlich der Konstablerwache sowie auf die Rampe westlich des Theaterplatzes in der Gutleutstraße verzichtet und stattdessen eine provisorische Wendeanlage eingerichtet. Für den Vorlaufbetrieb mussten allerdings auch neue Fahrzeuge angeschafft werden, da bislang keine geeigneten 2-Richtungs-Wagen vorhanden waren. Die Bahnsteige wurden von Anfang an mit der 1967 festgelegten Standardhöhe von 87 cm gebaut, jedoch wurde für die nur 2,35 m breiten Pt-Wagen an die endgültige Bahnsteigkante eine Verbreiterung von 15 cm angeschraubt, wie es später auch auf der C-Strecke geschah. Der zentrale Abschnitt der B-Strecke zwischen Konstablerwache und Theaterplatz (heute Willy-Brandt-Platz) wurde am 26. Mai 1974 in Betrieb genommen und von der Linie B1, die aus der ehemaligen Straßenbahnlinie 7 hervorgegangen war und bis zur Gießener Straße führte, bedient. Die nördliche Endhaltestelle lag zwischen den heutigen Haltestellen Gießener Straße (die damals den Zusatz Marbachweg trug) und Theobald-Ziegler-Straße. Die Linie B1 wurde am 6. März 1977 entlang der Gießener Straße auf eigenem Gleiskörper bis Preungesheim verlängert, wobei die 1974 errichtete Endstation entfiel. Da der Stationsabstand bis zur Ronneburgstraße nun aber mit rund 800 m zu lang war, wurde im Dezember 1981 eine Haltestelle an der Theobald-Ziegler-Straße eingerichtet. Der oberirdische Teil der U5 verfügt bis heute über keine Hochbahnsteige, so dass hier nur Fahrzeuge mit Klapptrittstufen eingesetzt werden können.

Der Tunnelbau war inzwischen in westliche Richtung bis zum Hauptbahnhof fortgesetzt worden. Dort entstand unter der Regie der *Deutschen Bundesbahn* gemeinsam mit dem viergleisigen S-Bahnhof auch ein viergleisiger U-Bahnhof, da sich hier eines Tages die B-Strecke mit der D-Strecke treffen sollte. Auch zwischen Theaterplatz und Hauptbahnhof waren einige Häuser zu unterfahren, wofür zum Bau von zwei jeweils 350 m langen Röhren wieder die NÖT angewandt wurde. Nördlich der Station Hauptbahnhof wurde der Tunnel in offener Bauweise in der Düsseldorfer Straße bis zum Platz der Republik verlängert, wo eine spätere Verzweigung der B-Strecke bzw. die Trennung von B- und D-Strecke vorgesehen war. Vorerst sollte dieses Bauwerk als Abstell- und Kehranlage dienen. Als die Linie B1 schließlich im Mai 1978 rechtzeitig zur Inbetriebnahme der S-Bahn Rhein-Main zum Hauptbahnhof verlängert wurde, bekam

**Dom/Römer** – Eingang vor dem Dom (*Foto Fritz D. Kegel, 1979*)
*– entrance in front of the cathedral*

*operated with tram vehicles, but as soon as the extension to Bornheim had been completed, route B was to become a real metro line. For this reason, the second ramp previously planned north of Konstablerwache, as well as the ramp west of Theaterplatz on Gutleutstraße, was cancelled, and a temporary reversing facility built instead. For the temporary tram operation through the B tunnel, new vehicles had to be ordered, as the existing fleet did not include any adequate bidirectional vehicles. The platforms were built to the 1967 standard of 87 cm above the rail top, but as the new Pt-cars were only 2.35 m wide, the platform edges had to be fitted with 15 cm extensions, as was done later on route C. The central section of route B between Konstablerwache and Theaterplatz (now Willy-Brandt-Platz) was opened on 26 May 1974, and introduced line B1, the successor of the old tram line 7. The northern terminus of line B1 lay between the present stops at Gießener Straße (which then carried the appendage Marbachweg) and Theobald-Ziegler-Straße. On 6 March 1977, line B1 was extended on a separate right-of-way along Gießener Straße to its present terminus at Preungesheim, while the 1974 terminus was closed. The resulting distance of 800 m between Gießener Straße and Ronneburgstraße was then considered too long, and eventually an intermediate stop at Theobald-Ziegler-Straße was opened in December 1981. The surface section of line U5 still lacks high platforms, so vehicles with folding steps have to be used.*

**Theaterplatz** (heute Willy-Brandt-Platz)
– von 1974 bis 1978 Endstation der Linie B1 *(Foto Stadtbahnbauamt/VGF)*
*– from 1974 until 1978, the terminus of line B1*

**Preungesheim** – seit 1977 Endstelle der Linie U5, damals mit ‚Pt'-Wagen ohne Verbreiterungen (*Foto Fritz D. Kegel, 1979*)
*– since 1977, the terminus of line U5, then operated with 'Pt' cars still without the side bulges*

sie gleichzeitig mit den Umbenennungen auf der A-Strecke die Bezeichnung U5.

Von Anfang an war geplant, die B-Strecke vom Hauptbahnhof entlang der Mainzer Landstraße weiter nach Westen zu führen. Nach einer Rampe im Bereich Güterplatz sollte die Bahn ähnlich wie in der Eschersheimer Landstraße (A-Strecke) ebenerdig verlaufen. Nach der schlechten Akzeptanz einer derartigen Streckenführung wegen ihrer starken Trennwirkung wurde dieses Vorhaben vorerst zurückgestellt, außerdem wurden die westlichen Stadtteile später auch durch die S-Bahn schnellbahnmäßig angeschlossen. In den frühen achtziger Jahren tauchte eine Verlängerung der B-Strecke wieder auf, nun mit einer 3,6 km langen Tunnelstrecke bis zur Mönchhofstraße, denn ab dort stand bereits der Straßenbahn ein eigener Gleiskörper mit Ampelvorrangschaltung zur Verfügung. Konkrete Planungen sahen unterirdische Stationen am Güterplatz, östlich des S-Bahnhofs Galluswarte, an der Schwalbacher Straße, an der Rebstöcker Straße und schließlich an der Mönchhofstraße vor. Die oberirdischen Haltestellen Waldschulstraße, Linnegraben und Jägerallee wurden bereits 1983-85 im Hinblick auf den späteren Stadtbahnbetrieb umgebaut. Zwischen Jägerallee und Birminghamstraße entstand sogar eine Überführung, um eine Schnellstraße kreuzungsfrei in die Mainzer Landstraße einzufädeln. Die darauffolgende Strecke zwischen Nied und Höchst müsste erst für den Stadtbahnbetrieb ausgebaut werden. Da mit der Straßenbahnlinie 11 heute auch wieder eine direkte Verbindung in die Innenstadt angeboten wird, sind die Planungen einer Stadtbahnverlängerung bis auf Weiteres nicht mehr aktuell.

Im Nordosten der Stadt wurde in den sechziger Jahren auf dem freien Gelände zwischen Seckbach, Preungesheim und Bad Vilbel ein neuer Stadtteil für bis zu 100.000 Einwohner geplant. Dieser sollte durch einen Ast der Stadtbahn-Strecke B

*Tunnel construction had meanwhile continued westwards to the city's main railway station. At Hauptbahnhof, the 'Deutsche Bundesbahn' built a 4-track S-Bahn station together with a 4-track underground station for the Stadtbahn – routes B and D were to intersect at this point in the future. Between Willy-Brandt-Platz and Hauptbahnhof, the single-track tunnels pass under several buildings, so for a 350 m section of both tubes the NATM had to be used. North of Hauptbahnhof, a cut-and-cover tunnel continues along Düsseldorfer Straße to Platz der Republik; it was designed to accommodate the future junction for routes B and D, but in the meantime it was to function as a reversing and stabling facility. When line B1 was extended to Hauptbahnhof in May 1978 – in time for the inauguration of the S-Bahn system – it was renamed U5, in line with the changes in line designations on route A.*

*Beyond Hauptbahnhof, an underground extension west along Mainzer Straße had been planned from the start. After a ramp at Güterplatz, the route was to continue on an alignment like that on route A along Eschersheimer Landstraße. Due to the negative reception of that section, which was perceived as a physical barrier between neighbourhoods, the western extension was temporarily shelved. Meanwhile, the western districts had also been linked by the S-Bahn. During the early 1980s, the western extension re-appeared in the plans, now with a 3.6 km tunnel all the way to Mönchhofstraße, from where a separate right-of-way with priority at traffic lights had already been built for the tram. Detailed plans included five underground stations: one at Güterplatz, one east of Galluswarte S-Bahn station, and the others at Schwalbacher Straße, Rebstöcker Straße and Mönchhofstraße. The surface stops at Waldschulstraße, Linnegraben and Jägerallee had already been upgraded between 1983 and 1985, making them suitable for future Stadtbahn operation.*

an die Innenstadt angeschlossen werden. Über einen Abzweig sollte auch der erst 1977 eingemeindete Stadtteil Bergen erreicht werden. Für den ersten ca. 3 km langen Abschnitt (Linie B2) dachte man anfangs an eine etwas nördlicher verlaufende Trassierung entlang der Günthersburgallee oder Burgstraße, jedoch 1968 beschloss man, die Tunnelstrecke entlang der zentralen Achse des Stadtteils Bornheim, nämlich der Berger Straße zu bauen. Da die erwähnten Wohnbauprojekte jedoch noch keine konkreten Formen angenommen hatten, sollte die Stadtbahn vorerst an der Seckbacher Landstraße enden. Auf den Bau der Nordoststadt wurde schließlich verzichtet, und auch einer Verlängerung der Stadtbahn nach Bergen wurde später nie die nötige Priorität eingeräumt. Heute wird eventuell eine kurze Neubaustrecke bis Atzelberg für möglich gehalten.

Bis auf die Stationen und den Anschluss an den Tunnelstutzen nördlich von Konstablerwache wurde die Bornheimer U-Bahn ab Sommer 1971 bergmännisch per NÖT aufgefahren, wobei die beiden eingleisigen Streckentunnel wegen der Enge der Berger Straße in übereinanderliegenden Röhren aufgefahren wurden, zuerst die untere Röhre und anschließend direkt darüber die obere. Ursprünglich hatte man für diesen Abschnitt die offene Bauweise vorgesehen, aber die bisherigen positiven Erfahrungen mit der NÖT veranlassten die Ingenieure zu einer Planungsänderung, da so die Beeinträchtigungen an der Oberfläche reduziert werden konnten. Durch die Doppelstockbauweise konnten großzügige U-Bahnhöfe mit drei Ebenen errichtet werden. Auf der Ebene -2 halten die Züge stadtauswärts und auf der Ebene -3 stadteinwärts. In dieser Konzeption ähneln sich die Stationen Merianplatz, Höhenstraße

**Jägerallee** – stadtbahnmäßig ausgebauter Abschnitt
– *Stadtbahn-style section* (*Foto Stephan Kyrieleis, 05/1991*)

**Jägerallee** > **Birminghamstraße** – schnellbahnartiges Überwerfungsbauwerk
– *metro-like flyover*

*Between Jägerallee and Birminghamstraße, a viaduct had even been built to provide for a grade-separated road linking Mainzer Landstraße to a dual carriageway. The tram route between Nied and Höchst would still need to be upgraded before being used by Stadtbahn trains. As the present tram line 11 provides a direct link into the city centre, a western extension of route B is currently not considered a priority.*

*In the northeast of the city, in the area between Seckbach, Preungesheim and Bad Vilbel, a new district for some 100,000 people was planned during the 1960s. This area was to be served by a branch off route B, while another branch was to link Bergen, a district only annexed by Frankfurt in 1977. The alignment of the first 3 km section starting at Konstablerwache was initially meant to run further north along Günthersburgallee or Burgstraße, but in 1968 its definitive route along Berger Straße, the main street in the district of Bornheim, was chosen. As the aforementioned housing schemes had not made any progress, a temporary terminus for the Stadtbahn was fixed at Seckbacher Landstraße. The 'Nordoststadt' project was eventually cancelled, and a Stadtbahn extension to Bergen never gained the necessary priority either; present plans include a possible 1-stop extension to Atzelberg.*

*From summer 1971, the NATM was used to construct the underground route through Bornheim, except for the stations and the section that linked with the existing tunnel stub at Konstablerwache; due to the narrow Berger Straße, the two running tunnels were built on top of each other, with the lower tube being excavated first, and the upper one immediately afterwards. The cut-and-cover method had initially been envisaged for this route, but after the successful implementation of the NATM on other sections, it was applied here, reducing the impact of the construction work on the surface. The double-deck tunnels allowed for the construction of spacious 3-level stations, with outbound trains stopping on level -2, and inbound on level -3. The basic layout of Merianplatz, Höhenstraße and Bornheim Mitte stations is thus quite similar, although there are differences in both the colour schemes and the locations of the exits. Northeast of Bornheim Mitte station, the two tubes become aligned parallel to each other before reaching the terminus at Seckbacher Landstraße in a long left-hand bend. The terminus has an island platform, allowing trains to reverse there, although beyond the station there are four sidings. Two of these sidings were meant to be used as running tracks for a future extension to Seckbach and Bergen. At the same time, a grade-separated junction was built to access the maintenance yard at Sausee, which*

und Bornheim Mitte, sie unterscheiden sich allerdings in der Anordnung der Zugänge und in der farblichen Ausgestaltung. Nordöstlich der Station Bornheim Mitte kommen die beiden Tunnelröhren in Parallellage und erreichen nach einer langen Linkskurve die Endstation Seckbacher Landstraße, die mit einem Mittelbahnsteig ausgestattet wurde, so dass direkt am Bahnsteig gewendet werden kann, auch wenn hinter der Station eine viergleisige Kehranlage eingerichtet wurde. Zwei dieser Gleise sind für eine spätere Verlängerung nach Seckbach bzw. Bergen vorgesehen. Gleichzeitig entstand ein kreuzungsfreier Abzweig zum damals bereits geplanten Betriebshof Ost (Sausee) bis zum Tunnelmund jenseits der heutigen Autobahn A661. Der Betriebshof konnte erst 2003 in Betrieb genommen werden, und seit Juni 2008 findet auf diesem Abschnitt auch probeweise Linienbetrieb statt, indem die Züge der U4 über das Betriebshofgelände bis Schäfflestraße an der U7 durchgebunden werden.

Mit Vollendung der Bornheimer U-Bahn wurde am 31. Mai 1980 die Linie U4 zwischen Hauptbahnhof und Seckbacher Landstraße eingerichtet. Gleichzeitig wurde die U5 zur Konstablerwache zurückgenommen, da die U4 mit 2,65 m breiten Fahrzeugen des neuen Typs ‚U3' betrieben wurde und die 1974 angebrachten Bahnsteigverbreiterungen nun abmontiert waren. Die U5 endete aus Preungesheim kommend fortan am westlichsten Gleis des dreigleisigen U-Bahnhofs Konstablerwache. Mit der U4 hatte Frankfurt nun eine richtige U-Bahn-Linie, die völlig kreuzungsfrei und unabhängig von Straßenbahnlinien zwischen Hauptbahnhof und Seckbacher Landstraße verkehrte. Allerdings wurde auch diese Strecke über Oberleitung mit Strom versorgt und nicht über seitliche Stromschiene, wie es lange Zeit in Deutschland von einer U-Bahn erwartet wurde.

Nach 1980 blieb die B-Strecke lange unverändert, da der Bau der C-Strecke und die Verlängerung der A-Strecke nach Sachsenhausen Vorrang hatten.

Die 1,8 km lange Verlängerung der Linie U4 vom Hauptbahnhof zur Bockenheimer Warte wurde bereits im März 1989 in Angriff genommen, doch verzögerten sich die Bauarbeiten immer wieder, so dass dieser Abschnitt erst am 10. Februar 2001 in Betrieb gehen konnte. Bei Baubeginn stieß man im Bereich der Messe auf Boden- und Grundwasserkontaminationen, die vermutlich aus einer Druckfarbenfabrik stammten, die sich im 19. Jahrhundert an dieser Stelle befand. Später mussten die Rohbauarbeiten neu ausgeschrieben werden, nachdem ein Bauunternehmen als Folge der Verzögerungen ausgestiegen war. Der als DI bezeichnete Abschnitt gehört planerisch zur D-Strecke, die Mitte der siebziger Jahre als Verbindung von Niederrad am Südufer des Mains über Hauptbahnhof, Messe, Ginnheim, Nordweststadt und Riedberg bis Kalbach entworfen wurde. Da die Planungen für eine zweite unterirdische Mainquerung heute nicht mehr verfolgt werden, wird dieser Abschnitt auf unbestimmte Zeit Teil der B-Strecke bleiben. Durch diese Verlängerung wurde das Frankfurter Messegelände an das Stadtbahnnetz angeschlossen, außerdem entstand so eine weitere Umsteigemöglichkeit zu den Linien der C-Strecke (U6, U7). Während die beiden U-Bahnhöfe und die nördlich an den Endbahnhof Bockenheimer Warte anschließende viergleisige Kehranlage in offener Bauweise errichtet wurden, baute man die eingleisigen Streckentunnel trotz der Breite der zu unterfahrenden Straßen wiederum per NÖT. Zwischen Neubaustrecke und C-Strecke wurde eine Gleisverbindung geschaffen. Nördlich des Bahnhofs Festhalle/Messe wurde baulich die Möglichkeit eines späteren Abzweigs Richtung Westen offen gelassen, allerdings wird nun das Gebiet Rebstock seit 2003 von einer Straßenbahn-Neubaustrecke erschlossen.

Am 14. Oktober 2004 beschloss die Stadtverordnetenversammlung die verkehrstechnische Erschließung des Neubaugebiets Riedberg, was die 2,4 km lange DII-Strecke, d.h. den

*had already been planned; the tunnel mouth is located at the eastern side of motorway A661. The maintenance yard was only brought into service in 2003, and since June 2008, the access tracks have been used on a trial basis by scheduled U4 trains, which now run across the depot area to terminate at Schäfflestraße, an existing stop on line U7.*

*With the completion of the underground route through Bornheim on 31 May 1980, a new line called the U4 was introduced between Hauptbahnhof and Seckbacher Landstraße, while line U5 was curtailed at Konstablerwache. Line U4 was operated with new rolling stock of class 'U3', which is 2.65 m wide; the platform side extensions added in 1974 thus had to be removed. Line U5 from Preungesheim now terminated at the westernmost track at Konstablerwache. Line U4 thus became Frankfurt's first real metro line, as it was totally grade-separated and segregated from any tram-like lines; but it was also operated with an overhead instead of a third rail power supply, as had long been expected from an 'U-Bahn' in Germany.*

*After 1980, route B remained unchanged for a long period, as the construction of route C and the southern extension of route A to Sachsenhausen were given priority.*

*Construction on a 1.8 km U4 extension from Hauptbahnhof to Bockenheimer Warte started in March 1989, but due to a series of problems, it did not open until 10 February 2001. In the area of the present fairgrounds, contaminated groundwater and soil was encountered, possibly the residue of a paint factory which stood on this terrain during the 19th century. Later, new construction contracts had to be awarded after one of the contractors withdrew due to the long delays caused by the cleaning which had become necessary. The section referred to as DI is part of route D, which was added to the master plan in the mid-1970s, meant to run from the south bank of the Main River via Hauptbahnhof, Messe, Ginnheim, Nordweststadt and Riedberg to Kalbach. As plans for a second river crossing are no longer being pursued, this section will remain incorporated into route B for the time being. With this extension, the Frankfurt exhibition centre [Messe] was linked by the Stadtbahn, while a second interchange between route B and route C (U6, U7) was created. The two stations, as well as the tunnel with four sidings beyond Bockenheimer Warte, were built by cut-and-cover, but the running tunnels between the stations were once again excavated using the NATM, despite the large width of the roads the tunnels follow. Between the new section and route C, a track link was established. At the northern end of Festhalle/Messe station, provisions were made for a future*

**Bockenheimer Warte** – seit 2001 Endstation der Linie U4
*– since 2001, line U4's terminus*

Lückenschluss zwischen Bockenheimer Warte und Ginnheim mit den U-Bahnhöfen Franz-Rücker-Allee und Ginnheim einschloss. Über die bestehende U1-Strecke sollte die U4 dann von Ginnheim zum Nordwestzentrum und von dort weiter über den Riedberg und Kalbach nach Nieder-Eschbach fahren. Gleichzeitig sollte die Linie U1 vom Nordwestzentrum als Linie U8 auf der Strecke der U4 ins Stadtzentrum durchgebunden werden. Die derzeitige Straßenbahnlinie 16 wäre dadurch auf diesem Abschnitt entfallen, was wegen der größeren Stationsabstände bei der Stadtbahn heftige Proteste der örtlichen Bevölkerung weckte. Die Tunnelröhren sollten bergmännisch aufgefahren werden, die Stationen jedoch in offener Bauweise entstehen. Der Baubeginn war für Mitte 2007 vorgesehen, die Inbetriebnahme für 2013. Mitte 2006 wurden diese Planungen jedoch von der aktuellen Stadtregierung auf Eis gelegt, und die oberirdische Strecke über den Riedberg soll nun stattdessen an die A-Strecke angeschlossen werden (▶ S. 22/23).

Als die Linie U5 mit Inbetriebnahme der U4 im Jahr 1980 zur Konstablerwache zurückgezogen wurde, gab es bereits starke Proteste, da man nun von Preungesheim, Eckenheim und dem Nordend nur noch mit Umsteigen zum Hauptbahnhof kommen konnte. Ab 1983 stand dafür neben der U4, die in Richtung Hauptbahnhof am selben Bahnsteig gegenüber fährt, allerdings auch die S-Bahn zur Verfügung. Obwohl eine Verbreiterung der Wagen schon damals vorgeschlagen wurde, war diese Option anfangs wegen des zu geringen Gleisabstands auf den oberirdischen Strecken der U5 noch nicht möglich. Da der Druck aus der Bevölkerung anhielt, wurden allmählich die notwendigen Anpassungen an den Gleistrassen vorgenommen und die ‚Pt'-Wagen um 11,5 cm im Türbereich verbreitert, so dass die U5 ab 1998 wieder bis zum Hauptbahnhof durchgebunden werden konnte.

Die Zukunft der Linie U5 ist trotzdem ungewiss. Ursprünglich sollte die 1974 in Betrieb genommene Rampe am Scheffeleck nur provisorischen Charakter haben, der Tunnel sollte unter der engen Eckenheimer Landstraße mindestens bis zum Alleenring, d.h. etwa bis zur Haltestelle Deutsche Nationalbibliothek, verlängert werden. Um auch diese Linie behindertengerecht auszubauen, werden derzeit verschiedene Möglichkeiten diskutiert:

1) Tunnelverlängerung bis zum Marbachweg und Hochbahnsteige entlang der sonst stadtbahnmäßigen Strecke nach Preungesheim;
2) Hochbahnsteige entlang der bestehenden Strecke, also im Fall der Haltestellen Musterschule und Glauburgstraße im Straßenraum;
3) Umstellung der gesamten Strecke auf Niederflurstraßen-

*western branch, but this is now very unlikely as the Rebstock area has been served by a new tram line since 2003.*

*On 14 October 2004, the city council approved the transport scheme for the new development on the Riedberg, including the 2.4 km DII section between Bockenheimer Warte and Ginnheim, with two new underground stations at Franz-Rücker-Allee and Ginnheim. Over the existing U1 route, U4 trains were to continue to Nordwestzentrum and from there via Riedberg and Kalbach to Nieder-Eschbach. At the same time, line U1 was to be extended as line U8 from Nordwestzentrum into the city centre. As this would have meant abandoning the present tram line 16 on this section, there were heavy protests from the local population due to the longer distances between stations on the planned Stadtbahn compared to the tram. The running tunnels were to be built using the NATM, while the stations were to be excavated by cut-and-cover. Construction was scheduled to start in mid-2007 for completion in 2013. In mid-2006, however, this project was shelved by a newly-elected city government, and the surface extension to Riedberg will instead be linked to route A (▶ p. 22/23).*

*There had already been heavy protests when line U5 was cut back to Konstablerwache with the opening of line U4 in 1980, as the city's main railway station was now only accessible from Preungesheim, Eckenheim and Nordend by changing to line U4, which in the direction of Hauptbahnhof was possible across the platform; since 1983, the S-Bahn has been an additional option to get to the railway station. The widening of the cars had already been proposed then, but due to the narrow gap between tracks on some sections on the surface, this was not possible at the time. With pressure from passengers continuing, the necessary track modifications were made, and the 'Pt'-cars were fitted with 11.5 cm wide extensions in the door areas, allowing U5 trains to finally return to Hauptbahnhof in 1998. But the future of line U5 is still uncertain. When the ramp at Scheffeleck opened in 1974, it was to be a temporary solution, and the tunnel was to be extended at least as far as the so-called Alleenring, i.e. up to the present stop at Deutsche Nationalbibliothek. In order to make this line fully accessible too, various options are being discussed:*

*1) a tunnel extension up to Marbachweg, and high platforms along the surface route to Preungesheim, where a separate right-of-way is available;*
*2) high platforms at all stops along the existing line, even at Musterschule and Glauburgstraße, where the tracks are embedded in the roadway;*

**Schäfflestraße** – Wagen vom Typ ‚U3' (links) auf dem Kehrgleis
*– class 'U3' car (left) on the reversing siding*

**Schäfflestraße** – Linie U4 bei der Ausfahrt aus dem Betriebshofgelände
*– line U4 leaving the depot area*

**Schäfflestraße** – probeweise endet seit Juni 2008 jeder zweite Zug der Linie U4 an der Haltestelle Schäfflestraße im Stadtteil Riederwald.
*– on a trial basis, every other train on line U4 now terminates at Schäfflestraße in the Riederwald neighbourhood.*

bahnbetrieb mit unterirdischer Endstelle im U-Bahnhof Konstablerwache;

4) wie 3) jedoch oberirdische Einbindung in das Straßenbahnnetz, z.B. durch Fortführung bis zum Zoo.

Gegen die Variante 1) sprechen vor allem die hohen Kosten, gegen die Variante 2) städtebauliche Aspekte sowie Sicherheitsfragen, da die beiden umstrittenen Haltestellen starken Schülerverkehr aufweisen und Hochbahnsteige direkt zwischen den Fahrbahnen eine erhöhte Gefahr darstellen. Die Variante 3) würde die unbefriedigende Situation des gebrochenen Verkehrs der U5 zwischen 1980 und 1998 wiederherstellen. Gegen eine Umstellung auf Niederflurstraßenbahn wird trotz vorgesehener Doppeltraktionen mit der unzureichenden Kapazität im Vergleich zur Stadtbahn argumentiert. Allerdings könnte die Nachfrage mit Inbetriebnahme der neuen Straßenbahnstrecke nach Preungesheim Ost, die derzeit im Bau ist, sinken. Gleichzeitig ist seit Langem eine Verlängerung von Preungesheim bis zum Frankfurter Berg (1,6 km) vorgesehen.

Im Westen ist ein Abzweig der B-Strecke ins Europaviertel geplant. Dieses Neubaugebiet entsteht auf dem Gelände des ehemaligen Güterbahnhofs südlich des Messegeländes. Unklar ist weiterhin, ob die Stadtbahn hier oberirdisch oder unter der Erde verkehren soll. Zur Ausfädelung aus der bestehenden Strecke kann die Anlage nördlich des Hauptbahnhofs genutzt werden. In jedem Fall würde im Bereich des Güterplatzes ein unterirdischer Bahnhof entstehen, daran anschließend könnte die Bahn an die Oberfläche kommen oder entlang der Europaallee unterirdisch weiterfahren. Bei der Anlage dieses neuen Straßenzugs wurden allerdings keinerlei Vorleistungen für die Stadtbahn erbracht.

*3) the conversion of the entire line to low-floor operation, with an underground terminus at Konstablerwache;*

*4) like 3) but with a surface link to the existing tram network, and with a possible extension to Zoo;*

*The main argument against option 1) are the high costs, while option 2) is undesirable both because of the visual impact the high platforms may have on the urban environment, as well as for safety reasons, as a large number of young students use the two stops in question, and the high platforms right between the car lanes constitute an additional danger. Option 3) would bring back the unsatisfactory solution experienced on line U5 between 1980 and 1998. The arguments against conversion to low-floor operation include insufficient capacity, even if operated with double tram units. Passenger numbers on line U5, however, may decrease once the new tram line to Preungesheim Ost, which is currently under construction, has been completed. On the other hand, the long-envisaged 1.6 km extension from Preungesheim to Frankfurter Berg would bring additional passengers.*

*In the west, a route B branch into the Europaviertel is planned; the Europaviertel is a new development on the terrain of the former freight yard to the south of the exhibition centre. It is still unclear whether the Stadtbahn will run through this area underground or on the surface. The branch can diverge from the existing route at the junction already built north of Hauptbahnhof. All options include an underground station at Güterplatz, after which the line would either emerge from the tunnel or continue underground along Europaallee. However, no provisions were made for the future Stadtbahn when this new road was laid out.*

**_ Bockenheimer Warte**

Der derzeitige Endbahnhof der Linie U4 wurde von den Architekten Nieper und Partner gestaltet. Die knapp 9 m hohe Halle wird durch eine doppelte Stützenreihe gegliedert. An den in Sichtbeton belassenen Wänden hängen große Fotografien mit Motiven aus der Nachbarschaft: Senckenbergmuseum, Palmengarten und Universität. Der Bahnsteig lag ursprünglich auf einer Höhe von 80 cm, wurde jedoch kurz nach Eröffnung auf 87 cm angehoben, um einen ebenen Einstieg in die Fahrzeuge des Typs ‚U3' zu ermöglichen.

Der nördliche Teil des Stationsrohbaus wurde bereits mit der C-Strecke mitgebaut, hier besteht ein Übergang zu den Linien U6 und U7 (▶ S. 84), entweder direkt über eine Festtreppe bzw. einen Aufzug, oder mit Rolltreppen über das Zwischengeschoss ⑤. Am Südende des Bahnhofs liegt ein weitläufiger Zugangsbereich unter der Senckenberganlage ①②. Neben der viergleisigen Abstellanlage nördlich des Bahnhofs (mit Archivräumen für die Stadt- und Unibibliothek darüber) gibt es auch südlich ein mittiges Aufstellgleis, sowie eine Gleisverbindung zur C-Strecke.

*The present U4 terminus was designed by 'Architekten Nieper und Partner'. The 9 m high station hall is structured by two rows of columns. The walls were left in bare concrete, but are decorated with large photographs relating to the Senckenbergmuseum, the Palmengarten and the University, all in the vicintiy. The platform was initially 80 cm high, but was raised to 87 cm shortly after the station had opened to provide level access into the 'U3' vehicles.*

*The northern part of the station shell had already been built together with route C. Transfer to lines U6 and U7 (▶ p. 84) is provided directly via fixed stairs or a lift, as well as by escalators via the mezzanine ⑤. A large entrance area is located at the southern end below Senckenberganlage ①②.*

*Besides the four sidings to the north of the station (with storage space used by the University and city libraries above them), there is a southern siding between the running tracks, as well as a track link to route C.*

_ **Festhalle/Messe**
Dieser U-Bahnhof wurde von der Architektengemeinschaft G. Balser entworfen. Die 8 m hohe Halle ähnelt einer Ausstellungshalle. Die Wand hinter dem Gleis Richtung Bockenheimer Warte ist durch große Farbflächen (Idee: Gerhard Lienemeyer) gegliedert, die auf die bunten Flaggen anspielen, die vor dem Messeeingang hängen. Zwei 12 m hohe Glaskegel, deren Form wohl durch die Spitze des Messeturms ② inspiriert wurde, dienen als Zugänge und ermöglichen Tageslichteinfall. Vom südlichen führt ein Aufzug ① direkt auf den Bahnsteig.

*The underground station Festhalle/Messe [Festival Arena/Exhibition Centre] was designed by the 'Architektengemeinschaft G. Balser' with an 8 m high station box resembling an exhibition hall. The wall behind the track towards Bockenheimer Warte is divided into large coloured fields (an idea by Gerhard Lienemeyer), an allusion to the flags hoisted up outside the exhibition centre. Two 12 m high glass cones – a shape most likely inspired by the top of the Messeturm ② – serve as accesses and allow daylight into the station; the southern cone accommodates a direct lift ① from the surface to the platform.*

①

②

**_ Hauptbahnhof**
Der viergleisige U-Bahnhof liegt auf der Ebene -2 vor dem Hauptbahnhof. Er wurde zusammen mit dem unterirdischen S-Bahnhof (-3; ▶ S. 118) unter der Regie der *Deutschen Bundesbahn* errichtet. An der Beschilderung ① kann man erkennen, dass auch im weitläufigen Zwischengeschoss die DB AG die Hausherrin ist. Das Wandbild ① zeigt die Stadtgeschichte Frankfurts in komprimierter Form.

Als Vorleistung für die einst geplante D-Strecke wurde der U-Bahnhof großzügig mit zwei Mittelbahnsteigen und vier Gleisen gebaut, wobei das äußere Gleis Richtung Bockenheimer Warte aus Richtung Willy-Brandt-Platz nicht erreicht und somit nicht genutzt werden kann. Richtung Innenstadt fährt die U5 ② vom inneren und die U4 ③ vom äußeren Gleis ab. Die Hintergleiswände sind mit aktuellen Frankfurter Stadtansichten ⑤ geschmückt.

③

*The 4-track underground station at Hauptbahnhof [Central Station] is located on level -2 in front of the station building. It was built by the 'Deutsche Bundesbahn' together with their 4-track underground S-Bahn station (▶ p. 118). The kind of signs ① indicates that the mezzanine is still part of the DB's domain. The mural in the background shows a condensed version of Frankfurt's history ①.*
*In provision for the future route D, the Stadtbahn station was laid out with two island platforms and four tracks. The outer track towards Bockenheimer Warte is not accessible from Willy-Brandt-Platz and therefore remains unused. Towards the city centre, line U5 ② departs from the inner track, and line U4 ③ from the outer. The walls behind the tracks are decorated with contemporary images of Frankfurt ⑤.*

④

⑤

①

②

**_ Willy-Brandt-Platz**
[bis | *before* 01-07-1993 ‚Theaterplatz']

Die Bahnsteige der B-Strecke (Ebene -4) sind nur über die der A-Strecke (-3, ▶ S. 26) ② erreichbar. Die große Tiefenlage wurde durch den gleichzeitigen Bau eines Autotunnels auf der Ebene -2 notwendig.
Durch den Einsatz von kleinteiligen Waschbetonplatten an den Wänden sollte eine attraktivere Gestaltung erreicht werden als bei den älteren Stationen der A-Strecke, aus heutiger Sicht wirkt die Station wohl etwas schmucklos.
Von 1974 bis 1978 war ‚Theaterplatz' die Endstation für die Linie B1, die mit Verlängerung zum Hauptbahnhof zur Linie U5 wurde. Der am Schauspielhaus gelegene Eingang ① wurde 1987/88 umgebaut.

③

*At Willy-Brandt-Platz, the platforms for route B (level -4) are only accessible via the route A platforms (-3, ▶ p. 26) ②. The great depth was necessitated by a road tunnel on level -2 built at the same time.*
*The walls are decorated with small exposed aggregate concrete tiles, which were originally meant to give the station a more pleasant design than that used on the early underground stations on route A, but which today make the station look rather plain.*
*From 1974 until 1978, 'Theaterplatz' was the terminus for line B1, which was renamed U5 when it was extended to Hauptbahnhof. The entrance next to the theatre complex ① was redesigned in 1987/88.*

④

①

②

_ **Dom/Römer** [bis | *until* 2002 ‚Römer']

Dieser U-Bahnhof liegt im Herzen von Frankfurts Altstadt, zwischen dem Römerberg mit dem alten Rathaus und dem Dom (▶ S. 52).
Anders als bei den Nachbarbahnhöfen, wo man Waschbetonplatten verwendete, wurden hier die Gleishinterwände mit rötlichem hessischem Sandstein, der für die Frankfurter Architektur typisch ist, verkleidet.

Wegen seiner Unübersichtlichkeit war der Bahnhof jedoch bereits Ende der achtziger Jahre fällig für eine Umgestaltung ②, besonders auch im Bereich der Zwischenebene. Eine weitere Modernisierung, z.B. durch Anbringen geistreicher Sprüche ①, die auf die benachbarte Kunsthalle Schirn Bezug nehmen, wurde 2003 vorgenommen.

③

*The underground station Dom/Römer is located right in the heart of the old town between the old city hall, called Römer, and the cathedral [Dom] (▶ p. 52).*
*Instead of the exposed aggregate concrete used in the neighbouring stations, red sandstone from the region, typical for Frankfurt's architecture, was employed to clad the walls in this station. Due to the station's unattractive layout, with many areas difficult to overlook, it was partially refurbished in the late 1980s ②, e.g. in the mezzanine. Another modernisation scheme was carried out in 2003, and since then, witty statements referring to a nearby art museum have been displayed, like 'U-Bahn-Fahren ist keine Kunst' [literally 'Travelling on the metro is not art', although idiomatically it also means 'It's easy to travel on the metro'] ①.*

④

⑤

①

②

**_ Konstablerwache**

Neben Hauptwache und Hauptbahnhof ist Konstablerwache der wichtigste Umsteigepunkt im Schnellbahnnetz. Die Linien U4 und U5 halten auf der Ebene -2, darunter kreuzen die C-Strecke (▶ S. 88) sowie die S-Bahn (▶ S. 120). An der Oberfläche verkehrt außerdem die Straßenbahnlinie 12. Über ein Zwischengeschoss erreicht man die Zeil, Frankfurts Haupteinkaufsstraße ①.
Der dreigleisige U-Bahnhof der B-Strecke verfügt stadtauswärts über einen von beiden Linien benutzten Seitenbahnsteig ③, stadteinwärts jedoch über einen Mittelbahnsteig, wobei die U4 innen und die U5 außen ④ halten. Zwischen 1980 und 1998, als die U4 als artreine U-Bahn verkehrte, endete die U5 auf dem westlichsten Gleis, von wo sie auch wieder zurück nach Preungesheim fuhr.
Gestalterisch ist der U-Bahnhof Konstablerwache eher unauffällig, die Außenwände sind mit Waschbetonplatten verkleidet, die Stützen zwischen den Gleisen sind, wie einst für Umsteigestationen vorgesehen, rot gestrichen. Der Bereich der Treppenabgänge ② zu den anderen Linien ist in verschiedenen Rosatönen gefliest.

③

*Together with Hauptwache and Hauptbahnhof, Konstablerwache is the busiest interchange station on the entire urban rail network. Lines U4 and U5 stop on level -2, with route C (▶ p. 88) and the S-Bahn (▶ p. 120) crossing one level deeper, and tram line 12 operating on the surface. Frankfurt's main shopping street, the Zeil ①, is accessible via the mezzanine.*
*The 3-track station for route B has a single side platform for outbound trains ③, and an island platform for inbound trains, with line U4 running on the inner track and line U5 on the outer ④. Between 1980 and 1998, line U5 terminated on the westernmost track before returning from there to Preungesheim.*
*The design of Konstablerwache station is rather inconspicuous, with the side walls covered only with exposed aggregate concrete slabs. The columns between the tracks are painted red, a design initially meant for all the interchange stations. The area around the stairs that lead down to the other lines is tiled in pink and purple tones ②.*

④

## _ Merianplatz

Nach den eher unauffälligen Stationen des ersten Abschnitts der B-Strecke wagte man für die Bahnhöfe der Bornheimer U-Bahn wieder kräftige Farben. Statt wie früher auf der A-Strecke mit Paneelen wurden nun die Wände mit 30x45 cm großen Keramikfliesen verkleidet, da diese langlebig und pflegeleicht sind. In jedem der vier U-Bahnhöfe dominiert eine andere Grundfarbe, was die Orientierung der Fahrgäste erleichtert. Das Farbkonzept stammt von Friedrich Ernst von Garnier. Im U-Bahnhof Merianplatz herrscht die Farbe Grün vor. Die beiden Bahnsteige liegen übereinander, stadtauswärts oben ①. An beiden Enden gibt es kleine Zwischenebenen ④, wobei die untere Bahnsteigebene (-3) ②③ nur über die Ebene -2 zugänglich ist.

*After the rather humble designs of the early stations on route B, strong colours came back with the construction of the so-called 'Bornheimer U-Bahn'. Unlike the route A stations and their panels, the new stations were clad in large ceramic tiles (30x45 cm) both durable and easy to clean. A basic colour was chosen for each of the four underground stations to help passengers recognise their station, the colour scheme being conceived by Friedrich Ernst von Garnier.*
*Green is the dominant colour in the Merianplatz station. The two platforms lie on top of each other, with the outbound track on the upper level ①. There are small mezzanines at each end of the station ④. The lower level (-3) ②③ is only accessible via level -2.*

①

②

③

④

①

②

## _ Höhenstraße

Wie bei den beiden benachbarten U-Bahnhöfen liegen die Bahnsteige übereinander auf den Ebenen -2 ③ und -3 ⑤, allerdings konnte in diesem Fall wegen der Lage der Station an der Kreuzung der Berger Straße mit dem breiten Alleenring (Habsburgerallee/Höhenstraße) ① (*Foto Philipp Krammer*) mittig eine großzügige Treppenanlage ② errichtet werden. Gleichzeitig dient das Zwischengeschoss als Fußgängerunterführung. Hier gab es in den ersten Jahren eine Spiegelreliefwand mit farbigen Lichteffekten zu sehen. Im Bahnhof Höhenstraße dominiert die Farbe Rot, die abschnittsweise über Orange in Gelb übergeht.
In allen vier Bahnhöfen der Bornheimer U-Bahn wurden nachträglich Aufzüge eingebaut ④.

*Like in the two neighbouring stations, the platforms in Höhenstraße station lie on top of each other on levels -2 ③ and -3 ⑤. However, as this station is located at the intersection of Berger Straße and the wide Alleenring (Habsburgerallee/Höhenstraße) ①, it was possible to build a larger staircase ②. The mezzanine, which also functions as an underpass for pedestrians, used to boast an art installation, with a wall made of mirrors which created special light effects. Höhenstraße station is dominated by red tiles mixed with some orange and yellow areas.*
*All four stations in Bornheim have been retrofitted with lifts ④.*

③

⑤

④

**_ Bornheim Mitte**
Der wichtigste Bahnhof auf der Bornheimer Strecke ist farblich durch den Grundton Gelb zu unterscheiden, allerdings kommen am Ende der Bahnsteige rötliche und bräunliche Töne hinzu. Konzeptionell gleicht dieser U-Bahnhof der Station Merianplatz, mit Zwischenebenen an beiden Enden, und einer unteren Bahnsteigebene ③④, die nur über die obere zugänglich ist ②.
An der Station Bornheim Mitte kann man zur Straßenbahnlinie 12 und zu mehreren Buslinien umsteigen.

*The busiest station on the Bornheim route can be distinguished by its yellow tiles, which are mixed with reddish and brownish tones towards the end of the platforms. The station layout of Bornheim Mitte is similar to that of Merianplatz, with small mezzanines at both ends, and the lower platform level ③④ only accessible via the upper one ②.*
*At Bornheim Mitte, transfer is provided to tram line 12 as well as several bus lines.*

①

②

**_ Seckbacher Landstraße**

Anders als bei den benachbarten Bahnhöfen liegen in der Station Seckbacher Landstraße die beiden Streckengleise wieder auf derselben Ebene, dazwischen ein Mittelbahnsteig. Diese Anordnung war einerseits durch die breitere Straße möglich, andererseits aber für einen Endbahnhof auch wünschenswert, denn so können die Züge auch am Bahnsteig wenden, auch wenn sich dahinter eine Wendeanlage befindet.
Seit Juni 2008 enden nicht mehr alle Züge der Linie U4 hier, etwa jeder zweite fährt (probeweise) über den Betriebshof Ost bis zur Schäfflestraße im Stadtteil Riederwald weiter ⑤ (▶ S. 56/57).
Im U-Bahnhof Seckbacher Landstraße dominiert die Farbe Blau, unterbrochen von wenigen Streifen in Grün. Vom nördlichen Ende des Bahnsteigs führt ein Schrägaufzug ①④ ins kleine Zwischengeschoss, und von dort ein Vertikalaufzug an die Oberfläche ②. Hier kann zu den Buslinien Richtung Atzelberg und Bergen umgestiegen werden – dorthin sollte ursprünglich auch die U-Bahn verlängert werden.

③

*Unlike the previous stations, the two tracks in Seckbacher Landstraße station lie on the same level, with an island platform between them. Only possible because of the larger width of the road above, this arrangement was necessary to allow trains to reverse at the platform, even though there are several sidings beyond the station. Since June 2008, not all U4 trains have terminated here, as, on a trial basis, every other train now continues to Schäfflestraße in Riederwald via the eastern Stadtbahn depot ⑤ (▶ p. 56/57).*

*Seckbacher Landstraße station is dominated by the colour blue, mixed with a few green stripes. From the northern end of the platform, an inclined lift ①④ leads to a small mezzanine. A vertical lift continues from there to the surface ②, from where several bus lines run to Atzelberg and Bergen, destinations previously planned to be served by the Stadtbahn.*

④

⑤

①

②

Die Linie U5 verlässt nördlich der Station Konstablerwache den Tunnel über die Rampe Scheffeleck ①, quert die Eschenheimer Anlage niveaugleich ② und fährt als Straßenbahn weiter durch die Eckenheimer Landstraße. Wie an der Gethsemane-Kirche zwischen Musterschule und Glauburgstraße ④ liegen die Gleise im Straßenpflaster, die Trasse wird von den Autos mitbenutzt. An den Haltestellen **Musterschule** ③ und **Glauburgstraße** ⑤ (und S. 69 ①) gibt es bislang keinerlei Bahnsteige, die Fahrgäste müssen von der Straßenebene einsteigen. Der Bau von Hochbahnsteigen ist wegen der Enge der Straße hier sehr umstritten, weshalb die Zukunft der U5 noch unklar ist.

③

*North of Konstablerwache station, line U5 emerges from the tunnel on the Scheffeleck ramp ①; it then crosses a street called Eschenheimer Anlage at grade ② before continuing on-street along Eckenheimer Landstraße. Like at Gethsemane Church ④, between Musterschule and Glauburgstraße, the tracks are embedded in the roadway and the alignment is shared by cars. The stops at* ***Musterschule*** *③ and* ***Glauburgstraße*** *⑤ (and p. 69 ①) have no platforms at all, so passengers need to board from street level. The proposed construction of high platforms is very controversial, so line U5's future is still unclear.*

④

⑤

①

Szenen wie in Bild ① an der Haltestelle **Glauburgstraße** (stadteinwärts) sind in anderen Stadtbahnstädten wie Hannover oder Düsseldorf keine Seltenheit, jedoch verblüffen sie in Frankfurt doch umso mehr, da das Verkehrssystem auch von den Bevölkerung als „U-Bahn" bezeichnet wird.
Ursprünglich sollte entlang der Eckenheimer Landstraße in einer späteren Phase ein Tunnel gebaut werden, mindestens bis zur Haltestelle **Deutsche Nationalbibliothek** ② (bis 2006 ‚Nibelungenallee/Deutsche Bibliothek'), ab wo ein eigener Gleiskörper in Mittellage zur Verfügung steht. Wünschenswert wäre aber sicherlich eine Verlängerung des Tunnels bis hinter die Kreuzung mit dem Alleenring (Adickesallee/Nibelungenallee), der eine wichtige Ost-West-Straßenverbindung darstellt. Die Rampe könnte an der ‚Städtischen Pietät' ③ im südwestlichen Bereich des Hauptfriedhofs liegen.

*Scenes like that in photo ① at **Glauburgstraße** (inbound direction) are rather frequent in other Stadtbahn cities like Hanover or Düsseldorf, but they surprise one even more in Frankfurt as the system is referred to by the local population as the 'U-Bahn'.*

*The initial plans envisaged a tunnel extension along Eckenheimer Landstraße, at least to the **Deutsche Nationalbibliothek** stop ② (until 2006 'Nibelungenallee/Deutsche Bibliothek'), from where a separate right-of-way is available. It would certainly be desirable to extend the tunnel beyond the busy intersection with the so-called 'Alleenring' (Adickesallee/Nibelungenallee), a major east-west road link. The ramp could be located in the area of the 'Städtische Pietät' ③, at the southwestern corner of the city's main cemetery.*

②

③

Zwischen den Haltestellen **Hauptfriedhof** und Eckenheimer Landstraße/Marbachweg ist die Trasse der Stadtbahn vom übrigen Verkehr durch Bodenmarkierungen abgetrennt ①. Auf diesem Abschnitt liegt der wohl am einfachsten ausgeführte „U-Bahnhof" der Welt, **Versorgungsamt** ②, nur knapp 250 m von der nächsten Haltestelle entfernt. Auch hier muss an beiden Seiten von der Straßenebene aus eingestiegen werden.
Ein weiteres Kuriosum der Frankfurter Stadtbahn findet man nördlich davon an der Kreuzung **Eckenheimer Landstraße/Marbachweg**: die U5 hält an der gleichnamigen Station südlich der Kreuzung in der Eckenheimer Landstraße ③, biegt dann in den Marbachweg ein ④, wo unmittelbar die nächste Station **Marbachweg/Sozialzentrum** ⑤ folgt. Der Abstand zwischen den jeweiligen Bahnsteigenden beträgt nur 70 m! Die in Bild ④ nach links laufenden Gleise führen zum Eckenheimer Depot, wo weiterhin einige Züge der U5 nächtigen.

*Between the **Hauptfriedhof** [main cemetery] and Eckenheimer Landstraße/Marbachweg stops, the alignment is separated from road traffic by road markings ①. This section includes what is probably the simplest 'metro station' in the world, **Versorgungsamt** ②; it lies only 250 m from the neighbouring stops, and boarding is done from street level in either direction.*
*Another curiosity of the Frankfurt Stadtbahn is found a bit further north at the **Eckenheimer Landstraße/Marbachweg** road intersection: line U5 stops at the station of the same name located on Eckenheimer Landstraße ③, then turns into Marbachweg ④ to stop again at **Marbachweg/Sozialzentrum** ⑤ – the distance between the respective platform ends being only 70 m!*
*The tracks continuing towards the left in photo ④ lead to the Eckenheim depot, which is still used to stable some U5 trains during night-time hours.*

Ab der Haltestelle Marbachweg/Sozialzentrum ist auch die Linie U5 stadtbahnmäßig trassiert, der Bau von Hochbahnsteigen wäre hier unkompliziert. Bild ① zeigt die schön bepflanzte Strecke entlang des Marbachwegs am Nordrand des Hauptfriedhofs. An der Haltestelle **Gießener Straße** ②, deren Bahnsteige ums Eck versetzt liegen, biegt die U5 in die Gießener Straße ein. Bei ihrer Inbetriebnahme 1974 endete sie kurz hinter der Kurve in einer heute nicht mehr existierenden Anlage. Die Strecke wurde 1977 in westlicher Seitenlage der Gießener Straße bis zur heutigen Endstation verlängert. Der Halt **Theobald-Ziegler-Straße** ③ wurde erst im Dezember 1981 eingefügt. An der **Ronneburgstraße** ④ kann zur Buslinie 39 umgestiegen werden. Über den Halt **Sigmund-Freud-Straße** erreicht die U5 schließlich ihren Endpunkt **Preungesheim**, eine dreigleisige Stumpfendstelle ⑤. Seit Langem ist eine 1,5 km lange Verlängerung entlang der Homburger Landstraße bis zum S-Bahnhof Frankfurter Berg geplant.

*From the stop at Marbachweg/Sozialzentrum, the U5 alignment has Stadtbahn standard, and the construction of high platforms would not present any difficulties. Photo ① shows the route on Marbachweg, lined with flowers along the northern side of the main cemetery. At the* ***Gießener Straße*** *stop ②, which has platforms located on either side of the street corner, line U5 turns into Gießener Straße. When it first opened in 1974, a since-abandoned terminus lay a short distance further north. In 1977, the route was extended along the western side of Gießener Straße to its present terminus. The* ***Theobald-Ziegler-Straße*** *stop ③ was only added in December 1981. At* ***Ronneburgstraße*** *④, transfer is provided to bus line 39. Via* ***Siegmund-Freud-Straße****, line U5 finally reaches its present 3-track terminus at* ***Preungesheim*** *⑤, although a 1.5 km extension along Homburger Landstraße to the S-Bahn station Frankfurter Berg has been planned for a long time.*

**Habsburgerallee** – auf der C-Strecke gibt es insgesamt zwölf richtige U-Bahnhöfe.
*– on route C, there is a total of twelve full-scale metro stations.*

## _ C-Strecke

Die C-Strecke der Frankfurter Stadtbahn besteht aus den Linien U6 und U7, die zwischen Industriehof und Zoo eine gemeinsame Stammstrecke bilden. Daran schließen sich an beiden Enden jeweils unterschiedlich lange Außenäste an. Die C-Strecke ist bis auf die Haltestelle Fischstein (U6), die in naher Zukunft umgebaut werden soll, voll stadtbahnmäßig ausgebaut, d.h. die oberirdischen Außenstrecken liegen durchgehend auf eigenem Gleiskörper und es stehen 100 m lange Hochbahnsteige zur Verfügung. Während auf der Linie U7 meist ‚U2e'-Züge (meist in 3-fach-Traktion, in den HVZ aber auch als 100 m lange 4-fach-Traktionen) zu sehen sind, wird die U6 bis auf Weiteres von ‚Ptb'-Wagen mit Klapptrittstufen, wie sie auch auf der U5 verkehren, betrieben.

Die Linien U6 und U7 verkehren zwischen 4:00 morgens bis 1:00 nachts, und zwar früh morgens bis etwa 5:30 und abends ab 20:30 im 20-Minuten-Takt und von 6:30 bis 10:00 bzw. von 13:30 bis 19:30 im 7/8-Minuten-Takt, dazwischen wird alle 10 Minuten gefahren. Samstags besteht tagsüber durchgängig ein 10-Minuten-Takt, sonntags fahren die Bahnen bis 11:00 nur alle 20 Minuten, dann bis 12:30 alle 15 Minuten und erst nachmittags im 10-Minuten-Takt. Durch Überlappung der beiden Linien wird auf dem zentralen Abschnitt zwischen Industriehof und Zoo wochentags tagsüber somit alle 3-5 Minuten gefahren.

## _ *Route C*

*Route C of the Frankfurt Stadtbahn comprises lines U6 and U7, which share the same tracks between Industriehof and Zoo. At either end of the route, there are two branches of different lengths. Except for the Fischstein stop, which is planned to be rebuilt in the near future, route C has full Stadtbahn standard, i.e. all surface routes are on a separate right-of-way, and all stops are equipped with 100 m long high-level platforms. While line U7 is normally operated with 3-car trains of class 'U2e' (during peak hours 100 m long 4-car trains can also be seen), line U6 is served by 'Ptb' vehicles with folding steps, the same rolling stock as on line U5.*

*Lines U6 and U7 operate between 04:00 and 01:00: every 20 minutes in the early mornings until 05:30 and in the evenings after 20:30; every 7/8 minutes from 06:30 to 10:00 and from 13:30 to 19:30; and every 10 minutes at other times. On Saturdays, there is a 10-minute headway during daytime hours. On Sundays, trains only run every 20 minutes before 11:00, then every 15 minutes until 12:30, and finally every 10 minutes in the afternoon. With the two lines overlapping on the central section, there is a train every 3 to 5 minutes between Industriehof and Zoo during daytime hours.*

15,1 km (ca. 8,2 km unterirdisch | *underground*), 26 Haltestellen | *stations*

11-10-1986 Hausen/Heerstraße – Kirchplatz – Zoo
30-05-1992 Zoo – Eissporthalle – Enkheim
29-05-1999 Zoo – Ostbahnhof

## _ Geschichte der C-Strecke

Die C-Strecke war von Anfang an als Ost-West-Achse in den Stadtbahnplanungen enthalten, schließlich folgt sie auf ihrem westlichen Abschnitt zwischen Innenstadt und Bockenheim der Strecke der ersten Frankfurter Pferdebahn von 1872. Die ersten Rohbauarbeiten wurden bereits im Zuge des Baus der A-Strecke im Stationsbereich Hauptwache Mitte der sechziger Jahre, also gut 20 Jahre vor Inbetriebnahme der C-Strecke, ausgeführt. Zu jener Zeit war auch schon klar, dass die S-Bahn der *Deutschen Bundesbahn* entlang der Zeil, Frankfurts Haupteinkaufsstraße zwischen Hauptwache und Konstablerwache, in einem gemeinsamen Tunnelbauwerk, nämlich zwischen den Gleisen der Stadtbahn verkehren sollte.

Ähnlich wie bei den anderen Tunnelstrecken dachte man anfangs an einen Straßenbahnvorlaufbetrieb, der Innenstadttunnel sollte ursprünglich in der Bockenheimer Landstraße westlich der Station Alte Oper sowie in der Pfingstweidstraße östlich der Station Konstablerwache mit provisorischen Rampen enden, so dass bestehende Straßenbahnstrecken an den Tunnel angeschlossen werden konnten. Nach den Beschwerden entlang der Eschersheimer Landstraße, wo man die oberirdische Führung der A-Strecke als Trennwand zwischen den Stadtteilen empfand, war an einen ähnlichen Ausbau der Bockenheimer Landstraße durch das Westend nicht mehr zu denken, so dass 1970 eine Verlängerung des Tunnels bis in den Bereich Bockenheimer Warte in die Planungen aufgenommen wurde. Von hier sollten die Bahnen oberirdisch in der Adalbertstraße Richtung Westbahnhof weiterfahren. Nachdem Anfang 1976 mit den Rohbauarbeiten an der C-Strecke im Bereich Alte Oper begonnen worden war, wurden 1977 derartige Proteste gegen den Bau einer langen Rampe in der Adalbertstraße erhoben, dass bereits ein Jahr später eine verlängerte Tunnelstrecke entlang der Leipziger Straße bis zur Rampe Industriehof genehmigt wurde, wodurch der gesamte Stadtteil Bockenheim zentral erschlossen werden konnte. Obwohl der Westbahnhof nun nicht durch die Stadtbahn angeschlossen wurde, verzichtete man ebenfalls auf einen Umsteigebahnhof am Kreuzungspunkt mit der Main-Weser-Bahn (S6).

Am östlichen Ende stellte sich der Bau einer Rampe unmittelbar vor der Station Zoo als problematisch heraus, so dass die Züge vorerst unterirdisch enden sollten, bis schließlich eine Rampe jenseits des Ostbahnhofs in der Hanauer Landstraße fertig gestellt sein würde.

Anfang der achtziger Jahren waren dann alle Abschnitte zwischen Industriehof und Zoo (5,4 km) im Bau. Die Rampe Industriehof wurde so ausgeführt, dass eine spätere Tunnelverlängerung und eine dreigleisige unterirdische Verzweigungsstation Industriehof möglich ist. Westlich der Main-Weser-Bahn beginnen die beiden per NÖT aufgefahrenen Streckentunnel, die erst nebeneinander angeordnet sind, jedoch kurz vor der Station Leipziger Straße übereinander zu liegen kommen (stadteinwärts oben). Trotz der beengten Straßenverhältnisse konnte so auch der eben erwähnte U-Bahnhof in offener Bauweise erstellt werden. Etwa auf halber Strecke zwischen den Stationen Leipziger Straße und Bockenheimer Warte kommen die beiden Streckentunnel wieder in Parallellage. Trotz dieser Anordnung der Tunnelröhren mussten entlang der Leipziger Straße einige Gebäude unterfahren werden. Am östlichen Ende der Station Bockenheimer Warte entstand ein großzügiges Zwischengeschoss und gleichzeitig ein Teil des Rohbaus für den zukünftigen Bahnhof der D-Strecke, der schließlich 2001 in Betrieb

## *_ The History of Route C*

*From the beginning, route C was included in the overall Stadtbahn plans as an east-west route. On its western section between the city centre and Bockenheim it follows Frankfurt's first horse tram line opened back in 1872. The first construction work on route C was already carried out during the mid-1960s in the area of Hauptwache station when route A was built, i.e. some 20 years before route C was finally opened. At that time, it had already been decided that the S-Bahn was to share the same tunnel along Frankfurt's main shopping street, the Zeil, between Hauptwache and Konstablerwache, with the S-Bahn running on the central tracks and the Stadtbahn on the outer.*

*Like the other tunnels, the C tunnel was initially meant to be used by trams in the first stage, with a western ramp on Bockenheimer Landstraße just west of Alte Oper station, and an eastern ramp on Pfingstweidstraße east of Konstablerwache, where the existing tram lines were to be connected to the underground route. After the complaints regarding Eschersheimer Landstraße, where the surface section on route A was perceived as a barrier, a similar alignment along Bockenheimer Landstraße was discarded, and an extended tunnel up to Bockenheimer Warte was added to the project. From there, the trams were to run on the surface along Adalbertstraße towards Westbahnhof. With construction work having started on route C in the area of Alte Oper in early 1976, heavy protests arose against the long ramp planned on Adalbertstraße; within just a single year, a new tunnel route along Leipziger Straße all the way to Industriehof had been approved, thus serving the central areas of the district of Bockenheim. Although the Stadtbahn now bypassed the Westbahnhof, an interchange at the point where the Stadtbahn route intersects with the Main-Weser-Bahn (S6) was not planned either.*

*At the eastern end of the C tunnel, the construction of a ramp west of Zoo station turned out to be complicated, so that an underground terminus was chosen instead, a temporary solution until a ramp could be built on Hanauer Landstraße at the eastern side of Ostbahnhof.*

*In the early 1980s, all the sections between Industriehof and Zoo (5.4 km) were under construction. The ramp at Industriehof was built so as to allow for a future underground extension with a 3-track underground station. The two NATM tubes start west of the Main-Weser railway line; lying parallel at first, they get aligned on top of each other just before Leipziger Straße station (inbound track on the upper level) — this allowed the station to be built by cut-and-cover despite the narrowness of the street it lies under. About halfway between Leipziger Straße and Bockenheimer Warte stations, the two running tunnels return to a parallel alignment. Along Leipziger Straße, the tunnels run below several buildings despite this special alignment.*

*At the eastern end of Bockenheimer Warte station, a spacious mezzanine was built together with a part of the station box for route D, which was finally extended here in 2001 (line U4). East of the station on the southern side, there is a siding which was later used as the starting point for the track link*

**Zoo** – bis 1992 östliche Endstation der C-Strecke, bis 1998 mit Bahnsteigverbreiterung (*Foto Helmut Roggenkamp, 09/1986*)
*– until 1992, the eastern terminus of route C, and until 1998, with widened platforms*

ging. Östlich der Station befindet sich an der Südseite ein Abstellgleis, von dem aus seit Inbetriebnahme der D-Strecke (Linie U4) eine Gleisverbindung zwischen beiden Stammstrecken besteht. Der Teil des heute unter einem Gebäude liegenden Verbindungstunnels konnte im Zuge einer Neubebauung der Oberfläche in offener Bauweise errichtet werden.

Die weiteren Streckentunnel bis zur Alten Oper wurden wieder in geschlossener, die Stationen Westend und Alte Oper jedoch wieder in offener Bauweise aufgefahren. Im Bereich Westend unter der Bockenheimer Landstraße kam dabei nicht die NÖT, sondern der Messerschildvortrieb zur Anwendung. Dabei wird das Erdreich im Schutze eines Schildes von einem Bagger abgetragen und die so entstandene runde Röhre erst mit Beton abgestützt und anschließend mit Tübbings ausgekleidet. Unmittelbar östlich des U-Bahnhofs Alte Oper schließt der in offener Bauweise errichtete, bis zu 30 m breite Gemeinschaftstunnel Stadtbahn/S-Bahn an, der bis hinter den Bahnhof Konstablerwache reicht. Die S-Bahn-Gleise fädeln dabei im Verlauf der Großen Bockenheimer Straße (auch *Freßgass'* genannt) zwischen den Stadtbahngleisen ein, indem sie das stadteinwärtige Gleis der Stadtbahn unterqueren. Auf der gemeinsamen Strecke liegen die beiden Bahnhöfe Hauptwache und Konstablerwache, wobei die Bahnsteige der S-Bahn mit 210 m mehr als doppelt so lang sind wie die der Stadtbahn, weshalb der S-Bahnsteig an der Hauptwache am westlichen Ende einen eigenen Zugang besitzt. An der Konstablerwache teilt sich die Stadtbahn mit der S-Bahn je einen Mittelbahnsteig pro Fahrtrichtung, so dass man hier bequem zwischen den beiden Schnellbahnsystemen umsteigen kann. Eine ebenbürtige Anordnung findet man in Deutschland sonst nur am Bahnhof Wuhletal in Berlin (U5/S5). Während die Bahnsteige der C-Strecke und der S-Bahn an der Hauptwache auf der Ebene -2

*to route D. This linking tunnel, part of which now lies below a building, was built by cut-and-cover when the area was redeveloped.*

*The following running tunnels up to Alte Oper were again excavated below ground, while the stations of Westend and Alte Oper were realised by cut-and-cover. The NATM was not used for the section around Westend station, but by means of a tunnelling shield equipped with cutters the soil was cleared away with an excavator, then the tube was secured by shotcrete before being lined with precast concrete segments. The shared Stadtbahn/S-Bahn tunnel, which was built by cut-and-cover under the Zeil, starts just east of Alte Oper station; it is up to 30 m wide and reaches beyond Konstablerwache station. The S-Bahn tracks get aligned between the Stadtbahn tracks on Große Bockenheimer Straße (also known as Freßgass') by burrowing under the eastbound Stadtbahn track. The shared section includes the two stations Hauptwache and Konstablerwache. At 210 m, the S-Bahn platforms are over twice as long as the Stadtbahn ones; at Hauptwache, there is therefore a separate western entrance to the S-Bahn platform. At Konstablerwache, the S-Bahn and Stadtbahn share an island platform in each direction, thus providing convenient cross-platform transfer. In Germany, an arrangement of this kind is otherwise only found at Wuhletal (U5/S5) in Berlin. Whereas the platforms for route C and the S-Bahn lie on level -2 at Hauptwache, i.e. above the older route A, they are located on level -3 at Konstablerwache, i.e. below route B. The Zeil was once a busy road for both trams and cars, and the construction of a road tunnel above the rail tunnel was therefore initially considered, too. Eventually, the road tunnel was shelved and the Zeil, as well as the Freßgass', is now a very popular pedestrian zone.*

liegen, also über der älteren kreuzenden A-Strecke, befinden sie sich an der Konstablerwache auf der Ebene -3, also unter der kreuzenden B-Strecke. Entlang der Zeil herrschte früher reger Straßenbahn- und auch dichter Autoverkehr, weshalb ursprünglich über dem Schnellbahntunnel auch ein Autotunnel errichtet werden sollte. Auf diesen wurde schließlich jedoch verzichtet, und die Zeil sowie die *Freßgass'* präsentieren sich heute als überaus belebte Fußgängerzonen.

Unmittelbar östlich der Station Konstablerwache trennt sich die S-Bahn, die 1978 bis Hauptwache und 1983 bis Konstablerwache in Betrieb ging, wieder von der Stadtbahn, indem sie wiederum unter dem nach Osten führenden Stadtbahngleis hindurchtaucht. Für das Überwerfungsbauwerk sowie die anschließenden Streckentunnel wurde auf kurzen Abschnitten die geschlossene Bauweise unter der Bebauung gewählt, der Rest entstand in offenen Baugruben. Als zukünftiger Verzweigungsbahnhof wurde die vorläufige Endstation Zoo mit drei Bahnsteiggleisen ausgestattet, die Verzweigung östlich der Station unter dem Zoogelände wurde per NÖT gleich mitgebaut, wobei sich das stadtauswärts führende Gleis gabelt, während das vom Ostbahnhof kommende Gleis unter den beiden Streckengleisen von/nach Enkheim durchtaucht.

Anders als bei den früheren Strecken legte man beim Entwurf der C-Strecke großen Wert auf die Gestaltung der unterirdischen Bahnhöfe (Näheres dazu bei den einzelnen Stationen auf den folgenden Seiten). Für eine unbestimmte Übergangszeit sollte der C-Tunnel wie anfangs auch der B-Tunnel von Pt-Fahrzeugen befahren werden, weshalb an die späteren Bahnsteigkanten Verbreiterungen angebracht wurden, während die Bahnsteighöhe von Anfang an 87 cm betrug.

Gleichzeitig mit der Inbetriebnahme der C-Strecke sollte die Innenstadt nun endlich schienenfrei werden, d.h. auch die dort noch übriggebliebenen Straßenbahnstrecken sollten stillgelegt werden, was jedoch zu massiven Bürgerprotesten führte. Nachdem daraufhin die Stilllegungsgenehmigung für die Ost-West-Strecke durch die Altstadt vom zuständigen Regierungspräsidenten in Darmstadt verweigert worden war, wurde die C-Strecke am 11. Oktober 1986, zwei Wochen nach der angekündigten Eröffnung, ohne große Feierlichkeiten in Betrieb genommen, während die Straßenbahnstrecke zwischen Hauptbahnhof und Börneplatz bestehen blieb.

Während im Osten der Stadt nun am Zoo in die Stadtbahn umgestiegen werden musste, wurden im Westen zwei oberirdische Strecken an den Stadtbahntunnel angeschlossen. Der heutige Ast der U7 ging dabei auf eine Straßenbahnstrecke aus

*The S-Bahn was brought into service up to Hauptwache in 1978, and to Konstablerwache in 1983. Immediately east of Konstablerwache station, the S-Bahn tracks once again burrow under the eastbound Stadtbahn track. The junction, as well as short sections of the adjacent running tunnels, was built using the NATM, the rest being done by cut-and-cover. The temporary terminus at Zoo was built with three tracks, and the following junction below the zoo was completed at the same time; while the outbound track diverges into two branches, the inbound track from Ostbahnhof burrows under the running tracks to/from Enkheim.*

*Unlike with the older routes, the design of the underground stations on route C received special attention. Further details about station architecture can be found in the following pages. For a transitional period, route C was to be operated with 'Pt' cars, and therefore the definitive platforms had to be widened; the platform height was 87 cm from the start.*

*Coinciding with the opening of route C, the tramway lines through the city centre were to be abandoned, a plan that led to heavy protests. The competent authorities in Darmstadt thereupon refused to give permission for the closure of the east-west route through the old town between Hauptbahnhof and Börneplatz, and route C was finally opened on 11 October 1986, i.e. two weeks later than scheduled, without any major celebrations, while the tram route between Hauptbahnhof and Börneplatz remained in service, too.*

*While passengers at the eastern side of the city were now forced to transfer to the Stadtbahn trains at Zoo, at the western side two surface routes were connected to the new Stadtbahn tunnel. The present U7 branch is a former tramway route opened in 1913 and last served by line 18. The U6 branch had been served by trams since 1932, the last tram line before conversion to Stadtbahn being line 22. Initially, a third branch to Rödelheim and possibly to Sossenheim was planned, but this was later deleted, not least because of the parallel S-Bahn route.*

*The route along Ludwig-Landmann-Straße (U6) had already been upgraded on a separate right-of-way in the late 1970s, although only with low platforms. Except at Fischstein, Ebelfeld (merged with Heerstraße in 2004) and Heerstraße, provisions were made, however, to raise these to 87 cm in the future. From the terminus Heerstraße, a track leads to the central Stadtbahn workshops. As this access was then also used by 2.65 m wide Stadtbahn vehicles, no high*

‚U2'-Wagen und ‚Ptb'-Wagen wegen Bauarbeiten in der Schlossstraße unweit des Westbahnhofs abgestellt (*Foto Stephan Kyrieleis, 20-11-1998*)
– *'U2' and 'Ptb' cars stabled on Schlossstraße near Frankfurt West due to track maintenance work*

**Große Nelkenstraße** – bei laufendem Betrieb werden die Bahnsteigkanten für den Einsatz der ‚U2e'-Fahrzeuge abgesägt. (*Foto Stephan Kyrieleis, 18-09-1998*)
– *without service being interrupted, the platform edges were sawn off to enable the use of 'U2e' vehicles.*

dem Jahre 1913 zurück, die zuletzt von der Linie 18 befahren wurde. Auf dem Ast der U6 war seit 1932 eine Straßenbahn unterwegs, zuletzt die Linie 22. Anfangs war noch ein dritter Ast nach Rödelheim und eventuell weiter nach Sossenheim vorgesehen, der aber schließlich nicht zuletzt wegen der parallelen S-Bahn gestrichen wurde.

Die Strecke entlang der Ludwig-Landmann-Straße (U6) wurde bereits Ende der siebziger Jahre stadtbahnmäßig ausgebaut, allerdings vorerst natürlich mit Niedrigbahnsteigen, die bis auf Fischstein, Ebelfeld (2004 mit Heerstraße zusammengelegt) und Heerstraße für eine Erhöhung auf 87 cm vorbereitet waren. Von der Endhaltestelle Heerstraße führte nun ein Anschlussgleis zur neuen Stadtbahn-Zentralwerkstatt. Da diese Zufahrt auch von 2,65 breiten Stadtbahnfahrzeugen genutzt wurde, konnten auf dem U6-Ast vorerst keine Hochbahnsteige errichtet werden. Diese wurden bis auf Fischstein erst zwischen 1998 und 2004 nachgerüstet, nachdem auch die C-Strecke auf Betrieb mit breiteren Wagen umgestellt worden war. Langfristig könnte die U6 nach Westen verlängert werden. Nach knapp 1 km könnte an der Autobahn A5 eine Park-and-Ride-Anlage gebaut werden, und 2 km weiter westlich davon würde Steinbach am Taunus erreicht werden.

Der kurze Ast nach Hausen (U7) wurde ebenfalls in den späten siebziger Jahren in mehreren Etappen im Zuge von Straßenaus- und -umbauten neu trassiert. Der anschließende eingleisige Abschnitt entlang der Praunheimer Landstraße bis zur Brücke über die Nidda kurz vor dem alten Praunheimer Ortskern wurde nicht in das Stadtbahnnetz übernommen, da es zu keiner Einigung über den stadtbahngerechten Ausbau dieses Abschnitts kam. Stattdessen wurde im Bereich der ehemaligen Haltestelle Eichwäldchen der Linie 18 die heutige Endstation Hausen eingerichtet. Wegen der kurzen Stationsabstände entfiel der ehemalige Halt Ellerfeld zwischen Große Nelkenstraße und Hausen.

Von den beiden östlichen Anschlussstrecken galt immer die über Ostbahnhof entlang der Hanauer Landstraße Richtung Fechenheim führende als die wichtigere, da sich hier neben Wohngebieten auch ausgedehnte Gewerbegebiete befinden. Während der äußere Teil dieser Straßenbahnstrecke bereits in den sechziger Jahren auf einen eigenen Gleiskörper verlegt wurde, sollte der Stadtbahntunnel bis zum Ratswegkreisel führen, wo heute die Straßenbahnlinien 11 und 12 zusammenlaufen. Auf dieser Strecke würden unterirdische Bahnhöfe an der Schwedlerstraße sowie an den Riederhöfen liegen. Während man lange nach der besten Variante suchte, tauchte mittlerweile auch die Idee einer nordmainischen S-Bahn auf, die mit zusätzlichen Haltestellen dieselben Gebiete abdecken

**Hessen-Center** – ‚Pt'-Wagen 721 auf der ehemaligen Linie 23 während des Umbaus der Haltestelle für die U7 (*Foto Stephan Kyrieleis, 1992*)
– *'Pt' car 721 on the long-abandoned line 23, with the station being upgraded for Stadtbahn line U7*

**Schäfflestraße** > **Gwinnerstraße** – ‚P'-Wagen 697 auf der ehemaligen Linie 18 im Bereich des heutigen von der U4 genutzten Kehrgleises (*Foto Stephan Kyrieleis, 10/1991*)
– *'P' car 697 on the former line 18, in the area of the reversing siding currently used by line U4*

*platforms were initially able to be built along the U6 branch. Except for Fischstein, these were only erected between 1998 and 2004, once route C had also been converted for operation with wider cars. In the long term, line U6 may be extended further west; after about 1 km, a park-and-ride facility could be established where the route intersects with motorway A5; and about 2 km further on, line U6 would then reach the town of Steinbach am Taunus.*

*The short branch to Hausen (U7) was also modified in stages during the late 1970s together with road improvements. The following single-track section along Praunheimer Straße and up to the bridge across the Nidda, close to the Praunheim village centre, was not incorporated into the Stadtbahn scheme, as no agreement with the neighbours along the route could be reached. Instead, the present terminus Hausen was established near the location of the former tram stop Eichwäldchen on line 18. Due to the short distances between stops, Ellerfeld, a stop between Große Nelkenstraße and Hausen, was abandoned.*

*Of the two eastern feeder lines, the one via Ostbahnhof along Hanauer Landstraße towards Fechenheim had always been considered the more important, as besides residential areas, it would also serve large industrial estates. The outer section of this route had already been put on a separate right-of-way during the 1960s. The Stadtbahn tunnel was therefore planned to run up to Ratswegkreisel, the point where lines 11 and 12 currently converge. There would be two underground stations, at Schwedlerstraße and Riederhöfe. While the search for the best alignment was going on, the idea of an S-Bahn route north of the Main River emerged, which, with additional stations, would serve the same area. Despite all these uncertainties, the construction of the first Stadtbahn section to Ostbahnhof (700 m) began in March 1989. As the definitive alignment for a possible S-Bahn route had not yet been decided upon, the Stadtbahn station at Ostbahnhof was initially only built with a 75 m island platform. While this short section took until 1999 to build, the station was only fully completed in 2007. An extension to Fechenheim is currently not being given high priority, while the S-Bahn route has not been realised yet either.*

*With the Fechenheim branch postponed time and again, in the end it was the Enkheim branch that was dealt with first. According to the initial project, this route was to follow Wittelsbacher Allee, but in 1968, when route B was diverted along Berger Straße, route C was also moved further south to Rhönstraße. The construction of the 2.1 km extension with*

sollte. Trotz der lange ungeklärten Zukunft dieser Stadtbahnstrecke konnte im März 1989 wenigstens das nur 700 m lange Teilstück bis zum Ostbahnhof in Angriff genommen werden. Da die endgültige S-Bahn-Trasse jedoch auch noch nicht feststand, konnte der U-Bahnhof am Ostbahnhof vorerst nur in einer verkürzten Form mit einem 75 m langen Mittelbahnsteig gebaut werden. Die Eröffnung dieses Teilabschnitts fand allerdings erst 1999 statt, der komplette Ausbau konnte dann erst 2007 abgeschlossen werden. Ein Weiterbau wird derzeit nicht als vorrangig eingestuft, allerdings ist auch die nordmainische S-Bahn bislang nicht verwirklicht worden.

Während sich also der Bau des Astes nach Fechenheim immer weiter verzögert hatte, wurde schließlich der Ast nach Enkheim vorgezogen. Dieser sollte in den ersten Planungen entlang der Wittelsbacher Allee führen, wurde dann aber 1968, nachdem die B-Strecke in die Berger Straße verlegt worden war, ebenfalls nach Süden in die Rhönstraße verschoben. Baubeginn für die 2,1 km lange Strecke mit drei unterirdischen Bahnhöfen war im Februar 1985. Im Anschluss an die Tunnelstutzen östlich des U-Bahnhofs Zoo wurden die Streckentunnel per NÖT weitergebaut, wobei erst das Zoogelände und östlich des Parlamentsplatzes auch die dortige Bebauung unterfahren werden mussten. Die beiden eingleisigen Röhren vereinigen sich kurz vor der Station Eissporthalle, die wie die beiden anderen U-Bahnhöfe wiederum in offener Bauweise erstellt wurde. Wegen einer Geländestufe (Bornheimer Hang) ist die anschließende Tunnelausfahrt keine Rampe im eigentlichen Sinn.

Mit Inbetriebnahme der östlichen Tunnelstrecke am 30. Mai 1992 wurde die U7 vom Zoo bis Enkheim verlängert. Die oberirdische Trasse konnte dazu weitgehend von der Straßenbahn übernommen werden, nur zwischen Schäfflestraße und Gwinnerstraße wurde der Abzweig in die Borsigallee etwas begradigt. Die Straßenbahn fuhr bereits 1911 bis zur Gwinnerstraße, die Strecke für die ehemalige Linie 18 in der Borsigallee wurde dann 1952 bis zur Kruppallee und 1957 weiter bis Enkheim verlängert. Die über die Gwinnerstraße nach Bergen verkehrende Straßenbahnlinie (früher die Linie 20, zuletzt die Linie 12) wurde mit Ankunft der Stadtbahn eingestellt. Da ihre Trasse noch weitgehend erhalten ist und im oberen Teil sogar auf eigenem Gleiskörper abseits von Straßen verläuft, könnte die Strecke in Zukunft in irgendeiner Form wieder reaktiviert werden. Die oberirdischen Stationen der U7 wurden mit 100 m langen und 87 cm hohen Bahnsteigen ausgebaut, sie erhielten wie die unterirdischen Stationen anfangs noch seitliche Verbreiterungen. Erst seit Sommer 1998 wird die Linie U7 mit den 2,65 m breiten ‚U2e'-Wagen bedient, während auf der U6 die umgebauten ‚Ptb'-Wagen fahren.

**Eissporthalle/Festplatz** – auch auf der U7 sind vereinzelt ‚Ptb'-Wagen zu sehen.
– *'Ptb' cars are also sporadically used on line U7.*

*three underground stations started in February 1985. Connecting to the tunnel stubs east of Zoo station, the running tunnels were again built using the NATM; the tubes lie below the terrain of the zoo, and east of Parlamentsplatz below some buildings. The two single-track tunnels converge just before arriving at Eissporthalle station, which like the other two stations was built by cut-and-cover. Due to the incline at Bornheimer Hang, the following tunnel portal is not actually a ramp.*

*Line U7 was extended from Zoo to Enkheim together with the opening of the eastern tunnel extension on 30 May 1992. The surface route was largely taken over from the tramway, the only work necessary being the smoothening of the turn into Borsigallee between Schäfflestraße and Gwinnerstraße. With the tramway having reached Gwinnerstraße back in 1911, the former line 18 was extended to Kruppallee in 1952 and Enkheim in 1957. The tramway route along Gwinnerstraße to Bergen (once line 20, in the end line 12) was abandoned when the Stadtbahn arrived. As its alignment has largely been preserved and even runs on a separate right-of-way along its upper section, it may be revived in some form in the future. All the surface U7 stops were built with 100 m long and 87 cm high platforms. Like the underground stations, they were initially widened for the use of narrower rolling stock. Since summer 1998, line U7 has been operated with 2.65 m wide 'U2e' vehicles, while line U6 is still served by rebuilt 'Ptb' cars.*

**Bockenheimer Warte** – auf der U7 verkehren seit 1998 meist ‚U2e'-Wagen.
– *since 1998, line U7 has mostly been served by 'U2e' cars.*

**Ostbahnhof** – neuester U-Bahnhof auf der C-Strecke
– *newest underground station on route C*

①

②

**_ Heerstraße**

Der westliche Endpunkt der Linie U6 ①② wurde 2004 neu gebaut und dabei mit dem ehemaligen Halt Ebelfeld zusammengelegt. Nördlich der Haltestelle Heerstraße führt ein Verbindungsgleis zur Stadtbahn-Zentralwerkstatt. Eine Verlängerung durch weitgehend unbebautes Gebiet nach Steinbach am Taunus ist möglich.
Die oberirdische Trasse der U6 wurde bereits in den siebziger Jahren auf einen eigenen Gleiskörper gelegt, wie hier zwischen Heerstraße und Friedhof Westhausen ③.

*The western U6 terminus at Heerstraße ①② was rebuilt in 2004 by merging the former Heerstraße stop with the neighbouring Ebelfeld stop. North of the terminus, a service track leads to the Stadtbahn's workshops.*
*An extension of line U6 through largely undeveloped land to Steinbach am Taunus is possible.*
*The surface U6 route was already put on a separate right-of-way in the 1970s, like here between Heerstraße and Friedhof Westhausen ③.*

③

**_ Friedhof Westhausen**

Hier gibt es am stadtauswärtigen Ende Abgänge ④ zu einer Straßenunterführung, am stadteinwärtigen hingegen ebenerdige Zugänge zu den 2001 errichteten Hochbahnsteigen.

*At Friedhof Westhausen, the northern ends of the platforms are accessible via a road underpass ④, whereas at the southern side, ramps lead to platforms raised in 2001.*

**_ Stephan-Heise-Straße**

Die im Jahr 2000 gebauten Hochbahnsteige ⑤ sind am südlichen Ende (S. 79 ①) über einen Fußgängertunnel und am nördlichen ebenerdig zugänglich.

*The high platforms at Stephan-Heise-Straße ⑤ were built in 2000, and are accessible from the southern side via a pedestrian tunnel (p. 79 ①), and at the northern end via ramps.*

④

⑤

## _ Hausener Weg

Ähnlich wie bei Stephan-Heise-Straße ① gab es an der Station Hausener Weg ② früher am Nordende Zugänge über eine Unterführung, welche zwar noch besteht, aber seit dem Bau von 100 m langen Hochbahnsteigen im Jahr 2000 nicht mehr von der Station aus erreicht werden kann. Am Südende führen Treppenabgänge zum Nidda-Ufer.

*Like at Stephan-Heise-Straße ①, Hausener Weg station ② used to have accesses via a pedestrian tunnel located at the northern end. This tunnel still exists, but is no longer connected to the platforms, which were extended to 100 m in 2000. At the southern end, stairs lead down to the Nidda River.*

## _ Fischstein

Westlich der Haltestelle Fischstein kreuzt die U6 an der Russisch-Orthodoxen Kirche ③ einen großen Kreisverkehr, dessen Lage es nicht ermöglicht, die Station an dieser Stelle mit 100 m langen und 87 cm hohen Bahnsteigen auszustatten, weshalb hier bislang von der Straßenebene ④⑤ eingestiegen werden muss. In naher Zukunft soll nun eine neue Station etwas nach Osten verschoben errichtet werden. Anschließend kann auch die Linie U6 mit Fahrzeugen ohne Klapptrittstufen betrieben werden.

*West of Fischstein, line U6 passes a Russian Orthodox Church ③; the large roundabout next to it is the reason why the station is yet to be upgraded with platforms 100 m long and 87 cm high. Boarding is therefore still done from street level ④⑤. A new station to be built slightly further east in the near future will allow line U6 to also be operated with vehicles without folding steps.*

①

### _ Hausen

Anders als auf der U6 wurden die beiden Stationen des U7-Astes bereits 1986 zu Beginn des Stadtbahnbetriebs mit 105 m langen und 87 cm hohen Hochbahnsteigen ausgestattet. Dieser wirkt am Endpunkt Hausen ① mit nur 3,3 m Breite etwas eng.
Der frühere Straßenbahnhalt Ellerfeld gleich südlich der Autobahn ② entfiel beim Umbau auf Stadtbahnbetrieb, da der Abstand zur nächsten Haltestelle zu kurz war.

*Unlike the U6 stops, the stations on the U7 branch were already equipped with 105 m long and 87 cm high platforms in 1986 when Stadtbahn operation began. At the Hausen terminus ①, the island platform is only 3.3 m wide. The former tram stop Ellerfeld, located just south of the motorway ②, was cancelled when the route switched to Stadtbahn operation as it was too close to the neighbouring stations.*

②

### _ Große Nelkenstraße

Dies ist die einzige Station auf der C-Strecke mit versetzt angeordneten Bahnsteigen; diese liegen jeweils vor dem Bahnübergang (stadtauswärts ③, stadteinwärts ④). Anders als bei den unterirdischen Stationen, die eine provisorische Verbreiterung erhielten, baute man hier Bahnsteige für die 2,35 m breiten ‚Pt'-Wagen, weshalb die Kanten 1998 abgesägt werden mussten (▶ S. 75).

*Große Nelkenstraße is the only station on route C with staggered platforms, each of which is located before a level crossing (outbound ③, inbound ④). Unlike the underground stations on route C, which were temporarily widened, the platforms here were initially laid out for 2.35 m wide 'Pt' cars, so in 1998 the edges had to be sawn off (▶ p. 75).*

③

④

**_ Industriehof/Neue Börse**
Direkt westlich der Station Industriehof ① laufen die Linien U6 und U7 zusammen. Diese Haltestelle wurde 1998 zur Einführung der breiteren ‚U2e'-Fahrzeuge mit Hochbahnsteigen ausgestattet ②④. Direkt südöstlich der Station befindet sich die Tunnelrampe ③. Diese wurde so ausgeführt, dass hier eines Tages eine dreigleisige unterirdische Verzweigungsstation gebaut werden könnte, was aber mittelfristig nicht vorgesehen ist. Der erst seit einigen Jahren verwendete Namenszusatz ‚Neue Börse' könnte demnächst wieder verschwinden, da die Börse plant, ins benachbarte Eschborn umzuziehen. Vor der Einfahrt in den Tunnel zweigen zwei Gleise ab ③, die einen Anschluss an das Straßenbahnnetz darstellen. Über die Gleise der Linie 16 erreichen die in Heddernheim beheimateten Fahrzeuge der A-Strecke so die Stadtbahn-Zentralwerkstatt in Rödelheim.

*Lines U6 and U7 converge just west of Industriehof station ①, which was rebuilt with high platforms ②④ in 1998, when the wider 'U2e' cars were first introduced. The ramp to the C tunnel starts immediately southeast of the station ③. The layout of the ramp would allow a future 3-track underground station to be built at Industriehof, although this option is not considered in the mid-term plans. The appendage 'Neue Börse', which has been used for a few years, may disappear in the near future as the Frankfurt Stock Exchange plans to move to nearby Eschborn.*
*The two tracks which diverge right before the tunnel ramp ③ provide a link to the tramway network. The link is required to take the vehicles stabled at the Heddernheim depot on route A to the central Stadtbahn workshops at Rödelheim via the tram tracks otherwise used by line 16.*

**_ Kirchplatz**

Der Name der westlichsten unterirdischen Station der C-Strecke bezieht sich auf die evangelische St. Jakobskirche ① im Stadtteil Bockenheim. Inspiriert von diesem Bauwerk dominieren im U-Bahnhof Rundbögenformen, sowohl an der Decke als auch an den Wänden. Nachbildungen von Kirchenfenstern auf Emailplatten ⑤ und Bilder anderer Gotteshäuser runden den sakralen Charakter ab. Rubinrote Kanten und Rahmen aus Keramikfliesen gliedern den ansonsten grauen Raum.

Der westliche Teil (etwa 2/5) der Station ④ wurde per NÖT aufgefahren, der Rest in offener Bauweise gebaut. Im Zwischengeschoss ② wurde ein 16 m langes Mosaikbild mit einer Ansicht des alten Bockenheim angebracht. Von dort führen zwei Abgänge, jeweils mit zwei Fahrtreppen und einer festen Treppe, auf den Bahnsteig. Der Einbau eines Aufzugs ist für 2009 geplant.

*The name of the westernmost underground station on route C, Kirchplatz [church square], refers to the Protestant St. Jacob's Church ① in the district of Bockenheim. Inspired by this building, the station features rounded arches, on both the ceiling and the walls. Copies of church windows on enamelled panels ⑤, along with images of other places of worship, add to the religious atmosphere of the station. Ruby-red edgings made of ceramic tiles give structure to the otherwise grey space.*
*The western part of the station (i.e. about two fifths of it) ④ was excavated using the NATM, whereas the rest was built by cut-and-cover. In the mezzanine ②, a 16 m mosaic depicts the old Bockenheim town centre. From there, two separate flights of stairs, each with a pair of escalators, lead down to the platform. The retrofitting of the station with a lift is planned for 2009.*

①

②

**_ Leipziger Straße**

Der U-Bahnhof im Herzen des Stadtteils Bockenheim unterscheidet sich von den übrigen der C-Strecke durch seine übereinander angeordneten Bahnsteigebenen, was wegen der geringen Breite der Leipziger Straße ① erforderlich war. Stadtauswärts halten die Züge auf der untersten Ebene (-3) ③, die mit blauen Fliesen verkleidet ist. Eine Ebene höher (-2, gelb) kann man Richtung Stadtzentrum einsteigen. Im Bereich der westlichen Treppenanlage gibt es zwischen beiden Ebenen eine achteckige Öffnung ②, eine Form, die sich auch in der Anordnung der Deckenbeleuchtung widerspiegelt.

Auf beiden Ebenen hängen an den Wänden Bilder mit Eingängen zu den ältesten U-Bahnen Europas, nämlich London, Paris, Berlin, Budapest ④, Wien ⑤ und Madrid, womit Frankfurt klar seinen Anspruch zum Ausdruck brachte, zu den Städten mit richtigen U-Bahnen zu gehören (siehe S. 7).

③

*Leipziger Straße station is located in the centre of the district of Bockenheim. Unlike the other stations on route C, its two platforms lie one on top of the other due to the narrowness of Leipziger Straße ①. Outbound trains stop on the lowest level (-3) ③, which is clad in blue tiles. One level up (-2, yellow) is for inbound trains. Near the western staircase, there is an octagonal opening between the two levels ②. The octagonal shape is also visible in the arrangement of the lights on the ceiling.*

*The decoration of both platform levels with some entrances to Europe's oldest metro systems, notably London, Paris, Berlin, Budapest ④, Vienna ⑤ and Madrid, underlines Frankfurt's claim to be a city with a real U-Bahn system (see p. 7).*

④

⑤

①

②

**_ Bockenheimer Warte**

Dieser U-Bahnhof wurde mit dem Namen ‚Universität' geplant und gehört zu den am meisten frequentierten außerhalb der Innenstadt. Seit 2001 kann man hier über das östliche Zwischengeschoss ② oder über eine direkte Treppe bzw. einen Aufzug in die Linie U4 (▶ S. 58), die eine Ebene tiefer abfährt, umsteigen. Von diesem Zwischengeschoss führen mehrere Ausgänge an die Oberfläche, darunter der ‚ausbrechende U-Bahn-Wagen' ① von Prof. Zbigniew Pininski. Die östlichsten Zugänge beiderseits der Bockenheimer Landstraße konnten in neue Gebäude integriert werden. Der westliche Ausgang (mit Schrägaufzug) führt zum namensgebenden Landwehrturm aus dem 15. Jahrhundert (▶ S. 105). Über der Station liegt ein Magazin der Universitätsbibliothek. Die Hintergleiswände zieren großflächige Fotos mit Szenen aus der Goethe-Universität, dazwischen spiegeln sich die wartenden Studenten auf dem Bahnsteig. Manche Stützen auf dem Bahnsteig und im Verteilergeschoss sind nichttragend und dienen nur der Raumgestaltung, eine Idee des Architektenbüros Nieper und Partner.

③

*Bockenheimer Warte station was planned as 'Universität'; it is among the busiest stations outside the city centre. Since 2001, transfer to line U4 (▶ p. 58), which departs from the lower level, has been possible either via direct stairs or a direct lift, or with escalators by taking a detour via the eastern mezzanine ②. From this mezzanine, several exits lead to the surface, among them 'The Escaping Metro Carriage' ① by Professor Zbigniew Pininski. The easternmost exits on either side of Bockenheimer Landstraße were integrated into new buildings.*
*The western exit, which has an inclined lift, leads to the Bockenheimer Warte, a 15th century defence tower (▶ p. 105). The space above the station is used by the University library for storage. The walls behind the tracks are decorated with large images of scenes from the Goethe University, the mirrors between them reflecting the students waiting on the platform. Some of the columns on the platform and the mezzanine are non-supporting and merely decorative (an idea of the architects Nieper & Partner).*

④

⑤

①

②

**_ Westend**
Der vom Architekturbüro A.C. Walter und Partner entworfene U-Bahnhof gehört sicherlich zu den gestalterischen Höhepunkten der Frankfurter Stadtbahn. Inspiriert durch den nahe gelegenen Palmengarten werden die Zugänge an beiden Bahnsteigenden ②④ von mächtigen pflanzenartigen Säulen dominiert. Von den beiden Emporen bekommt der Fahrgast einen guten Überblick ⑤ über die vergleichsweise sehr hohe Bahnsteighalle. Die in verschiedenen Pastelltönen gehaltenen Farbstreifen an den Wänden gingen ursprünglich ineinander über, mussten aber nach einer Verunstaltung durch Graffiti in vereinfachter Form renoviert werden. In den Jahren 2009/10 ist der Einbau von Aufzügen vorgesehen.

③

*Westend station was designed by the architects A.C. Walter & Partner, and is without doubt one of the most appealing on the Frankfurt Stadtbahn system. Inspired by the nearby Palmengarten, the access areas at either end of the platform are dominated by massive plant-like columns ②④. Due to the comparatively high ceiling, passengers can overlook the entire station from the galleries ⑤. The pastel-coloured stripes on the walls originally blended into each other, but due to vandalism, they had to be restored in a simplified form. In 2009/2010, the station will be retrofitted with lifts.*

④

⑤

## _ Alte Oper

Der als ‚Opernplatz' geplante U-Bahnhof am westlichen Rand der Innenstadt bildet mit dem U-Bahnhof Westend eine gewisse gestalterische Einheit (ebenfalls ein Werk des Architekturbüros A.C. Walter), allerdings wurde hier die Bahnsteighalle stützenlos ③ ausgeführt und die markanten Säulen mit Pilzköpfen ④ sind nur am westlichen Bahnsteigende zu sehen. Trotz der geringeren Höhe wirkt der Bahnhof durch den hellen Anstrich der Decke sehr geräumig. Bei den abstrakten Formen an den Wänden herrschen warme Erdtöne vor. Am östlichen Ende setzt sich der Bahnsteig einige Meter bis zu den Aufgängen fort ②. Vom östlichen Zwischengeschoss wurde ein direkter Zugang zum Opernfoyer geschaffen. Der Einbau von Aufzügen ist in naher Zukunft geplant.

*Alte Oper station lies at the western edge of the city centre and was originally planned as 'Opernplatz'. In some respects, this station is similar to the neighbouring Westend station, both having been designed by the architects A.C. Walter & Partner, but it was built without supporting pillars ③, and the characteristic columns are only found at the western exit ④. The ceiling is lower than at Westend, but with its yellowish paint, it still gives the impression of a very spacious station. Warm earthly tones dominate the abstract shapes on the walls. At the eastern end, the platform is extended a few metres ② to allow passengers to reach the exit. From the eastern mezzanine, a direct entrance into the opera house was built. Lifts will be added in the near future.*

**_ Hauptwache**
Auf der C-Strecke wurde der U-Bahnhof Hauptwache zwar erst 1986 von der Stadtbahn in Betrieb genommen, der Rohbau entstand jedoch schon Mitte der sechziger Jahre im Zuge des Baus der A-Strecke (▶ S. 27). Die C-Linien halten hier an Seitenbahnsteigen, die S-Bahn (▶ S. 119) dazwischen bereits seit 1978 an einem Mittelbahnsteig ④. Die Wände der Bahnsteigebene wurden mit farbigen Paneelen verkleidet.
Die so genannte B-Ebene ① wurde Anfang der achtziger Jahre nach einem Entwurf des Architekten Laske neu gestaltet. Dabei wurde der Bereich eines Abgangs zum Bahnsteig Richtung Westen mit Bildern alter Straßenbahnwagen ② verschönert.

*Hauptwache underground station on route C was only opened in 1986, but the station shell had already been realised in the 1960s together with the A tunnel (▶ p. 27). The C lines use side platforms, whereas since 1978, the S-Bahn (▶ p. 119) has been stopping at an island platform ④ located between the C tracks. The walls on the platforms are clad with colourful panels. The mezzanine ① was refurbished in the 1980s following a design by the architect Laske. Among other things, one of the accesses to the westbound platform was decorated with pictures of old tram vehicles ②.*

**_ Konstablerwache**

Mitten im Stadtzentrum kann man am selben Bahnsteig von der Stadtbahn in die S-Bahn (▶ S. 120) umsteigen ②, wobei die Stadtbahn auf den äußeren Gleisen hält. Vom östlichen Ende der Bahnsteige führen Treppenaufgänge zu den Bahnsteigen der B-Strecke (U4/U5, ▶ S. 63) hinauf. Weitere Aufgänge verbinden die Bahnsteige mit einer Zwischenebene ①, in der wie an der Hauptwache mehrere Läden untergebracht sind. Die Bahnsteigkanten der S-Bahn setzen sich nach Westen fort, da diese mit einer Standardlänge von 210 m etwa doppelt so lang sind wie die der Stadtbahn.

Die Wände hinter den Gleisen der Stadtbahn ③ wurden farblich nach einer Idee von F.E. von Garnier gestaltet. Die bei genauem Hinsehen erkennbaren Buchstaben stellen einen Auszug eines Texts einer Ratsverordnung von 1756 über das Benehmen auf den Straßen dar – der Bezug zur Gegenwart steht außer Frage:

„.... nachdrücklich von Obrigkeits wegen verwarnet, sich des übermäßigen Trinckens und Zechens bis in die sinckende Nacht [...] in den Häusern sowohl, als auf den Gassen, zu enthalten."

*Right in the heart of the city, interchange between route C and the S-Bahn (▶ p. 120) is provided on the same platform ②, with the Stadtbahn stopping on the outer tracks. Stairs lead up to the route B platforms (U4/U5; ▶ p. 63) from the eastern ends of the two island platforms. Further exits connect the platforms with a mezzanine ①, which, like at Hauptwache, accommodates several shops. The platform edges used by the S-Bahn extend further west, as with the standard length of 210 m they are about double the length of those for the Stadtbahn.*

*The walls behind the Stadtbahn tracks boast a colourful design ③ created by F. E. von Garnier. A closer look reveals a series of words reproducing the text of a 1756 ordinance on behaviour on public roads – its message without doubt still valid today:*

*"... the citizens are strongly advised by the authorities to refrain from drinking and boozing into the deep night [...], inside their houses as well as out in the streets and alleys."*

①

②

## _ Zoo

Diese dreigleisige Anlage verfügt über einen stadteinwärtigen Mittelbahnsteig, sowie einen mittig angeordneten Seitenbahnsteig ③ stadtauswärts. Direkt östlich des Bahnhofs verzweigt sich die C-Strecke unterhalb des Zoogeländes in einen Ast zum Ostbahnhof (U6) und einen nach Enkheim (U7).
Es lag auf der Hand, den Tierpark als Motiv für die Gestaltung des Bahnhofs zu nehmen, was auch auf allen Ebenen klar sichtbar ist. Im östlichen Zwischengeschoss ② findet man Tiermotive auf weißen Emailplatten, auf der Bahnsteigebene wurden solche im Stil der naiven Malerei von Hildegard Lackschewitz direkt auf die Betonwände aufgetragen. Selbst als Bahnhofsmobiliar dienen Schildkröten und Elefanten. Wie Westend und Alte Oper stammt das Gestaltungskonzept vom Architekturbüro A.C. Walter.

③

*The 3-track Zoo station has both an inbound island platform, as well as a side platform ③ for outbound trains, with, rather unusually, doors opening on the left side. Just to the east of the station, route C diverges beneath the terrain of the zoo into a branch to Ostbahnhof (U6) and another to Enkheim (U7). The theme of the station is clearly recognisable: the eastern mezzanine ② shows animals on white enamelled panels, and on the platform level they cover the walls, with naïve paintings created on concrete by Hildegard Lackschewitz. Turtles and elephants also function as benches on the platforms. Like Westend and Alte Oper, the overall design was conceived by A.C. Walter.*

④

⑤

①

②

## _ Ostbahnhof

Hier wurde erstmals in Frankfurt ein U-Bahnhof mit Tageslichteinfall über eine Glaspyramide ①④ errichtet. Das Gestaltungskonzept des Bahnhofs stammt von Willy Orth. Auf der Bahnsteigebene dominiert die Farbe Grau, ergänzt durch Schwarz-Weiß-Fotografien an den Wänden, die die Geschichte der Mainbrücken (in Bild ⑤ die Deutschherrnbrücke für die Eisenbahn) veranschaulichen. In der Zwischenebene ② wird durch farbige Wandfliesen die Frankfurter Skyline angedeutet. Wegen der lange unklaren Lage des geplanten unterirdischen S-Bahnhofs konnte der U-Bahnhof anfangs nur auf einer Länge von 75 m fertig gestellt werden, weshalb die Züge mangels Durchrutschweg mit 10 km/h in den Bahnhof einfahren mussten. Erst am 26. Juni 2007 konnte der Bahnsteig auf 105 m verlängert werden. Dieser Teil ③ wurde als Betonkasten bei laufendem Bahnbetrieb unter die Gleise der DB geschoben (Vorpressbauweise). Hinter dem Bahnhof befindet sich keine Wendeanlage. Am Ostausgang besteht nun eine bessere Umsteigemöglichkeit zur Straßenbahnlinie 11, für die eine neue Haltestelle eingerichtet wurde.

③

*Ostbahnhof [eastern railway station] was designed by Willy Orth, and was the first underground station in Frankfurt to have daylight coming down to the platform level ①④, which is dominated by the colour grey. The walls are enhanced with black-and-white photographs illustrating the history of the Main bridges (photo ⑤ shows a railway bridge called Deutschherrnbrücke). In the mezzanine ②, a colourful silhouette hints at Frankfurt's American-style skyline.*
*Due to the undefined location of the future underground S-Bahn station, the Stadtbahn station was initially only built 75 m long, so for safety reasons the trains had to enter the station with a maximum speed of 10 km/h. By 26 June 2007, the platform had been extended to 105 m ③ by driving a precast concrete box beneath the DB tracks with the help of hydraulic presses. Beyond the station, there are no sidings. At the new eastern exit, a tram stop was added on line 11 to improve transfer between tram and Stadtbahn.*

④

⑤

**_ Habsburgerallee**
Während die Stationen des zentralen Abschnitts der C-Strecke von bekannten Architekten gestaltet wurden, übernahm das Stadtbahnbauamt diese Aufgabe bei den drei Bahnhöfen der Ostverlängerung selbst. Durch die achteckigen Mittelstützen, die sich nur farblich unterscheiden, entstand auf diesem Abschnitt eine gestalterische Einheit. Im U-Bahnhof Habsburgerallee zieren Esel, die allerlei Lasten tragen ④, die Außenwände, ein Werk von Manfred Stumpf. Am östlichen Ende führen die Aufgänge in ein großzügiges Zwischengeschoss ② unter der Kreuzung Rhönstraße/Habsburgerallee ①. In der kleineren westlichen Zwischenebene ist eine Fotocollage mit Ansichten aus dem Stadtteil Ostend ⑤ zu sehen.

*While the stations on the central section of route C were designed by renowned architects, the three underground stations on the eastern extension were planned by the Stadtbahn construction office. With their octagonal columns, coloured differently in each station, the three stations have a similar basic design.*

*The walls in Habsburgerallee station are decorated with a large number of donkeys carrying all sorts of loads ④, a work of art created by Manfred Stumpf. At the eastern end, there is a large mezzanine ② below the Rhönstraße/Habsburgerallee road intersection ①. The smaller western mezzanine is decorated with a photo collage showing images of the Ostend district ⑤.*

①

②

**_ Parlamentsplatz**

Dieser U-Bahnhof ist baulich weitgehend mit der benachbarten Station Habsburgerallee identisch. Im mittleren Bereich der Bahnsteighalle sind die Außenwände mit Schwarzweißbildern ④ geschmückt, die in abstrahierter Form aus einem Prospekt eines Supermarkts stammen, eine Idee von Udo Koch.

*Parlamentsplatz underground station is laid out like the neighbouring Habsburgerallee station. The centre part of the side walls on platform level is decorated with black-and-white shapes ④ which, in an abstract form, were taken from a supermarket's advertising leaflet; this work of art was created by Udo Koch.*

③

④

⑤

①

②

**_ Eissporthalle/Festplatz**
Der Haupteingang am westlichen Ende des Bahnhofs, der wegen der hier vorbeiführenden Straße als ‚Ratsweg' geplant wurde, ist der einzige der Frankfurter Stadtbahn mit einem richtigen Eingangsgebäude ①②, in dem die Fahrkartenautomaten und Informationstafeln untergebracht sind. Von hier führen die Abgänge ohne Zwischengeschoss direkt auf den Bahnsteig. Die Eissporthalle sowie der Festplatz, auf dem zweimal jährlich die ‚Dippemess' stattfindet, sind über den östlichen Ausgang ④ erreichbar. An den mit roten Emailplatten verkleideten Wänden hängen Schwarz-Weiß-Fotografien von Gerald Domenig mit Szenen aus der Eissporthalle und ihrer Umgebung.

③

*From the western side, Eissporthalle/Festplatz station is accessible from a road called Ratsweg, a name initially planned for the station, too. This access is the only one on the Frankfurt Stadtbahn with a surface entrance pavilion ①②; it accommodates ticket machines as well as information panels. Without a mezzanine, the stairs and escalators lead directly to the island platform. The ice stadium, as well as the Festplatz, the terrain where the Dippemess festival is held twice a year, is accessible via the eastern exit ④. The red enamelled panels on the station walls are enhanced with black-and-white photographs by Gerald Domenig showing scenes in and around the ice stadium.*

④

⑤

**_ Johanna-Tesch-Platz**

Zwischen Eissporthalle und Johanna-Tesch-Platz verlässt die U7 den Tunnel am Bornheimer Hang fast eben ①. Die Stadtbahntrasse führt in nördlicher Seitenlage der Straße Am Erlenbruch oberirdisch weiter. An der Haltestelle Johanna-Tesch-Platz, die sonst dem Standardtyp der Enkheimer Strecke entspricht ②, gibt es westlich der Autobahnbrücke einen Minibahnsteig für die Linie 12, die bei der Fahrt vom und zum Depot hier hält.

*Between the ice stadium and Johanna-Tesch-Platz, line U7 emerges from the tunnel on an almost flat alignment. The Stadtbahn then continues on the surface along the northern side of Am Erlenbruch road. At Johanna-Tesch-Platz, otherwise a standard surface station, there is a small platform for tram line 12 on the western side of the motorway viaduct; this platform is only used by trams entering or leaving the depot.*

**_ Schäfflestraße**

Diese Haltestelle ③ liegt direkt nach der Zufahrt zum Betriebshof Ost. Hier endet seit 15. Juni 2008 probeweise die U4, sie wendet auf einem an der Nordseite anschließenden 100 m langen Kehrgleis (▶ S. 56).

*Schäfflestraße station ③ is located next to the access to the depot. Since 15 June 2008, it has been the terminus for some U4 trains, which reverse in a 100 m siding located on the northern side (▶ p. 56).*

**_ Gwinnerstraße**

Nach einem verkehrsreichen Bahnübergang ④ erreicht die U7 die Station Gwinnerstraße ⑤, die direkt am Abzweig der ehemaligen Strecke nach Bergen liegt, weshalb eine Wiederinbetriebnahme schwierig wäre.

*After passing a busy level crossing ④, line U7 arrives at Gwinnerstraße ⑤, located directly at the point where the former tram route to Bergen used to diverge; the re-opening of that line would therefore be complicated.*

**_ Kruppstraße**

Bis zur Endstation liegt die Trasse der U7 in Mittellage der Borsigallee. An der Kruppstraße ①② befindet sich ein großes Parkhaus am derzeitigen Ende der östlichen A66.

*Line U7 continues on the centre strip of Borsigallee all the way to the terminus. The large park-and-ride facility at Kruppstraße ①② is ideally located at what is currently the end of the A66 motorway.*

**_ Hessen-Center**

Das Hessen-Center ist eines der größten Einkaufszentren im Großraum Frankfurt.
An den meisten Haltestellen der Strecke nach Enkheim werden die Autos durch Ampeln zurückgehalten, so dass die Fahrgäste auf der gesamten Länge des Bahnsteigs direkt die Straße überqueren können ③.

*Hessen-Center is one of the biggest shopping malls in the Frankfurt metropolitan area. At most stops along the Enkheim route, when a Stadtbahn train stops, cars have to wait at special traffic lights, so passengers can cross the road along the full length of the platform ③.*

**_ Enkheim**

An der Endstation fahren Busse durch ein massives Portal ⑤ quasi auf den Mittelbahnsteig, so dass die Fahrgäste hier bequem umsteigen können ④.

*At Enkheim, the terminus, convenient transfer ④ is provided by connecting buses which enter the station through a massive portal located at the eastern end ⑤.*

Wagen 1001 – Prototyp-Wagen in den Farben, wie er auf der Internationalen Verkehrsausstellung 1965 gezeigt wurde, im Verkehrsmuseum Frankfurt in Schwanheim (*Foto Stephan Kyrieleis, 12/1996*)
*– Car 1001 – prototype vehicle on display at the Verkehrsmuseum Frankfurt in Schwanheim, in a special livery as shown at the International Transport Fair in 1965*

Wagen 603 – neueste Fahrzeuggeneration des Typs ‚U5-25' auf Probefahrt an der Verzweigung Industriehof (*Foto Thomas Lusmöller, 06/2008*)
*– Car 603, which belongs to the latest rolling stock generation of class 'U5-25', on a test run at the Industriehof junction*

## _ Stadtbahn-Fahrzeuge

Nach Auslieferung des ersten Fahrzeugs des Typs ‚U5' im Mai 2008 verkehren auf dem Frankfurter Stadtbahnnetz, das eine Standardspurweite von 1435 mm aufweist und mit 600 V Gleichstrom über eine Oberleitung versorgt wird, derzeit fünf verschiedene Fahrzeugtypen. Um Verwechslungen mit den einzelnen Linien zu vermeiden, werden diese hier unter Anführungsstrichen geschrieben, zumal es auch kaum Übereinstimmung der Wagentypenbezeichnung mit der bedienten Linie gibt (z.B. Typ ‚U3' > Linie U4). Charakteristisch für das Frankfurter Stadtbahnnetz ist die Vielzahl unterschiedlicher Bahnsteighöhen (0/15/56/80/87 cm, früher auch noch 32 cm), sowie die unterschiedlichen Fußbodenhöhen (87/97 cm) und Breiten (2,35/2,65 m) der eingesetzten Fahrzeuge, ein Zustand, der nach langen provisorischen Zwischenstadien erst allmählich und mit großem Aufwand vereinheitlicht werden kann.

Als 1968 die erste unterirdische Strecke der Frankfurter Stadtbahn in Betrieb ging, fuhren neben den neuen Fahrzeugen vom Typ ‚U2' auch tunneltauglich gemachte Straßenbahnfahrzeuge des Typs ‚Mt' mit Beiwagen ‚mt' im Tunnel. Da diese Einrichtungsfahrzeuge nur 2,35 m breit waren, wurden an der Türseite Verbreiterungen, sog. Blumenkästen, angebracht. Sie waren mit Klapptrittstufen ausgestattet, wodurch der Einstieg sowohl vom Straßenniveau als auch von 32 bzw. 56 cm hohen Bahnsteigen möglich war. Die ‚Mt'-Wagen (Nr. 618-645) waren mit entsprechenden Beiwagen noch bis 1978 auf den Linie A3 und A4 im Einsatz, danach kamen sie ins städtische Straßenbahnnetz zurück.

Für den eigentlichen Stadtbahn-Betrieb wurden zwei Prototyp-Fahrzeuge (1001 und 1002; später als Typ ‚U1' mit den Nummern 301 und 302 eingeordnet) entwickelt. Dabei hatte man sich in Frankfurt nicht wie in München oder Nürnberg für eine Wagenbreite von 2,90 m entschieden, sondern für 2,65 m, da solche Fahrzeuge laut BOStrab ab 1965 auch im Straßenraum einsetzbar waren und immerhin in der Breite auch den Berliner Großprofilzügen entsprachen. Statt der in Berlin üblichen Doppeltriebwagen handelte es sich beim Typ ‚U1' jedoch um einen 21,8 m langen sechsachsigen Gelenktriebwagen, der außerdem mit Klapptrittstufen ausgestattet war, da auch an niedrigen Bahnsteigen gehalten werden musste. Die beiden Prototypen waren selten im Fahrgasteinsatz zu sehen und wurden schließlich 1976 außer Dienst gestellt. Wagen 1001 ist heute in den ursprünglichen Farben von 1965 im Straßenbahn-Museum in Schwanheim zu sehen.

## *_ Rolling Stock*

*The Frankfurt Stadtbahn system has 1435 mm standard gauge and a 600 V dc power supply via overhead catenary. With the first vehicle of class 'U5' having been delivered in May 2008, the Stadtbahn fleet now comprises five different types of cars. The rolling stock designations are written with quotation marks in this book to avoid confusion with the line numbers, particularly as in most cases the designation of the car type does not coincide with the line it serves (e.g. class 'U3' runs on line U4). A special feature of the Frankfurt Stadtbahn system has always been the variety of different platform heights (0/15/56/80/87 cm, previously also 32 cm), as well as the different car floor heights (87/97 cm) and car widths (2.35/2.65 m); they are all gradually being brought to the same standard now, although at a high cost.*

*When the first underground section opened in Frankfurt in 1968, the tunnel was not only used by new trains of class 'U2', but also by rebuilt tram vehicles of type 'Mt' with 'mt' trailers (the t stands for tunnel). As these vehicles were only 2.35 m wide, extensions had to be added to their sides. The cars were equipped with folding steps to allow access from street level as well as from 32 and 56 cm high platforms. On lines A3 and A4, the 'Mt' vehicles (no. 618-645) and their respective trailers remained in service until 1978, when they were transferred to the surface tram network.*

*For Stadtbahn operation, two prototype cars were developed (no. 1001 and 1002; later classified as 'U1' and numbered 301 and 302). Unlike in Munich or Nuremberg, the car width was fixed at 2.65 m instead of 2.90 m, so these vehicles were also permitted to run on streets, and 2.65 m was still equivalent to the large-profile U-Bahn stock in Berlin. Instead of the permanently coupled pairs typically used in Berlin, however, the 'U1' car was designed as a 21.8 m articulated six-axle vehicle; it was equipped with folding steps to allow boarding from low platforms. The two prototype cars were rarely seen in regular passenger service, and were finally withdrawn in 1976. Car 1001 is on display in its 1965 livery at the Tramway Museum in Schwanheim.*

## _ Betriebshöfe

Der erste Betriebshof für die Stadtbahn wurde in **Heddernheim** im Depot der Städtischen Straßenbahn, das bereits seit 1910 in Betrieb war, eingerichtet. Hier sind alle Fahrzeuge der A-Strecke beheimatet. Am 28. September 1980 kam es zu einem Brandanschlag, bei dem fünf Wagen zerstört und weitere schwer beschädigt wurden. Die Linien der A-Strecke (U1-U3) fahren nördlich der Station Heddernheim über das Gelände des Betriebshofs und verzweigen sich am nördlichen Rand. Die ausgedehnten Abstellgleise sind von den Streckengleisen nur aus südlicher Richtung angebunden.

Der **Betriebshof Ost** (Sausee) zwischen Seckbach und Riederwald ging nach langen Verzögerungen schließlich am 12. Juli 2003 in Betrieb. Er ist vom Norden her durch einen Tunnelabzweig an die bisherige Endstelle der U4, Seckbacher Landstraße, angeschlossen. An der Südseite münden zwei Verbindungsgleise westlich der Haltestelle Schäfflestraße in die Strecke der Linie U7 ein. Über diese beiden Verbindungen wird seit 15. Juni 2008 probeweise die Linie U4 verlängert. Im Betriebshof Ost finden neben den Fahrzeugen der B- und C-Strecke auch die Straßenbahnen der Linien 12 und 14 ihr Zuhause.

Neben den beiden Betriebshöfen gibt es noch begrenzte nächtliche Abstellmöglichkeiten in Bommersheim an der U3, zwischen Römerstadt und Niddapark (U1), sowie im Straßenbahndepot Eckenheim (U5).

Für größere Reparaturen und Hauptuntersuchungen werden alle Fahrzeuge in die **Stadtbahn-Zentralwerkstatt** (StZW) in Rödelheim gebracht. Diese ist über ein Verbindungsgleis an die Endstation der Linie U6, Heerstraße, angeschlossen. Um dorthin zu kommen, sind alle Fahrzeuge laut BOStrab für den Straßenbahnbetrieb zugelassen, da sie auf ihrem Weg von den Betriebshöfen auf herkömmlichen Straßenbahngleisen im Straßenraum verkehren müssen bzw. mussten.

Betriebshof Ost (Sausee)

Heddernheim

## _ *Depots*

*The first Stadtbahn depot was established at **Heddernheim**, where a depot for the municipal tramway had already existed since 1910. All cars for route A are stabled there. On 28 September 1980, five cars were destroyed and many more damaged in an arson attack. North of Heddernheim station, the A lines (U1-U3) run through the depot before diverging in different directions. The numerous sidings are only accessible from the southern side.*

*The **Betriebshof Ost** [eastern depot] at Sausee, between Seckbach and Riederwald, was opened on 12 July 2003 after long delays. From the northern side, it is linked to the traditional U4 terminus at Seckbacher Landstraße via an underground branch, while at the southern side, the access tracks diverge from the U7 route west of the Schäfflestraße stop. Since 15 June 2008, a trial service with an extended line U4 has been provided over these access tracks. The eastern depot is the base for all vehicles used on routes B and C, as well as for the tram cars operating on lines 12 and 14.*

*Besides the two main depots, there are limited stabling facilities at Bommersheim on line U3, between Römerstadt and Niddapark on line U1, and in the tramway depot Eckenheim on line U5.*

*Major repair work and regular overhauls are performed at the **Stadtbahn-Zentralwerkstatt** (StZW) in Rödelheim. These central workshops are accessible from the U6 terminus at Heerstraße. All the Stadtbahn cars are licensed as tram vehicles to operate on-street as they have or had to use conventional tramway tracks to get there.*

**Wagenpark**
***Rolling Stock***

| Typ *Class* | Wagennummer *Car Number* | Baujahr *Year* | Hersteller *Manufacturer* | Anmerkungen *Notes* |
|---|---|---|---|---|
| < **U1** > | 301-302 | 1965-66 | DUEWAG | Prototyp 1001 (1967 > Museum) & 1002 (1979 ausgemustert \| *scrapped*) |
| < **U2** > | 303-332 | 1968-69 | DUEWAG | |
| < **U2** > | 333-347 | 1971 | DUEWAG/Wegmann | |
| < **U2** > | 348-367 | 1975-76 | DUEWAG/Wegmann | |
| < **U2** > | 368-399 | 1977-78 | DUEWAG | |
| < **U2** > | 400-406 | 1984 | DUEWAG | Ersatz für bei Brand zerstörte Wagen \| *replacement for cars destroyed in fire* |
| < **Ptb** > | 651-680 | 1972 | DUEWAG | 1. Serie mit Klapptrittstufen geliefert \| *1st series delivered with folding steps* |
| < **Ptb** > | 681-716 | 1972-73 | DUEWAG | 2. Serie nachträglich mit Klapptrittstufen \| *2nd series retrofitted with folding steps* |
| < **Ptb** > | 717-750 | 1977-78 | DUEWAG | 3. Serie nachträglich mit Klapptrittstufen \| *3rd series retrofitted with folding steps* |
| < **U3** > | 451-477 | 1979-80 | DUEWAG/Wegmann | für Linie U4 \| *for line U4* |
| < **U4** > | 501-518 | 1994-95 | DUEWAG (Siemens) | |
| < **U4** > | 519-539 | 1996-98 | DUEWAG (Siemens) | |
| < **U5** > | 601- | 2008-15 | Bombardier | Flexity Swift |

‚U2'-Wagen 343 in rot-weißem Originalanstrich 1985 in der U-Bahn-Station Hauptwache *(Foto Alexander Piesenecker)*
– *'U2' car 343 in original red-and-white livery at Hauptwache in 1985*

Auch 2008 waren noch vereinzelt ‚U2'-Wagen in Orange/Elfenbein unterwegs, wie hier Wagen 361 in Weißkirchen Ost.
– *In 2008, a few 'U2' cars in orange-and-ivory livery were still in service, like car 361 at Weißkirchen Ost.*

Nach den Erfahrungen im Probebetrieb mit den Prototyp-Fahrzeugen wurden für die Serienproduktion einige Änderungen vorgenommen. Der nun als ‚**U2**' bezeichnete Wagen ist mit 23,00 m (24,30 m über Kupplung) länger als die Vorgänger und hat eine stark veränderte Stirnfront. Die Wagenhöhe beträgt 3,28 m, die Breite 2,65 m. Der Wagenboden wurde von 93 auf 97 cm erhöht, dazu kam statt Klapptrittstufen eine feste Trittstufe bei 68 cm Höhe, die den Einstieg an den meist 56 cm hohen Bahnsteigen ermöglichte (zwischen Zeilweg und Hohemark gab es lange trotz ‚U2'-Einsatzes nur 32 cm hohe Bahnsteige). Die Höchstgeschwindigkeit ist auf 80 km/h ausgelegt. Nur die beiden äußeren Drehgestelle sind angetrieben.

Der ursprüngliche Außenanstrich war rot mit weißer Bauchbinde. Zwischen 1981 und 1987 erhielten alle Fahrzeuge einen neuen Anstrich in ‚Reinorange', ‚Hellelfenbein' und ‚Beigegrau', und seit 1996 werden sie in der neuen VGF-Farbe ‚Subaru Vista Blue' lackiert. In den achtziger Jahren wurden im Zuge von Hauptuntersuchungen an den Wagenenden Fenster eingebaut, um so das Sicherheitsgefühl der Fahrgäste zu erhöhen.

1998 wurde schließlich in den Wagen 368-399 die Trittstufe entfernt und so für den Einsatz an den 87 cm hohen Bahnsteigen auf der C-Strecke umgebaut. Diese Fahrzeuge gehören seither zum Typ ‚U2e' (ebener Fußboden auf 97 cm Höhe). Bei

*With the experience gained from the tests with the prototype cars, several modifications were made before serial production started. The resulting '**U2**' car is 23.00 m long (24.30 m over couplers), and thus slightly longer than its predecessor; it also has a heavily modified front. The car height is 3.28 m, and width 2.65 m. The car floor was raised from 93 to 97 cm, and the folding steps were replaced by a 68 cm fixed step, which allowed access from 56 cm high standard platforms (for a long time the platforms between Zeilweg and Hohemark were only 32 cm high, despite the use of 'U2' cars). Their maximum speed is 80 km/h. The two end bogies are motorised.*

*The original livery was red with a white stripe along the lower side. Between 1981 and 1987, all 'U2' cars were repainted in orange, ivory and grey, and since 1996, most of them have been changed to the new VGF colour 'subaru vista blue'. During the 1980s, windows were added at the car ends to create a safer atmosphere for passengers.*

*In 1998, the intermediate step was removed from cars no. 368 to 399, which have since been used on route C, where platforms are 87 cm high. These modified cars are now referred to as subclass 'U2e', which has a level car floor at 97 cm. The rest of the 'U2' cars were rebuilt in 1999, with the in-car step being raised from 68 to 87 cm, thus leaving a step of 10 cm inside*

Entwicklung der Einstiegssituation beim ‚U2'-Wagen (Bahnsteighöhe in Klammer) | *Evolution of the access into the 'U2' vehicle (platform height in brackets)*
① U2 (56 cm; *Foto Hans-Ulrich Riedel*) | ② U2h (80 cm) | ③ U2h (56 cm) | ④ U2e (87 cm)

Direkter Vergleich zweier ‚U2'-Wagen in Ginnheim, links Wagen 382 in Orange/ Hellelfenbein, rechts Wagen 357 im neuen Türkis (*Foto S. Kyrieleis, 11/1997*).
– *Direct comparison between two 'U2' cars at Ginnheim: on the left, car 382 in orange-and-ivory, on the right, car 357 in the new turquoise livery.*

Fast baugleicher ‚U2'-Wagen in San Diego (Kalifornien, USA). Mangels Hochbahnsteige steht an der vorderen Tür ein Lift zur Verfügung.
– *Almost identical 'U2' cars are in service in San Diego (California, USA): as there are no high platforms, a lift is available at the train's first door.*

den übrigen ‚U2'-Fahrzeugen wurde dann 1999 die Trittstufe von 68 auf 87 cm erhöht, wobei nun im Wageninnern eine 10 cm hohe Stufe bleibt (‚U2h'). Auf der A-Strecke konnte so von 80 cm hohen Bahnsteigen quasi eben eingestiegen werden, gleichzeitig aber auch von weiterhin nur 56 cm hohen. Mittlerweile sind fast alle Bahnsteige der A-Strecke auf 80 cm erhöht worden. Zwischen 2001 und 2004 wurden in mehreren Wagen an einer Tür pro Seite die Haltestange entfernt, um so Rollstuhlfahrern oder Personen mit Kinderwagen das Einsteigen an einer 120 cm breiten Tür zu erleichtern.

Die Wagen 314, 317, 318, 320 und 323 wurden 1980 bei einem Brand im Betriebshof Heddernheim zerstört und Wagen 355 ist nach einer Entgleisung seit Dezember 2005 außer Dienst.

Fast baugleiche Fahrzeuge des Typs ‚U2' findet man auch im kalifornischen San Diego im Einsatz, wohin von 1981 bis 1990 solche Wagen mit festen Stufen geliefert wurden, sowie in den kanadischen Städten Edmonton und Calgary, wo seit 1978 bzw. 1981 Fahrzeuge an Hochbahnsteigen halten. In weiterentwickelter Form kam der ‚U2'-Wagen dann auch noch in anderen US-Städten in Einsatz, z.B. Sacramento, Salt Lake City oder Denver.

*the car ('U2h'). Whereas access into the vehicles is almost at level from 80 cm high platforms, this arrangement still allows boarding from 56 cm high platforms, too. Meanwhile, most platforms on route A have been raised to 80 cm. Between 2001 and 2004, at one door per side the grab pole was removed in many of the 'U2' cars, thus improving access through the 120 cm wide doors for those with prams or in wheelchairs.*

*Cars no. 314, 317, 318, 320 and 323 were destroyed in a fire at the Heddernheim depot in 1980, while car no. 355 was withdrawn from service after a derailment in December 2005.*

*Almost identical 'U2' vehicles, equipped with fixed steps, were delivered to San Diego (California) between 1981 and 1990; high platforms have been served by the same type of rolling stock in the Canadian cities of Edmonton since 1981, and Calgary since 1990. A later version of the class 'U2' car can be seen in other U.S. cities like Sacramento, Salt Lake City and Denver.*

**Hauptbahnhof** – Bis zur Inbetriebnahme des Betriebshofs Ost 2003 fuhren die ‚U2'-Wagen vom Betriebshof Gutleut über die Straßenbahngleise Richtung Industriehof (*Foto Stephan Kyrieleis, 1998*).
– *Before the eastern depot opened in 2003, 'U2' cars had to use tram tracks to get from the Gutleut depot to Industriehof.*

Veränderungen im Innenraum des ‚U2'-Wagens | *Changes made to the interior of the class 'U2' vehicle*

Bis 1998 fuhren die ‚Pt'-Wagen auf der C-Strecke ohne Verbreiterungen (Heerstraße; *Foto Stephan Kyrieleis, 01/1997*).
– *Until 1998, the 'Pt' cars operated without the side bulges (Heerstraße).*

Auch 2008 waren noch vereinzelt ‚Ptb'-Wagen in Orange/Elfenbein unterwegs, wie hier Wagen 742 am Halt Friedhof Westhausen.
– *In 2008, a few 'Ptb' cars in orange-and-ivory livery were still in service, like car 742 at Friedhof Westhausen.*

Während der Wagentyp ‚U2' bereits für einen späteren U-Bahn-Betrieb konzipiert worden war, stellte der Typ ‚P' einen eigentlichen Stadtbahn-Wagen dar, also eine Mischung aus Straßenbahn- und U-Bahn-Wagen, weshalb seine Breite auf 2,35 m beschränkt war. Diese achtachsigen 2-Richtungs-Fahrzeuge sind 27,40 m (über Kupplung 28,72 m) lang und 3,26 m hoch. Sie besitzen zwei Gelenke, wobei das Mittelteil über keine Türen verfügt. Bis zu drei Wagen können miteinander gekuppelt werden. Die Fußbodenhöhe beträgt 96 cm über Schienenoberkante, wodurch beim Einstieg an 87 cm hohen Standardbahnsteigen eine kleine Stufe entsteht.

Die ersten ‚P'-Wagen wurden ab 1972 mit der damals neuen Lackierung in ‚Reinorange', ‚Hellelfenbein' und ‚Beigegrau' für den Einsatz auf der B1-Strecke (heute U5) geliefert. Zur Unterscheidung von den gleichartigen Fahrzeugen, die später statt mit Klapptrittstufen mit festen Stufen gebaut wurden, erhielt die erste Serie die Bezeichnung ‚Pt' (für tunnelgängig). Ab 1980 hielten sie auf der U5 allerdings nur noch an einem Hochbahnsteig, nämlich an der Konstablerwache.

Für den Einsatz auf der C-Strecke ab 1986 wurden die Fahrzeuge der dritten Serie mit Klapptrittstufen bei gleichzeitiger Verkürzung der Falttüren ausgestattet, zur Verlängerung nach Enkheim später auch die der zweiten. Ein weiterer Umbau erfolgte 1998 bei den Wagen 692-750, die nun für den Mischbetrieb mit den breiteren ‚U3'- und ‚U2e'-Fahrzeugen auf der B- und C-Strecke verbreitert werden mussten. Durch Verschieben der Klapptrittstufen um einige Zentimeter nach außen wurde so aus dem Typ ‚Pt' der ‚**Ptb**' (für breit). Die übrigen ‚Pt'-Wagen gingen zurück ins Straßenbahnnetz, wo sie 2007 ausgemustert wurden.

*Whereas the 'U2' cars had been designed for future metro operation, the vehicles of class 'P' are the real Stadtbahn cars, i.e. they were a hybrid between a tram and a metro vehicle, and thus only 2.35 m wide. The eight-axle bidirectional cars are 27.40 m long (28.72 m over couplers) and 3.26 m high. They have two articulations, with the central section having no doors. Up to three cars can be coupled to operate as multiple units. The floor height is 96 cm above the rail top, so there is a small step when boarding from 87 cm high platforms.*

*The first 'P' cars were delivered in 1972 for use on line B1 (now U5); they carried the then new orange, ivory and grey livery. To distinguish these cars from later deliveries with fixed instead of folding steps, the initial series was now referred to as class 'Pt' (t for tunnel). From 1980, however, they only served one high platform station, that at Konstablerwache.*

*To operate on route C from 1986 on, the 'P' cars of the third series were retrofitted with folding steps, and the folding doors were shortened. When route C was extended to Enkheim, the cars of the second series were also modified. For lines U5 and U6, cars no. 692 to 750 were rebuilt once again in 1998 to be used on the routes also served by the wider 'U3' and 'U2e' cars, i.e. routes B and C. By moving the folding steps a few centimetres outwards, class 'Pt' became class* ***'Ptb'****. The remaining 'Pt' vehicles were transferred to the tramway network, but in 2007 they were permanently withdrawn from service.*

① Ursprünglicher und ② modernisierter Innenraum des ‚Ptb'-Wagens
– *① Original and ② refurbished interior of a 'Ptb' vehicle*
③ Klapptrittstufen beim ‚Ptb'-Wagen | *'Ptb' folding steps*
④ Einstieg von 87 cm hohen Bahnsteigen | *Access from 87 cm platforms*

Bis 2001 fuhren die ‚U3'-Wagen der Linie U4 am Hauptbahnhof vom inneren Gleis ab *(Foto Alexander Piesenecker, 05/1991)*.
– *Until 2001, the class 'U3' trains, which serve line U4, departed from the inner track at Hauptbahnhof.*

Im Sommer 2008 sind die ‚U3'-Züge, mittlerweile in Türkis, nun auch im Linienbetrieb außerhalb des Tunnels zu sehen (Kehrgleis Schäfflestraße).
– *In summer 2008, the class 'U3' trains, now all in a turquoise livery, can be seen outside the tunnel in regular service (siding at Schäfflestraße).*

Die B-Strecke, die 1980 von der Konstablerwache nach Bornheim verlängert wurde, erhielt von Anfang an 87 cm hohe Bahnsteige, weshalb hier der Einsatz der ursprünglichen ‚U2'-Wagen mit ihrer Stufe im Wageninnern ausgeschlossen war. Für diese Strecke wurde deshalb der neue Typ ‚**U3**' mit einer durchgehenden Fußbodenhöhe von 97 cm entwickelt. Er ist mit 24,49 m (25,68 m über Kupplung) etwas länger als sein Vorgänger, mit 2,65 m jedoch gleich breit, und mit 3,28 m gleich hoch. Durch das Wegfallen von Stufen bzw. Klapptrittstufen konnten die Drehgestelle und Türen optimal angeordnet werden, außerdem wurde mehr Platz für die elektrische Ausrüstung sowie für eine bessere Sitzverteilung gewonnen. Außen waren die ‚U3'-Wagen ursprünglich in Orange/Elfenbein gestrichen, inzwischen tragen jedoch alle Fahrzeuge die neue VGF-Hausfarbe. Sie unterscheiden sich vom ‚U2' durch die einteilige, hohe Frontscheibe. Im Bereich der elektrischen Ausrüstung wurde die Motorleistung erhöht und eine Thyristor-Steuerung eingebaut, die eine Rückgewinnung der Bremsenergie erlaubt. Der spätere Einbau von seitlichen Stromabnehmern wurde bei diesen Wagen baulich berücksichtigt.

Da sich die Inbetriebnahme des Betriebshofs Ost bis zum Jahr 2003 verzögerte, waren die ‚U3'-Wagen lange im Straßenbahndepot Eckenheim beheimatet, wohin sie genauso wie zur Zentralwerkstatt in Rödelheim nur auf Straßenbahngleisen gelangen konnten, und daher auch Kurvenradien von nur 25 m befahren mussten. Im Linienbetrieb hingegen waren die ‚U3'-Fahrzeuge bis Juni 2008 nur im Tunnel der U4 zu sehen. Während der Typ ‚U2' in Amerika triumphierte, kommen vom ‚U3' abstammende Fahrzeuge bei der Salzburger Lokalbahn zum Einsatz.

*Route B, which was extended from Konstablerwache to Bornheim in 1980, had been equipped with 87 cm high platforms right from the start. The use of the original 'U2' car, which had a step inside the vehicle, was thus not possible. The new class '**U3**' stock, with a continuous floor at 97 cm above the rail top, was therefore especially designed for route B. At 24.49 m (25.68 m over couplers), the 'U3' cars are slightly longer than their predecessors, but they are otherwise equal in size at 2.65 m wide and 3.28 m high. The omission of fixed or folding steps allowed the bogies and doors to be better located, resulting in more room for the electrical equipment and an improved seating arrangement. The 'U3' cars originally had an orange/ivory livery, but they have since all been repainted in the present VGF colour. A 'U3' car can be distinguished from a 'U2' car by its high single-pane front window. The motor power was increased, and a thyristor control allows brake energy recovery. Provisions were made for the later addition of contact shoes for third rail power collection.*

*With the completion of the eastern depot delayed until 2003, the 'U3' cars were stored for a long time at the Eckenheim tramway depot, which, like the central workshops, was only accessible via surface tram tracks. The trains thus had to negotiate curves with radii of only 25 m. Until June 2008, the 'U3' cars were only seen in regular service in the U4 tunnel. While the 'U2' cars became very successful in America, a derivative of the 'U3' is in service on the Lokalbahn in Salzburg (Austria).*

① Ursprünglicher und ② modernisierter Innenraum des ‚U3'-Wagens | ① *Original and* ② *refurbished interior of a 'U3' vehicle*
③ Mit dem ‚U3' verwandter Wagen in der unterirdischen Station am Salzburger Hauptbahnhof *(Foto Christian M. Fuchs)*
*'U3' derivative in the underground station at Salzburg Hauptbahnhof*

(Nieder-Eschbach) Der ‚U4'-Wagen bietet erstmals auf der A-Strecke einen stufenlosen Einstieg, allerdings nur an bereits auf 80 cm erhöhten Bahnsteigen.
– *The 'U4' is the first type of vehicle that provides stepless access on route A, but only at platforms already raised to 80 cm.*

(Gonzenheim) Die erste und zweite Serie des Typs ‚U4' kann man z.B. durch die leicht abgeänderten Scheinwerfer unterscheiden.
– *The first and second batch of class 'U4' can be distinguished by the slightly modified headlights, for example.*

Der Fahrzeugtyp ‚**U4**' entspricht in seiner Grundkonzeption als sechsachsiges Gelenkfahrzeug mit einem Laufdrehgestell unter dem Gelenk und zwei angetriebenen Drehgestellen an den Enden weitgehend den früheren Typen der Frankfurter Stadtbahn, weshalb er ursprünglich als ‚U3-2000' bezeichnet wurde. Die Fußbodenhöhe beträgt beim ‚U4' allerdings nur 87 cm (im Vergleich zu den 97 cm bei den Vorgängertypen), was an der nun gültigen Standardbahnsteighöhe von 80 cm praktisch einen ebenen Einstieg ermöglicht. Der ‚U4' ist 24,49 m lang (25,84 m über Kupplung), 3,59 m hoch und 2,65 m breit. Neu waren außerdem die doppelflügeligen Schwenkschiebetüren, vier pro Seite, nachdem bisher immer Falttüren verwenden worden waren. Statt wie früher Polstersitze wurden im ‚U4' gepolsterte Hartschalensitze verwendet, um Vandalismus vorzubeugen. Neuartig war auch die äußere Farbgebung, ein Türkiston, der als ‚Subaru vista blue' bezeichnet wird. An jedem Wagenende ist weiterhin ein Führerstand eingebaut, an dem die große gebogene Frontscheibe auffällt.

Diese Fahrzeuge, die hauptsächlich auf der Linie U2 zu sehen sind, wurden wie schon die ersten Frankfurter Stadtbahnwagen von der DUEWAG (Düsseldorfer Waggonfabrik) entwickelt und gebaut, diese traditionsreiche Firma wurde jedoch 1999 von Siemens übernommen.

*The basic concept of type '**U4**', an articulated six-axle vehicle, with a non-motorised bogie in the middle and two motorised end bogies, corresponds to the previous types on the Frankfurt Stadtbahn; it was therefore initially referred to as the 'U3-2000'. At 87 cm, the floor height above the rail top in the 'U4' cars is 10 cm lower, allowing quasi-level access from the now standard 80 cm high platforms. The 'U4' cars are 24.49 m long (25.84 over couplers), 3.59 m high and 2.65 m wide. Instead of the previously used folding doors, the 'U4' was equipped with outward sliding plug doors, while the upholstered seats were replaced by plastic ones with a thin textile cushion to reduce the effects of vandalism. The 'U4' trains arrived in VGF's new colour, a turquoise tone known as 'subaru vista blue'. At both ends of the cars there is a driver's cab with a distinctive large curved window. The 'U4' is mainly seen on line U2.*

*Like all the older cars, the 'U4' vehicles were developed and produced by DUEWAG (Düsseldorfer Waggonfabrik), a company with a long history of car manufacture which was taken over by Siemens in 1999.*

Innenraum des ‚U4'-Wagens
– *Interior of a class 'U4' vehicle*

Bei einer Bahnsteighöhe von 80 cm und einem Wagenfußboden 87 cm über Schienenoberkante kann man in den ‚U4' praktisch stufenlos einsteigen.
– *With a platform height of 80 cm and a car floor of 87 cm above the top of the rail, the 'U4' provides almost level access.*

‚U5'-Wagen 603 auf Probefahrt (Friedhof Westhausen) (*Foto Thomas Lusmöller*)
– *'U5' car 603 on a test run (Friedhof Westhausen)*

Innenraum des ‚U5' (*Fotos Andreas Behrndt*)
*Interior of a 'U5' car*

Nach den positiven Erfahrungen mit den Niederflur-Straßenbahnen des Typs ‚S' bestellte die VGF im März 2006 von Bombardier insgesamt 146 Fahrzeuge aus der Produktfamilie FLEXITY Swift. Es besteht eine Option auf 24 weitere Fahrzeuge. Die Produktion erfolgt an den Bombardier-Standorten Bautzen (Fahrzeugkasten und Innenausstattung), Siegen (Drehgestelle) und Mannheim (elektrische Ausrüstung).

Der Typ ‚**U5**' wird in zwei Varianten geliefert:
1) ‚U5-25' - ein 25 m langes sechsachsiges Gelenkfahrzeug mit vier Türen pro Seite, in der Konzeption also den bisherigen Fahrzeugen ähnlich. Davon werden 54 Wagen in einer ersten Serie ausgeliefert, das erste wurde im Mai 2008 in Frankfurt vorgestellt.
2) ‚U5-50' - eine 50 m lange Einheit, die aus zwei 25-m-Wagen besteht, die in der Mitte mittels einer Kurzkupplung und einem Personenübergang miteinander verbunden sind, so wie es bereits in Hannover bei der Langversion des TW2000 der Fall ist.

Beide Versionen des ‚U5' können mit dem ‚U4' im Zugverband eingesetzt werden. Der ‚U5' ist das erste Stadtbahn-Fahrzeug in Frankfurt mit Klimaanlage. Die Höchstgeschwindigkeit ist für 80 km/h ausgelegt. Angetrieben werden wie beim ‚U4' die beiden Enddrehgestelle mit jeweils vier 130 kW starken Drehstrom-Asynchron-Motoren. Die Fußbodenhöhe beträgt wie beim Typ ‚U4' 87 cm über Schienenoberkante, womit die neuen Wagen theoretisch auf allen Strecken eingesetzt werden können, sie werden aber vorerst vor allem auf der A-Strecke zu sehen sein. Sie sollen bis etwa 2015 alle ‚U2'- und ‚Ptb'-Fahrzeuge ersetzen, von denen die ältesten nun 40 Jahre alt sind.

*In March 2006, after a positive experience with the low-floor trams of type 'S', the VGF ordered a total of 146 vehicles of the FLEXITY Swift product family from Bombardier, with an option for another 24. They are being manufactured in Germany at Bombardier's plants in Bautzen (car bodies and interiors), Siegen (bogies) and Mannheim (electrical equipment).*

*The '**U5**' car is being delivered in two versions:*
*1) 'U5-25' – a 25 m six-axle articulated unit with four doors on each side, corresponding to the layout of previous car types. The initial series will consist of 54 cars, with the first car having been presented in Frankfurt in May 2008.*
*2) 'U5-50' – a 50 m unit made up of two 25 m cars connected by a gangway, similar to the long TW2000 in Hanover.*

*Both versions of the 'U5' can be coupled with 'U4' units. The ‚U5' is the first air-conditioned Stadtbahn vehicle in Frankfurt, and has a maximum speed of 80 km/h. Like with the 'U4', the two end bogies are each motorised with four 130 kW asynchronous ac engines. With a floor height of 87 cm, the cars could theoretically be used on every line, but initially they will mostly be seen on route A. All the 'U2' and 'Ptb' cars, the oldest of which are now 40 years old, are scheduled to be replaced with 'U5's by 2015.*

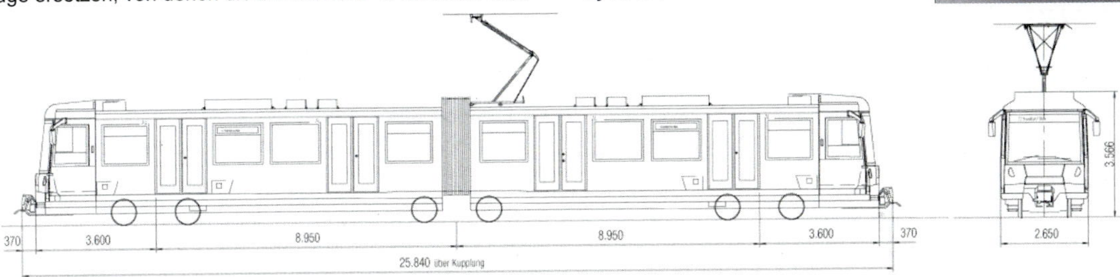


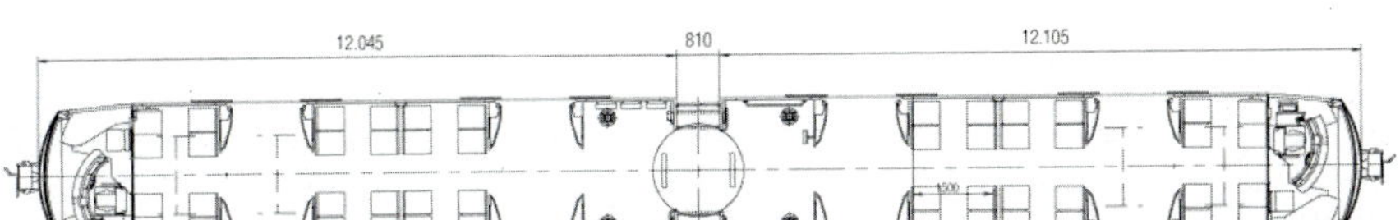


Typ ‚U5-25' (Abb. Bombardier)

**Willy-Brandt-Platz** – ‚S'-Wagen 219 auf der Linie 12 vor der Europäischen Zentralbank | *'S' car 219 on line 12, in front of the European Central Bank*

## _ Die Frankfurter Straßenbahn

Stadtbahn und S-Bahn haben in Frankfurt die Straßenbahn, die jahrzehntelang das wichtigste öffentliche Verkehrsmittel war, nur zum Teil ersetzt. Bereits 1872 verkehrte die erste Pferdebahnlinie zwischen Bockenheim und der Hauptwache. Ab 1884 fuhr eine der ersten elektrischen Straßenbahnen in Europa auf Meterspur von Sachsenhausen ins benachbarte Offenbach. Vier Jahre später übernahm die Stadt Frankfurt die normalspurigen Pferdebahnlinien und eröffnete 1899 die erste elektrische städtische Straßenbahnstrecke. In den nächsten Jahrzehnten wuchs das Straßenbahnnetz und hatte 1958 mit 329,5 km Gleislänge seine größte Ausdehnung erreicht. In den Folgejahren schrumpfte das Straßenbahnnetz mit jeder Eröffnung einer Stadtbahn- oder innerstädtischen S-Bahn-Strecke. Heute ist das Straßenbahnnetz mit einer Betriebsstreckenlänge von rund 64 Kilometern etwa genauso lang wie das Stadtbahnnetz. Trotz gemeinsam genutzter Infrastruktur (wie dem Betriebshof Ost und der Zentralwerkstatt) und der Verkehrsgesellschaft Frankfurt (VGF) als Betreiber werden beide Netze aufgrund unterschiedlicher Systemeigenschaften weitgehend getrennt betrieben. Die Straßenbahnwagen sind mit 2,35 m bzw. 2,40 m schmaler als die Stadtbahnwagen (2,65 m) und in Niederflurbauweise konstruiert. Dies ermöglicht engere Kurvenradien und niedrige Bahnsteige, die sich leichter in den Straßenraum integrieren lassen. Ein weiteres Unterscheidungsmerkmal zur Stadtbahn sind die dichteren Haltestellenabstände (mittlerer Haltestellenabstand 500 m gegenüber 700 m bei der Stadtbahn) sowie die Begrenzung der Zuglänge auf 75 m, auch wenn bislang außer auf der Stadionlinie 20 nur rund 30 m lange Einzelwagen eingesetzt werden. Zur Beschleunigung

## _ *The Frankfurt Tramway System*

*The Stadtbahn and S-Bahn have only partially replaced Frankfurt's tramway system, which for many decades had been the backbone of public transport in the city. Back in 1872, the first horse tram line was opened between Bockenheim and Hauptwache. In 1884, one of Europe's first electric tramways began operating on metre-gauge tracks from Sachsenhausen to the neighbouring city of Offenbach. Four years later, the city of Frankfurt took over all standard-gauge horse tram lines, and in 1899 it opened the first municipal electric tram line. During the following decades, the network was gradually expanded, and by 1958, it had reached its maximum extension with 329.5 km of tracks. In subsequent years, the network began to shrink with every new section of Stadtbahn or inner-city S-Bahn opened. At present, the tramway system has a total length of 64 km, and is thus similar in size to the Stadtbahn network. Both systems share the eastern depot as well as the central workshops, and both are operated by the VGF (Verkehrsgesellschaft Frankfurt), but because their technical specifications differ, they are operated separately. Depending on the type, the tramway cars are only 2.35 m or 2.40 m wide, and thus narrower than the Stadtbahn cars (2.65 m), and now all vehicles are of the low-floor type. The curves can be tighter, and no high platforms are required; the trams can therefore be better integrated into the public roadway. On the tramway system the average station distance is only 500 m, compared to 700 m on the Stadtbahn, and the train length is limited to 75 m, although currently only single vehicles about 30 m long are being used, except for the special stadium service (line 20). To accelerate tram operation, since*

**Bockenheimer Warte** – ‚R'-Wagen 028 auf der Linie 16 mit dem namensgebenden Turm; links der ehemalige Straßenbahnbetriebshof (bis 1978 Hauptwerkstatt)
*– 'R' car 028 on line 16, with the tower called Bockenheimer Warte; on the left, the former tramway depot (main workshop until 1978)*

der Straßenbahn hat man seit den 1970er Jahren große Teile der Trassen durch Markierungen vom Autoverkehr getrennt. Wo Platz vorhanden ist, hat man der Straßenbahn auch eigene Trassen eingeräumt, die teilweise im Vorgriff auf die geplante Umstellung auf Stadtbahnbetrieb ausgebaut wurden.

Galt die Straßenbahn bis Ende der 1980er Jahre als System, das schrittweise durch die Stadtbahn ersetzt werden sollte, ist sie heute fester Bestandteil des Frankfurter Nahverkehrssystems. Auslöser für den Richtungswechsel war der breite Bürgerprotest, der 1986 die gleichzeitig mit Eröffnung der Stadtbahnstrecke C erfolgte Stilllegung der verbliebenen Straßenbahnstrecken in der Innenstadt begleitet hatte. Damals verweigerte das zuständige Regierungspräsidium die Stilllegungsgenehmigung für die Altstadtstrecke zwischen Hauptbahnhof, Willy-Brandt-Platz und Börneplatz. Außerdem musste man feststellen, dass sich die Realisierung des geplanten Stadtbahnnetzes stark verzögert hatte. Mit dem 1990 erfolgten Beschluss zur Beschaffung neuer Straßenbahnwagen und zum Bau einer 740 m langen Verbindungsstrecke zwischen Börneplatz und Konstablerwache wurde daher die Entscheidung zum Erhalt und Ausbau der Straßenbahn getroffen.

Ganztägig verkehren in Frankfurt sieben Tramlinien. Dazu kommt an Wochenenden und Feiertagen der „Ebbelwei-Expreß", eine touristische Rundfahrtlinie mit knallbunt bemalten Oldtimer-Straßenbahnwagen. Kuriosum ist eine nur an Pfingsten und dem folgenden Dienstag verkehrende Sonderlinie, die als „Lieschen" bezeichnet wird. Auf der nur noch für diese Fahrten vorgehaltenen Strecke zwischen Stresemannallee/Mörfelder Landstraße und dem Oberforsthaus ist sie Zubringerlinie zum „Wäldchestag", einem großes Volksfest im Stadtwald.

*the 1970s many routes have been separated from car traffic by marking dedicated lanes; and where possible, the tracks were put on a separate right-of-way, often in provision for a future conversion to Stadtbahn operation.*

*Until the late 1980s, the tramway was still intended to gradually be replaced by the Stadtbahn, but nowadays it is once again seen as an integral part of the city's public transport system. This change of direction was triggered in 1986 by heavy protests from the local population against the plan to abandon all tramway routes through the city centre together with the opening of route C of the Frankfurt Stadtbahn. The competent authorities then refused to give permission for the closure of the tramway route from Hauptbahnhof via Willy-Brandt-Platz to Börneplatz. At the same time, the expansion of the Stadtbahn network was far behind schedule. A decision taken in 1990 to acquire new rolling stock and build a 740 m link between Börneplatz and Konstablerwache finally eliminated any doubt about the tramway's future.*

*The Frankfurt tramway network comprises seven full-time lines. On weekends and holidays, the 'Ebbelwei-Expreß' [apple wine express] can be seen on a circular tourist route with colourful vintage cars. Another curiosity is the 'Lieschen', a special service operated only at Whitsun and on the following Tuesday. It runs along a line maintained purely for that purpose, from Stresemannallee/Mörfelder Landstraße to Oberforsthaus, and serves during the 'Wäldchestag', a popular festival in the city forest.*

## _ Die heutigen Straßenbahnlinien

Mit jeweils rund 19 km und je einer Stunde Fahrzeit sind die Linien 11 und 12 die längsten Straßenbahnlinien der Stadt. Die Linie 11 durchquert die Stadt in West-Ost-Richtung vom Stadtteil Höchst bis nach Fechenheim. Dabei folgt sie der Mainzer Landstraße und fährt über Hauptbahnhof zur Altstadtstrecke und weiter über die Hanauer Landstraße nach Fechenheim.

Die Linie 12 fährt vom Stadtteil Schwanheim im Südwesten ebenfalls nach Fechenheim, endet aber bereits vor dem Ortskern an der Hugo-Junkers-Straße. Vom westlichen Endpunkt verläuft die Linie 12 erst zwischen dem südlichen Rand der Bebauung und dem Nordrand des Frankfurter Stadtwaldes, dann weiter auf eigenem Gleiskörper durch die Bürostadt Niederrad. Im älteren Teil des Stadtteils Niederrad trifft sie auf die Linien 21 und 15, quert den Main auf der Friedensbrücke und biegt kurz vor dem Hauptbahnhof auf die Altstadtstrecke in Richtung Osten ein, die sie gemeinsam mit der Linie 11 nutzt. Während die Linie 11 am Börneplatz geradeaus Richtung Ostend weiterfährt, biegt die Linie 12 in Richtung Konstablerwache ab. Dabei befährt sie die 740 m lange Neubaustrecke, die 1999 als Verbindung zwischen der Altstadtstrecke und dem damaligen Streckenende der Linie 12 in Betrieb ging. Mit einem Bogen über Bornheim und die Station Eissporthalle/Festhalle erreicht die Linie 12 ihr östliches Streckenende.

Die Linie 14 beginnt im Nordosten am Ernst-May-Platz in Bornheim und führt über Zoo und den S-Bahnhof Ostendstraße zur Ignatz-Bubis-Brücke. Nach der Mainquerung erreicht die Linie in Sachsenhausen den Lokal- und den Südbahnhof, wo die Strecke nach Süden abzweigt und über Louisa Bahnhof knapp 3 km durch den Stadtwald weiter bis zur Stadtgrenze Neu-Isenburg führt. In Neu-Isenburg findet sich ebenso wie an der Endstation in Schwanheim noch ein altes Bahnhofsgebäude aus der Zeit, als zwischen 1889 und 1929 diese Strecken von der Frankfurter Waldbahn-Gesellschaft mit Dampfbahnen betrieben wurden.

Nur „Dribbdebach“, also durch die südlich des Mains gelegenen Stadtteile, verkehrt die Straßenbahnlinie 15. Sie beginnt in Niederrad an der Wendeschleife Haardtwaldplatz und führt von dort zur Rennbahnstraße, wo sie sich den folgenden Streckenabschnitt über die Universitätsklinik zur Stresemannallee mit den Linien 12 und 21 teilt. Während aber die Linien 12 und 21 über die Friedensbrücke den Main in Richtung Hauptbahnhof überqueren, biegt die 15 in die Gartenstraße ein und fährt über Schweizer Platz weiter zum Südbahnhof. Montags bis freitags fährt die Linie 15 morgens und von Mittag bis zum frühen Abend von dort weiter bis zur Stadtgrenze Offenbach.

**Offenbach Stadtgrenze** – seit 1996 endet die Straßenbahn am westlichen Rand von Frankfurts Nachbarstadt.
*– since 1996, the tram has been terminating right on the border between Frankfurt and Offenbach.*

**Schwanheim** – Bahnhofsgebäude der Waldbahn von 1889
*– 'Waldbahn' station building from 1889*

## _ *The present tram lines*

*With some 19 km of route length each and one hour of travel time, lines 11 and 12 are the longest tram lines in Frankfurt. Line 11 crosses the city from west to east, linking Höchst to Fechenheim. It follows Mainzer Landstraße, before reaching the route through the city centre at Hauptbahnhof. Almost the entire eastern section runs along Hanauer Landstraße.*

*Line 12 starts in the southwest in Schwanheim and also terminates in Fechenheim, at the western side of the neighbourhood at Hugo-Junkers-Straße. From its western terminus, line 12 runs between the built-up area and Frankfurt's city forest, before continuing on a separate right-of-way through the Niederrad business park. It then converges with tram lines 21 and 15 in the older part of Niederrad, crosses the Main River on the Friedensbrücke, and finally joins line 11 on its way through the old town. While line 11 continues straight at Börneplatz, line 12 turns north towards Konstablerwache, taking advantage of the 740 m section opened between the cross-town route and the former line 12 terminus in 1999. Line 12 finally reaches its eastern terminus with a long detour via Bornheim and Eissporthalle/Festhalle Stadtbahn station.*

*Line 14 starts in the northeast at Ernst-May-Platz in Bornheim. It reaches the Ignatz-Bubis-Brücke via Zoo and Ostendstraße S-Bahn station, before crossing the Main River. On the south bank in Sachsenhausen it passes the S-Bahn stations Lokalbahnhof and Südbahnhof, before turning south towards Louisa, and continuing for 3 km through the Frankfurt city forest to terminate at the northern edge of Neu-Isenburg. At Neu-Isenburg, as well as at Schwanheim, the original station buildings have been preserved from the times when these routes were part of the 'Frankfurter Waldbahn-Gesellschaft', which operated steam trains between 1889 and 1929.*

*Line 15 only runs through the districts located south of the Main River. It starts at its western terminus Haardtwaldplatz in Niederrad, then joins lines 12 and 21 on Rennbahnstraße on their way via the University Hospital to Stresemannallee. Whereas the other lines cross the river on Friedensbrücke, line 15 turns into Gartenstraße towards Schweizer Platz before terminating at Südbahnhof. From Monday to Friday, line 15 continues to Offenbach Stadtgrenze during the morning peak hours and in the afternoons.*

*Since 1906, line number 16 has been associated with the link between Frankfurt and its smaller neighbour Offenbach. On 2 June 1996, line 16, like line 15, was cut back to Offenbach's city boundary. The route to Marktplatz, the last of Offenbach's tramway lines, was abandoned because ridership had fallen since the S-Bahn was extended to Offenbach in 1995, but also due to the relatively high fares for short trips, as the city boundary was at the same time the fare zone*

Seit 1906 steht die Liniennummer 16 für die Verbindung zwischen Frankfurt und seiner kleineren Nachbarstadt Offenbach. Seit dem 2. Juni 1996 endet die Linie 16, wie die Linie 15, in Offenbach direkt hinter der Stadtgrenze. Gründe für die Stilllegung des Streckenabschnitts bis zum Marktplatz, der letzten Straßenbahnstrecke Offenbachs, waren Fahrgastverluste durch die Inbetriebnahme der S-Bahn nach Offenbach 1995 und die hohen Fahrpreise für Kurzstreckenfahrgäste, da die Stadtgrenze gleichzeitig Tarifgrenze ist, sowie der Wunsch von Offenbacher Geschäftsleuten nach einer straßenbahnfreien Fußgängerzone. Der Linienweg der 16 beginnt im Nordosten in Ginnheim an der Endstation der Stadtbahnlinie U1 und führt über die Bockenheimer Warte, Messe und Hauptbahnhof zur Friedensbrücke. Nach der Mainquerung biegt die 16 hinter der Station Stresemannallee/Gartenstraße in die Gartenstraße ein und folgt bis zur Stadtgrenze Offenbach dem Linienverlauf der Linie 15.

Erst seit 13. Dezember 2003 fährt mit der Linie 17 die derzeit jüngste Straßenbahnlinie vom Rebstockbad durch das südliche Bockenheim, über den Westbahnhof und die Messe zum Hauptbahnhof, wo sie an der Südseite an der Haltestelle Pforzheimer Straße endet. Als Besonderheit wurden im Bereich der Stationen Kuhwaldstraße und An der Dammheide die Fahrbahnen beidseitig der in Mittellage liegenden Straßenbahntrasse angehoben und dienen bei haltender Tram als Bahnsteig.

Höchste derzeit in Frankfurt für die Straßenbahn vergebene Liniennummer ist die 21. Diese Linie startet in der Hauptverkehrszeit an der Wendeschleife im westlichen Stadtteil Nied und in der übrigen Zeit sechs Stationen später an der Mönchhofstraße. Bis zum Hauptbahnhof folgt sie dem Linienverlauf der 11. In der Hauptverkehrzeit fährt die Linie 21 aber in einer Fahrtrichtung (morgens aus Richtung Hauptbahnhof und nachmittags in Richtung Hauptbahnhof) über die Kleyerstraße, um die dortigen Arbeitsplätze besser anzubinden. Hinter dem Hauptbahnhof überquert die Linie 21, wie auch die Linien 12 und 16, den Main und erreicht die Station Stresemannallee/Gartenstraße. Auf dem Abschnitt über das Universitätsklinikum bis zur Niederräder Landstraße teilt sich die 21 die Strecke mit den Linien 12 und 15. Nach Passieren der Pferderennbahn endet die Linie in den ausgedehnten Gleisanlagen der Straßenbahnstation am Stadion.

Wurden Verstärkerzüge früher mit einem „V“ bzw. „Liniennummer + V“ bezeichnet, führen sie jetzt eigene Nummern. So verkehrt die Linie 19 nur an Schultagen mit je 2 Fahrten morgens und mittags zwischen Südbahnhof bzw. Stresemannallee/Gartenstraße und Schwanheim. Die Linie 20 verstärkt bei Großveranstaltungen im Stadion die Linie 21 auf dem Abschnitt zwischen Hauptbahnhof und Stadion. Sie ist die derzeit einzige Straßenbahnlinie, auf der Straßenbahnzüge in gekuppelter

**Festhalle/Messe** – die Linie 16 hält direkt am Osteingang zur Messe.
*– line 16 stops at the eastern entrance to the fairgrounds.*

**Baseler Platz** – die Linie 12 auf ihrem Weg Richtung Mainbrücke
*– line 12 on its way across the Main River*

*boundary. Another argument was that shop owners preferred a tram-free pedestrian zone. In the northeast, line 16 starts at the terminus of Stadtbahn line U1 in Ginnheim; from there, it runs via Bockenheimer Warte, Messe and Hauptbahnhof to Friedensbrücke. After crossing the Main River, line 16 joins line 15 on its way towards Offenbach.*

*Frankfurt's newest tram line, line 17, was opened on 13 December 2003, and runs from Rebstockbad via the southern parts of Bockenheim, Westbahnhof and Messe to Hauptbahnhof, where it terminates at the southern side on Pforzheimer Straße. As a special feature, raised car lanes at the Kuhwaldstraße and An der Dammheide stops function as low platforms.*

*The line with the highest number is currently line 21. During peak hours, this line starts in the district of Nied, and at other times, at Mönchhofstraße. Up to Hauptbahnhof it shares the line 11 alignment, but during peak hours, it is diverted along Kleyerstraße in one direction (outbound in the mornings, and inbound in the afternoons) to provide better service for the people working in this area. From Hauptbahnhof, line 21, together with lines 12 and 16, crosses the Main River, and from the stop at Stresemannallee/Gartenstraße, it joins lines 12 and 15 on their route via the University Hospital to Niederräder Landstraße. After passing the horse racecourse it terminates at Stadion, where several sidings are available for extra trams during events at the stadium.*

*Whereas in former times special services were labelled with a 'V', or the line number plus a 'V', these trams now carry separate numbers. Line 19 only operates on school days, with two trams in each direction in the mornings and at lunchtime between Südbahnhof (or Stresemannallee/Gartenstraße) and Schwanheim. Line 20 runs during special events at the stadium to reinforce line 21 between Stadion and Hauptbahnhof. It is the only line which can operate with double units,*

**Hauptbahnhof** – von der Straßenbahnhaltestelle führen Treppen direkt ins weitläufige Verteilergeschoss unterhalb des Bahnhofsvorplatzes.
*– from the tram stop, direct flights of stairs lead down to the large mezzanine beneath the railway station square.* (Foto Philipp Krammer)

Doppeltraktion zum Einsatz kommen. Dafür wurden anlässlich der Fußball-WM 2006 die Bahnsteige ausgebaut und die Stromversorgung verstärkt.

In Zukunft wird das Straßenbahnnetz weiter wachsen. Im Bau befindet sich eine 3,5 km lange Strecke (Linie 18), die über die Friedberger Landstraße zur Friedberger Warte und weiter zum Neubaugebiet Preungesheim Ost (‚Frankfurter Bogen') führt. Geplant ist zudem der Bau einer direkten Verbindung zwischen Neu-Isenburg und dem Hauptbahnhof über die Stresemannallee als Verlängerung der Linie 17. Diese Strecke soll später in einen Straßenbahnhalbring integriert werden, der Umsteigemöglichkeiten zu allen Stadtbahnlinien und Tangentialverbindungen zwischen vielen Stadtteilen böte.

*the platforms having been lengthened and the power supply upgraded for the 2006 FIFA World Cup Finals.*

*In the near future, the tramway network will be expanded. A 3.5 km route (line 18) is under construction along Friedberger Landstraße to Friedberger Warte and from there to a new residential area at Preungesheim Ost (the so-called 'Frankfurter Bogen'). Besides this extension, a direct link is planned between Neu-Isenburg and Hauptbahnhof via Stresemannallee, to be served by an extended line 17. This new section may later become part of a semicircular tram route, which would create the option of interchange to all Stadtbahn lines, as well as many tangential links between different neighbourhoods.*

**Römer** – die einzige erhaltene Straßenbahnstrecke durch die Innenstadt
*– only surviving tram route through the city centre*

Ebbelwei-Expreß auf der 1992 stillgelegten Strecke nach Bergen
(Foto Stephan Kyrieleis, 06/1990)
*– Ebbelwei-Expreß on the route to Bergen abandoned in 1992.*

**Schwanheim** – Das Verkehrsmuseum Frankfurt zeigt eine große Auswahl älterer Fahrzeuge, z.B. links ein Wagen von 1908 der Offenbacher Straßenbahn, daneben ein ‚D'-Wagen von 1914 aus Frankfurt.
– *The transport museum boasts a large selection of vintage tram cars, e.g. a 1908 vehicle from Offenbach, or a 'D' car built in 1914 for Frankfurt.*

**Ernst-May-Platz** – die ‚Pt'-Wagen sind seit 2007 auf dem Straßenbahnnetz nicht mehr in Betrieb. (*Foto Philipp Krammer*)
– *The 'Pt' cars were withdrawn from service on the tram system in 2007.*

## _ Straßenbahn-Fahrzeuge

Gab es früher bei der Straßenbahn eine große Typenvielfalt, kommen seit März 2007, als die VGF die letzten im Straßenbahnnetz eingesetzten Hochflurwagen des Typs ‚Pt' abstellte, nur noch zwei Fahrzeugtypen zum Einsatz. Im Stadtbahnnetz wird dieser Typ aber als ‚Ptb' weiterhin eingesetzt. Die Typenbezeichnungen begannen 1899 mit dem Typ ‚A', angehängte Kleinbuchstaben bezeichnen Unterbauarten. Die Ära der Niederflurtriebwagen begann in Frankfurt 1993 mit der Auslieferung der ersten Wagen des Typs ‚R'. Die erste Serie umfasste 20 Fahrzeuge. Es handelte sich dabei um die ersten Wagen mit 100% Niederfluranteil, die von DUEWAG (heute Siemens) gebaut wurden. Auf die Freude über dieses moderne Fahrzeug, das sich zum Bestellzeitpunkt erst im Reißbrettstadium befunden hatte, folgte im Betriebsalltag bald Ernüchterung. Die Bahnen quietschten und schlingerten in engen Kurven. Trotz Versuche, diese Probleme bei der zweiten Serie von weiteren 20 Fahrzeugen abzustellen, wurde die VGF mit dem Typ ‚R' nie richtig glücklich. Eine Option für den Kauf von weiteren 60 Bahnen nahm man daher nicht wahr. Stattdessen schaute sich im Jahr 2001 eine Kommission nach einem neuen, bereits bewährten Modell um. Fündig wurde man in Kassel, wo seit 1999 der bei Bombardier gebaute Typ ‚8NGTW' problemlos im Einsatz ist. Bombardier gewann auch in Frankfurt die Ausschreibung über 60 neue Straßenbahnwagen, so dass im Juni 2002 der Kaufvertrag abgeschlossen werden konnte. Die ersten Wagen des neuen Typs ‚S' wurden im Oktober 2003 der Öffentlichkeit vorgestellt. Ihr Niederfluranteil liegt bei 70% und sie können in Doppeltraktion fahren. Heute dominiert dieser Typ mit 65 Exemplaren das Straßenbahnnetz.

## _ *Tramway Rolling Stock*

*The Frankfurt tramway system was once served by a variety of tram vehicles, but since March 2007, when the VGF withdrew the last 'Pt' cars, only two different types have been in service. On the Stadtbahn network, the 'Ptb' cars are still in use, though. The type designations are in alphabetical order, with type 'A' starting in 1899. The small letters added refer to subclasses. The era of low-floor trams began in Frankfurt in 1993 with the delivery of the first 'R' cars. The first series comprised a total of 20 cars. This vehicle was the first 100% low-floor car developed and built by DUEWAG (now Siemens). When the order had first been made, the car had only existed on the drawing board, but its performance during actual everyday service caused any initial enthusiasm for the new vehicle to quickly melt away. The trams squealed and lurched uncomfortably around tight curves, and despite attempts to solve these problems for the second series of 20 cars, the VGF was never completely satisfied with the 'R' stock. An option for another 60 vehicles was therefore cancelled. Instead, in 2001 a study group looked for a proven vehicle and found one not far away in Kassel, where Bombardier's '8NGTW' had been in service without any problems since 1999. In June 2002, Bombardier was awarded a contract to build 60 cars for Frankfurt. The first cars of the new type 'S' were presented in October 2003. These cars are 70% low-floor and can run as double units. With a total of 65 trams, type 'S' now dominates Frankfurt's tram network.*

‚N'-Wagen 809 | *'N' car 809* (Zoo; *Foto Stephan Kyrieleis, 05/1985* )

Fahrzeugparade in der Stadtbahn-Zentralwerkstatt:
‚L'-, ‚M'-, ‚O'- und ‚Ptb'-Wagen (*Foto Stephan Kyrieleis*, 04-09-1999)
– *Tram parade in the Stadtbahn workshops: 'L', 'M', 'O' and 'Ptb' cars*

**Frankfurt West** – S-Bahnhof auf zwei Ebenen | *2-level S-Bahn station*

## _ S-Bahn Rhein-Main

Neben dem Stadtbahnnetz verfügt der Großraum Rhein-Main über ein dichtes Eisenbahnnetz, auf dem neun S-Bahn-Linien sowie zahlreiche Regionalbahn- und RegionalExpress-Züge verkehren. Frankfurt ist auch eine wichtige Drehscheibe im deutschen Fernbahnnetz. Hier lag bis zum Umzug nach Berlin im Jahr 2000 außerdem die Konzernzentrale der *Deutschen Bahn AG*. Die *S-Bahn Rhein-Main* ist ein Verkehrsbetrieb der *DB Regio Hessen*, einer Tochterfirma der *Deutschen Bahn AG*, und erbringt ihre Leistungen im Auftrag des RMV (*Rhein-Main Verkehrsverbund*).

Bis auf die Linie S7, die oberirdisch am Hauptbahnhof endet, fahren alle Frankfurter S-Bahn-Linien durch den City-Tunnel und verbinden so das westliche und nördliche Umland von Frankfurt direkt mit den östlich bzw. südlich gelegenen Gebieten. Lediglich die Linien S5 und S6 enden am Südbahnhof und stellen daher keine Durchmesserlinien dar.

Die ersten Züge erreichen von den Endpunkten die Hauptwache je nach Linie zwischen 4:13 und 5:51 Uhr, die letzten bis zu den Endpunkten durchfahrenden Züge verlassen das Stadtzentrum zwischen 0:08 und 1:21 Uhr.

Auf allen Linien wird ein 30-Minuten-Grundtakt angeboten, welcher je nach Linie und Abschnitt zu bestimmten Zeiten zu

S1 Wiesbaden – Höchst – Frankfurt – Offenbach – Rödermark - Ober-Roden (72 km)
S2 Niedernhausen – Frankfurt – Offenbach – Dietzenbach (55 km)
S3 Bad Soden – Frankfurt – Darmstadt (49 km)
S4 Kronberg – Frankfurt – Langen (34 km)
S5 Friedrichsdorf – Frankfurt Süd (29 km)
S6 Friedberg – Frankfurt Süd (39 km)
S7 Frankfurt Hbf – Riedstadt-Goddelau (35 km)
S8 Wiesbaden – Mainz – Flughafen – Frankfurt – Offenbach (– Hanau) (71 km)
S9 Wiesbaden – Flughafen – Frankfurt – Offenbach – Hanau (69 km)

*Besides the Stadtbahn network, the Rhine-Main area boasts an extensive railway network, which is served by nine S-Bahn lines as well as several regional rail lines (RB and RE). Frankfurt is also a major hub in the German long-distance network; before it moved to Berlin in 2000, the 'Deutsche Bahn AG' had its headquarters there. The 'S-Bahn Rhein-Main' is a part of 'DB Regio Hessen', a subsidiary of 'Deutsche Bahn AG'; it operates on behalf of the RMV (Rhein-Main Verkehrsverbund).*

*Except for line S7, which terminates on the surface at Hauptbahnhof, all the other S-Bahn lines run through the city tunnel, thus linking the western and northern regions of Frankfurt with those in the east and south; lines S5 and S6 terminate at Südbahnhof.*

*Depending on the line, the first trains arrive at Hauptwache from the outer termini between 04:13 and 05:51, while the last trains running through to the termini leave the city centre between 00:08 and 01:21.*

*All lines operate a basic 30-minute headway, which, depending on the line section, is reduced to 15 minutes at certain times. Some of the additional trains on lines S1 (starting at Höchst) and S8 (from Kelsterbach or the airport) terminate on the surface at Hauptbahnhof due to the limited capacity of the city tunnel. The same is true of the extra trains on*

einem 15-Minuten-Takt verdichtet wird. Auf der S1 (ab Höchst) und auf der S8 (ab Kelsterbach oder Flughafen) enden manche Verstärkerzüge wegen der Auslastung des City-Tunnels im oberirdischen Bereich des Hauptbahnhofs. Dasselbe gilt für alle Verstärkerfahrten der westlichen S2, im Osten hingegen beginnen und enden diese am Offenbacher Hauptbahnhof. Derzeit fahren in der Hauptverkehrszeit maximal 22 Züge pro Stunde und Richtung durch den City-Tunnel, d.h. alle 2-3 Minuten. Durch ein neues Signalsystem mit PZB (punktförmige Zugbeeinflussung) soll die Kapazität auf 24 Fahrten pro Stunde erhöht werden, was den Verstärkerfahrten der S2 zugutekommen würde. Alle Züge der S7 enden bis auf Weiteres im oberen Bereich des Hauptbahnhofs.

Von den 286 Streckenkilometern (303 km in offiziellen Angaben) und 115 S-Bahn-Stationen liegen etwa 63,4 km und 22 Stationen auf Frankfurter Stadtgebiet. Auf vielen Strecken hat die S-Bahn eigene Gleise oder diese werden nur von wenigen anderen Zügen mitbenutzt. Auf anderen, besonders auf der S6 nach Friedberg, führt der Mischbetrieb zu Engpässen, weshalb seit einigen Jahren ein viergleisiger Ausbau vorgesehen ist, in einer ersten Phase bis Bad Vilbel. Ähnliche Kapazitätsprobleme gibt es auf der S7 nach Riedstadt-Goddelau, da hier die zweigleisige Strecke den gesamten Fernverkehr von Frankfurt Richtung Mannheim, Stuttgart und Basel aufnehmen muss. Solange die geplante ICE-Neubaustrecke zwischen Frankfurt und Mannheim nicht verwirklicht ist, kann der 30-Minuten-Takt auf der S7 daher kaum verdichtet werden.

Das S-Bahn-Netz wird durch eine Reihe von wichtigen Regionalbahnlinien ergänzt, z.B:

1) Die RMV-Linie 13 zwischen Höchst und Bad Soden verkehrt tagsüber alle 60 Minuten, in den Hauptverkehrszeiten allerdings alle 30 Minuten. Sie wurde bis 1995 als Verlängerung der S3 betrieben. Diese Strecke wird derzeit von der Hessischen Landesbahn (HLB) mit diesel-elektrischen Triebwagen bedient.

2) Die RMV-Linie 12 (HLB) fährt im Halbstundentakt vom Frankfurter Hauptbahnhof nach Königstein am Taunus.

3) Die RMV-Linie 55 (DB) hält alle 30 Minuten an den Stationen der nordmainischen Strecke zwischen Frankfurt Ost und Hanau. Diese Züge fahren über Frankfurt Süd zum Hauptbahnhof durch. Die nordmainische Strecke soll mittelfristig als S-Bahn ausgebaut werden.

4) Die RMV-Linie 61 (DB) zwischen Dreieich-Buchschlag (Anschluss zur S3/S4) und Rödermark–Ober-Roden (S1) wird alle 30 Minuten bedient, wobei die Züge stündlich nach Dieburg weiterfahren. In der Hauptverkehrszeit werden einzelne Züge mit Halt in Neu-Isenburg über die Ferngleise zum Frankfurter Hauptbahnhof durchgebunden.

*the western S2, while on its eastern leg, these trains start and end at Offenbach Hauptbahnhof. At present, a total of 22 trains run through the city tunnel every hour in each direction during peak hours, i.e. a train every 2-3 minutes. A new signalling and train protection system will be installed to increase the capacity to 24 trains per hour, from which the now split S2 trains would benefit. For the time being, line S7 will terminate on the surface level at Hauptbahnhof.*

*The total route length is 286 km (official sources state 303 km), and there are 115 S-Bahn stations; 63.4 km and 22 stations are located within the Frankfurt city boundaries. Along many routes the S-Bahn has dedicated tracks, or the tracks are only shared by a few other trains. On others, however, notably line S6 to Friedberg, the mixed service leads to capacity constraints; the quadrupling of this route, in a first stage as far as Bad Vilbel, has therefore been planned for a long time. Similar problems occur on line S7 to Riedstadt-Goddelau, a double-track route which carries all long-distance trains from Frankfurt towards Mannheim, Stuttgart and Basle. Until the planned high-speed line between Frankfurt and Mannheim has been realised, the headways on line S7 can hardly be shortened.*

*The S-Bahn system is complemented by several important regional rail lines, like for example:*

*1) RMV line 13 between Höchst and Bad Soden, with a train every 60 minutes, and every 30 minutes during peak hours. Until 1995, this route was operated as an extension of line S3, but it is now served by the Hessischen Landesbahn (HLB) with diesel-electric units.*

*2) RMV line 12 (HLB) runs half-hourly from Frankfurt Hauptbahnhof to Königstein am Taunus.*

*3) RMV line 55 (DB) calls half-hourly at all stations between Frankfurt Ost and Hanau on the railway line on the north side of the Main River; this route is to be upgraded to S-Bahn standard in the future. From Frankfurt Ost, line 55 continues to Frankfurt Hauptbahnhof via Frankfurt Süd.*

*4) RMV line 61 (DB) between Dreieich-Buchschlag (interchange with lines S3/S4) and Rödermark–Ober-Roden (S1) is operated every 30 minutes, with every other train continuing to Dieburg. During peak hours, some trains are extended to Frankfurt Hauptbahnhof over the long-distance tracks, stopping at Neu-Isenburg.*

### Eröffnung der Bahnstrecken mit S-Bahn-Verkehr
### *Opening of the railway routes now served by the S-Bahn*

1839 Frankfurt – Hattersheim (*Taunus-Eisenbahn*) ▸ S1
1840 Hattersheim – Wiesbaden (*Taunus-Eisenbahn*) ▸ S1
1846 Frankfurt – Darmstadt (*Main-Neckar-Eisenbahn*) ▸ S3/S4
1848 Frankfurt Ost – Hanau (*Frankfurt-Hanauer Eisenbahn*) ▸ geplant | *planned*
1850 Frankfurt – Friedberg (*Main-Weser-Bahn*) ▸ S6
1860 Frankfurt – Bad Homburg (*Homburger Bahn*) ▸ S5
1858 Mainz – Bischofsheim (*Rhein-Main-Bahn*) ▸ S8
1863 Frankfurt – Kelsterbach – Bischofsheim (*Mainbahn*) ▸ S8
1873 Offenbach Ost – Hanau (*Kinzigtalbahn*) ▸ S8/S9
1874 Frankfurt-Rödelheim – Kronberg (*Kronberger Bahn*) ▸ S4
1877 Frankfurt-Farbwerke – Niedernhausen (*Main-Lahn-Bahn*) ▸ S2
1879 Frankfurt-Stadion – Riedstadt-Goddelau (*Riedbahn*) ▸ S7
1895 Bad Homburg – Friedrichsdorf (*Homburger Bahn*) ▸ S5
1896 Offenbach Ost – Rödermark Ober-Roden (*Rodgaubahn*) ▸ S1
1898 Offenbach-Bieber – Dietzenbach (*Rodgaubahn*) ▸ S2
1904 Mainz – Wiesbaden Ost (*Kaiserbrücke/Nordbrücke*) ▸ S8
1913 Bischofsheim – Mainz-Kastel (*Hochheimer Brücke*) ▸ S9
1970 Niederhöchstadt – Schwalbach (*Limesbahn*) ▸ S3
1972 Schwalbach – Bad Soden (*Limesbahn*) ▸ S3
1972 Frankfurt-Stadion – Flughafen (Airport) – Kelsterbach ▸ S8/S9

### S-Bahn Rhein-Main

~ 286 km – 115 Bahnhöfe | *Stations*

28-05-1978 Hauptwache – Hauptbahnhof
- Wiesbaden (S1)
- Niedernhausen (S2)
- Bad Soden (S3)
- Kronberg (S4)
- Friedrichsdorf (S5)
- Friedberg (S6)

01-06-1980 Hauptbahnhof – Flughafen – Mainz – Wiesbaden (S8)
28-05-1983 Hauptwache – Konstablerwache
27-05-1990 Konstablerwache – Südbahnhof
30-09-1990 Südbahnhof – Stresemannallee
31-05-1992 Ostendstraße – Mühlberg
28-05-1995 Mühlberg - Offenbach Ost – Hanau (S8/S9)
01-06-1997 Stresemannallee – Darmstadt (S3/S4)
01-12-1998 + Oberursel-Stierstadt (S5)
1999 + Kronberg Süd (S4)
11-01-1999 + Messe (S3-S6)
14-10-2001 + Bremthal (S2)
15-12-2002 Hauptbahnhof – Riedstadt-Goddelau (S7)
20-10-2002 + Langen-Flugsicherung (S3/S4)

15-12-2003 Offenbach Ost
- Rödermark–Ober-Roden (S1)
- Dietzenbach (S2)

13-05-2007 + Zeilsheim (S2)
2008 + Schwalbach Nord (S3)

**Hauptbahnhof** – Die S7 nach Riedstadt-Goddelau fährt von einem der oberirdischen Bahnsteige ab.
*– line S7 to Riedstadt-Goddelau departs from the surface area of the Central Station.*

**Friedrichsdorf** – nördlicher Endpunkt der S5 mit ET420 215 (3. Bauserie) im ursprünglichen Anstrich (*Foto Fritz D. Kegel, 1979*)
*– northern S5 terminus, with ET420 215 (3rd series) in original livery*

## _ Geschichte der S-Bahn Rhein-Main

Das Eisenbahnzeitalter begann in und um Frankfurt bereits im Jahre 1839, denn der erste Abschnitt der *Taunus-Eisenbahn* nach Wiesbaden wurde nur vier Jahre nach der ersten deutschen Eisenbahnstrecke zwischen Nürnberg und Fürth eröffnet. Am Frankfurter Ende hatte die Bahn ihren Ausgangspunkt im Bereich der Gallusanlage, also unweit des Willy-Brandt-Platzes. Jeweils direkt südlich und nördlich davon bauten wenig später die *Main-Neckar-Bahn* (1846) und die *Main-Weser-Bahn* (1850) ihre Kopfbahnhöfe. Diese drei Bahnen errichteten schließlich bis 1888 den 600 m weiter westlich gelegenen heutigen Hauptbahnhof, dessen dreischiffige Bahnsteighalle noch an die einst privaten Bahnen erinnert. Vom anderen Ende der Stadt fuhren die Züge der *Frankfurt-Hanauer Eisenbahn* ab 1848 von einem Kopfbahnhof, der etwa 400 m westlich des heutigen Ostbahnhofs (an der Einmündung des Röderbergwegs in die Hanauer Landstraße) lag, nach Hanau. Diese Strecke wartet jedoch bis heute darauf, in das S-Bahn-Netz aufgenommen zu werden. Trotz der Schwierigkeiten, die sich daraus ergaben, dass Frankfurt zu jener Zeit eine Freie Stadt war, die von mehreren Kleinstaaten umgeben war, entwickelte sich schnell ein dichtes Netz, von dem die Region Rhein-Main bis heute profitiert.

Bereits 1964 kam es zu einer Vereinbarung zwischen der Stadt Frankfurt und der *Deutschen Bundesbahn* bezüglich des Baus einer Verbindungsbahn (V-Bahn) durch die Innenstadt als Teil eines regionalen Schnellbahnnetzes. Dadurch konnte bei den Planungen für die Stadtbahn auf das zukünftige S-Bahn-Netz Rücksicht genommen werden, was sich ab 1965 bereits beim Bau des U-Bahnhofs Hauptwache konkretisierte. Hier wurde über der Station für die A-Strecke ein wesentlicher Teil der zukünftigen C-Strecke aber auch der S-Bahn-Station mitgebaut. Genau am Tag der Eröffnung der A-Strecke, am 4. Oktober 1968, unterzeichnete die Bundesbahn einen Finanzierungsvertrag mit der Stadt Frankfurt, fünf Tage später auch mit dem Land Hessen, so dass die Bauarbeiten für die S-Bahn Rhein-Main am 20. Januar 1969 offiziell beginnen konnten. In einer ersten Ausbaustufe sollten die Radialstrecken aus dem Norden und Westen in die Innenstadt geführt werden.

Der City-Tunnel beginnt im westlichen Gleisvorfeld des Hauptbahnhofs, wo die Gleise aus Richtung Höchst und Flughafen gemeinsam über eine zweigleisige Rampe in den Untergrund abtauchen, während die über den Westbahnhof kommenden Strecken über zwei getrennte Rampen in den Tunnel einfahren und so den viergleisigen S-Bahnhof

## *_ History of the S-Bahn Rhein-Main*

*The railway age began in and around Frankfurt back in 1839, when the first section of the 'Taunus-Eisenbahn' to Wiesbaden opened only four years after the trains had started running on Germany's first railway line between Nuremberg and Fürth. At the Frankfurt end, the railway's terminus was located at Gallusanlage, i.e. close to the present Willy-Brandt-Platz. Adjacent to it, on either side, the 'Main-Neckar-Bahn' (1846) and 'Main-Weser-Bahn' (1850) built their respective termini. In 1888, the three railway companies moved their termini about 600 m further west, where a shared main station [Hauptbahnhof] had been erected. The 3-nave structure is still reminiscent of the three original operators. On the other side of the city, the trains of the 'Frankfurt-Hanauer Eisenbahn' began to depart for Hanau from a terminal station located about 400 m west of the present Ostbahnhof (at the intersection of Röderbergweg and Hanauer Landstraße) in 1848; this route still awaits its integration into the S-Bahn network. Despite the fact that Frankfurt at that time was a Free Imperial City surrounding by several small states, a dense railway network was rapidly developed, and became the basis for the present rail system in the Rhine-Main region.*

*In 1964, an agreement was signed between the city of Frankfurt and the 'Deutsche Bundesbahn' to build a cross-city tunnel as the centrepiece of a regional rapid rail network. This agreement allowed for the coordinated planning of the Stadtbahn and S-Bahn, which was concretised from 1965 in the form of a joint station at Hauptwache; while route A was being built, a substantial part of the future route C and the S-Bahn was constructed at the same time. On the same day route A was inaugurated, 4 October 1968, the 'Deutsche Bundesbahn' signed a financing contract with the city of Frankfurt, and five days later with the state of Hesse too, with construction on the S-Bahn Rhein-Main officially starting on 20 January 1969. In a first stage, the radial routes from the north and west were to be extended into the city centre.*

*The city tunnel starts west of the main station; the tracks from Höchst and the airport enter the tunnel on a 2-track ramp, while the tracks from Westbahnhof use two separate ramps connected to the outer tracks in the 4-track Hauptbahnhof S-Bahn station. Between the ramps and the underground Hauptbahnhof stations, four single-track tubes were built by means of a tunnelling shield. The station proper was excavated by cut-and-cover in two stages at a depth of 20 m, as*

**Stadion** – Ein Zug der Linie S7 nach Riedstadt-Goddelau hält am S-Bahnhof Stadion, der für die Fußball-WM 2006 ausgebaut wurde.
*– S7 train to Riedstadt-Goddelau calling at Stadion, a station upgraded for the FIFA World Cup 2006*

Hauptbahnhof auf den Außengleisen erreichen. Zwischen Rampen und Hauptbahnhof wurden vier eingleisige Röhren im teilmechanisierten Schildvortrieb aufgefahren. Der Stationsbereich selbst entstand in 20 m Tiefe in offener Bauweise, wobei von der *Deutschen Bundesbahn* auch der U-Bahnhof vor dem Hauptbahnhof miterrichtet wurde. Da jeweils nur drei Gleise des Hauptbahnhofs außer Betrieb genommen werden konnten, musste der S-Bahnhof in zwei Phasen gebaut werden. Außerdem musste ein Teil der Fassade von 1888 abgetragen und nach Fertigstellung der unterirdischen Anlage wieder aufgebaut werden. Östlich des Hauptbahnhofs laufen je zwei Gleise zusammen und führen in zwei eingleisigen, per NÖT (Neue Österreichische Tunnelbauweise) unter der Bebauung vorgetriebenen Röhren zum S-Bahnhof Taunusanlage. Am Opernplatz beginnt der Gemeinschaftstunnel der S-Bahn mit der Stadtbahn. Die S-Bahn-Gleise unterqueren erst das nach Osten führende Stadtbahngleis und kommen dann zwischen den beiden Stadtbahngleisen zu liegen. Mit Inbetriebnahme der S-Bahn Rhein-Main am 28. Mai 1978 wendeten die Züge direkt am Mittelbahnsteig an der Hauptwache, da dahinter keine Kehranlage errichtet worden war, was bei anfangs sechs Linien im 20-Minuten-Takt bald zu betrieblichen Engpässen führte. Gleichzeitig mit den drei ersten Tunnelstationen der S-Bahn ging auch der neue Bahnhof Galluswarte in Betrieb, nachdem zwischen Tunnelrampen und Westbahnhof eigene Gleise für die S-Bahn gebaut worden waren. Der Westbahnhof wurde so umgebaut, dass eine kreuzungsfreie Ausfädelung möglich ist. An den übrigen Bahnhöfen, die teilweise auch von anderen Zügen benutzt werden, wurden die Bahnsteige auf nur 76 cm statt der sonst üblichen Standardhöhe von 95 cm auf reinen S-Bahn-Strecken erhöht. Die Bahnsteiglänge beträgt überall

*only three of the surface tracks could be taken out of service at a time. The 'Deutsche Bundesbahn' was also responsible for the construction of the 4-track Stadtbahn station located below the station square. Part of the façade, which dates from 1888, had to be demolished and reconstructed once the underground stations had been completed. To the east of Hauptbahnhof S-Bahn station, the four tracks converge into two, and in two single-track tubes built using the NATM (New Austrian Tunnelling Method) they continue below the buildings to the next station at Taunusanlage. Near Opernplatz, the S-Bahn tracks burrow under the eastbound Stadtbahn track before becoming aligned between the two Stadtbahn tracks in the shared tunnel. When the S-Bahn Rhein-Main officially started on 28 May 1978, the trains used to reverse at the island platform at Hauptwache as there were no sidings beyond the station. With six lines operating every 20 minutes, this situation soon led to capacity problems. Together with the city tunnel, a surface station opened at Galluswarte after separate tracks had been laid between the tunnel portal and Westbahnhof. The other stations are also served by other trains, so their platforms were only raised to 76 cm instead of the standard S-Bahn height of 95 cm. All platforms are 210 m long, which corresponds to a triple unit of class ET420; these trains had been in service on the future S-Bahn lines since 1975. The same type of train had been running in Munich for several years, and a few months later, it also started operating on the S-Bahn system in Stuttgart.*

*While the 'Deutsche Bundesbahn' took over the construction of the Stadtbahn station at Hauptbahnhof, the city in return built the shared 1.4 km tunnel along the Zeil. This cut-and-cover tunnel between Hauptwache and Konstabler-*

210 m, was einer 3-fach-Traktion (Langzug) der Baureihe ET420 entsprach, die bereits seit 1975 auf den späteren S-Bahn-Strecken im Regionalverkehr eingesetzt worden waren. Derselbe Fahrzeugtyp war schon seit einigen Jahren in München unterwegs und nur wenige Monate nach Frankfurt kam er auch bei der Stuttgarter S-Bahn zum Einsatz.

Während die Bundesbahn für den Bau des U-Bahnhofs am Hauptbahnhof verantwortlich war, baute die Stadt im Gegenzug den 1,4 km langen gemeinsamen Tunnel unter der Zeil auch für die S-Bahn mit. Hier kam die offene Bauweise zur Anwendung. Der Abschnitt von der Hauptwache bis zur Konstablerwache wurde von der S-Bahn 1983 genau fünf Jahre nach dem Start der S-Bahn in Betrieb genommen, während die Stadtbahn noch dreieinhalb Jahre länger auf sich warten ließ. Östlich der Station Konstablerwache wurde im anschließenden Tunnelstutzen eine Wendemöglichkeit eingerichtet.

Neben dem Innenstadttunnel umfasste das S-Bahn-Projekt auch den Bau eines direkten Flughafen-Anschlusses mit einer 7,5 km langen Schleife zwischen Stadion und Kelsterbach, die einen 2,2 km langen Tunnel und den dreigleisigen, unterirdischen Flughafenbahnhof enthielt. Dieser besitzt neben einem 210 m langen Seitenbahnsteig auch einen 410 m langen Mittelbahnsteig, da hier bis zur Eröffnung eines eigenen Fernbahnhofs 1999 auch Fernzüge hielten. Die Flughafenbahn wurde bereits 1972 in Betrieb genommen. Anschließend wurden zwischen Hauptbahnhof und dem Abzweig von der Mainbahn westlich der Station Stadion eigene S-Bahn-Gleise verlegt, so dass hier am 1. Juni 1980 der S-Bahn-Betrieb mit der Linie S15 aufgenommen werden konnte. Diese fuhr jedoch vorerst nicht in den City-Tunnel, sondern endete bis 1983 am Hauptbahnhof oben.

Wie die Flughafenbahn war auch die sog. Limesbahn (S3) bereits in Hinblick auf den S-Bahn-Betrieb einige Jahre vorher gebaut worden. Ab 22. Dezember 1970 wurde ein Pendelverkehr zwischen Niederhöchstadt und der neuen Station Schwalbach eingerichtet, und am 6. November 1972 wurde die durchgehende Strecke bis Bad Soden eröffnet. Diese ist wie der Abschnitt Niederhöchstadt – Kronberg bis heute eingleisig.

Die zweite Ausbaustufe der S-Bahn Rhein-Main umfasste den östlichen City-Tunnel mit einer unterirdischen Mainquerung. Aus finanziellen Gründen musste der Anschluss der östlichen und südlichen Radialstrecken noch zurückgestellt werden. Nördlich des S-Bahnhofs Ostendstraße wurden zwei Tunnelstutzen für einen Anschluss der nordmainischen Strecke nach Hanau mitgebaut. Nach heutigen Planungen soll die S-Bahn am Ostbahnhof unterirdisch halten und anschließend auf eigenen neu zu bauenden S-Bahn-Gleisen über Maintal nach Hanau fahren.

Im Bahnhof Ostendstraße kam erstmals in Frankfurt der Schildvortrieb im Stationsbereich zum Einsatz. Die daran anschließenden Tunnel bis zur Mainquerung sowie die kreuzungsfreie Verzweigung am Südufer wurden hingegen teils per NÖT und teils in offener Bauweise errichtet. Die Flussquerung selbst entstand 1982 mittels zwei je 62 m langen, am Ufer in Trockendocks hergestellten Betonkästen. Diese wurden eingeschwemmt, in eine 18 m tief in das Flussbett gegrabene Rinne abgesenkt und mit einer etwa 4 m dicken Erdschicht abgedeckt. An beiden Ufern wurden die Trockendocks dann zu Streckentunneln mit Wehrkammern gegen Wassereinbruch umgebaut.

Der nach Süden führende Ast erreicht am Südbahnhof die Oberfläche, wo die vier nördlichsten Gleise an die S-Bahn abgegeben wurden. Zwischen Südbahnhof und Stresemannallee entstand noch ein aufwändiges Tunnelbauwerk, um die S-Bahn von der Nord- auf die Südseite der Fernbahngleise zu bringen. Außerdem wurde in diesem Bereich eine Abstellanlage errichtet. 1990 endeten nun fünf S-Bahn-Linien am Südbahnhof und zwei fuhren weiter bis Stresemannallee.

*wache was brought into service by the S-Bahn in 1983, exactly five years after the start of the S-Bahn system, whereas the Stadtbahn tracks remained unused for another three and a half years. East of Konstablerwache, the tunnel stub was used as a reversing facility.*

*The S-Bahn scheme included not only the city tunnel, but also the 7.5 km airport loop between Stadion and Kelsterbach, with a 2.2 km tunnel and the 3-track underground airport station. Besides a 210 m side platform, this station also has a 400 m island platform, which was used by long-distance trains until the new airport station for long-distance trains was opened in 1999. The airport line had already been brought into service in 1972. Later, dedicated S-Bahn tracks were laid between Hauptbahnhof and the junction west of Stadion station, and S-Bahn line S15 was introduced on 1 June 1980; until 1983, it did not run through the city tunnel, but terminated on the surface at Hauptbahnhof.*

*Like the airport line, the so-called 'Limesbahn' (S3) was built in view of the future S-Bahn. On 22 December 1970, a shuttle service started between Niederhöchstadt and the new station at Schwalbach, the through route to Bad Soden being completed on 6 November 1972. Like the section Niederhöchstadt – Kronberg, this new line has remained single-track.*

*The second stage of the S-Bahn Rhein-Main project comprised the eastern section of the city tunnel and the crossing under the Main River. Due to financial problems, the connection of the eastern and southern radial routes had to be postponed. Just north of Ostendstraße station, two tunnel stubs were added for a future branch towards Hanau following the north bank of the Main River. According to the present plans, the S-Bahn is to stop underground at Ostbahnhof, from where a separate pair of tracks will be laid along the route via Maintal.*

*At Ostendstraße, a tunnelling shield was used to excavate a station for the first time in Frankfurt. The following tunnels up to the river as well as the junction on the south bank, however, were built partly by cut-and-cover, partly using the NATM. In 1982, the river crossing was realised with two concrete tunnel segments, each 62 m long and cast in drydocks by the river banks. They were then floated into the river, sunk into an 18 m deep trench previously excavated in the riverbed, and finally covered with a 4 m layer of soil. The two drydocks were converted into running tunnels equipped with flood gates.*

*The southern leg of the cross-city S-Bahn route emerges from the tunnel just before arriving at Südbahnhof, where*

**Hauptwache** – Ursprungszustand mit braunen Säulen und roten Umrandungen; der Bereich rechts zur Stadtbahn ist noch verschlossen (*Foto F. D. Kegel, 1979*).
*– original station with brown pillars and red handrails around them; the area on the right, now used by the Stadtbahn, was still covered up in 1979.*

Der östliche Abzweig der Stammstrecke sollte vorerst an der Station Mühlberg enden, jedoch war die Lage dieses Bahnhofs solange unklar, bis man sich auf die später verwirklichte Trassierung Richtung Offenbach einigen konnte. Im Bereich Oberrad waren in den siebziger Jahren weitreichende Wohnbauprojekte geplant, welche die neue S-Bahn berücksichtigen musste. Aus verschiedenen Gründen unterblieb diese Bebauung und die S-Bahn wurde in einer Kurve zur Fernbahnstrecke Frankfurt – Hanau geführt, wo sie nun in nördlicher Parallellage auf 1,2 km an der Oberfläche verkehrt. Auf diesem Abschnitt wurde der spätere Bau eines S-Bahnhofs Oberrad berücksichtigt. Von 1992 bis 1995 war nun Mühlberg Endbahnhof für die Linien S1 und S2. Im Anschluss daran stand eine Trassierung entlang der bestehenden Bundesbahntrasse über Offenbach Hauptbahnhof oder aber eine Tunnellösung durch das Offenbacher Stadtzentrum zur Debatte, wobei sich 1983 schließlich die zentralere Variante durchsetzte.

Der Baubeginn des 3,6 km langen Offenbacher City-Tunnels war am 23. März 1988. Die westliche Rampe liegt direkt an der Stadtgrenze zwischen Frankfurt und Offenbach. Der unterirdische Bahnhof Kaiserlei, der ein Entwicklungsgebiet im Westen Offenbachs erschließt, liegt an der Südseite des großen Kaiserlei-Kreisels, den die Autobahn A661 in Hochlage überquert. Die Fundamente von zwei Brückenpfeilern bestimmten die genaue Lage dieses Bahnhofs mit. Der Offenbacher Tunnel verläuft weiter unter der Berliner Straße und dann unter der Bieberer Straße und wurde auf voller Länge trotz der Tiefenlage von bis zu 20 m in offener Bauweise erstellt. In der engen Bieberer Straße musste die angrenzende Bebauung durch Bohrpfähle abgestützt werden, und im Bereich nahe des Ostbahnhofs mussten mehrere Gebäude abgefangen und unterfahren werden. Die drei unterirdischen Stationen wurden großzügig angelegt und gehören gestalterisch sicherlich zu den interessantesten im Rhein-Main-Gebiet. Auffallend ist vor allem die für die offene Bauweise untypische Gewölbeform. Am Bahnhof Offenbach Ost kommt die S-Bahn an der Südseite an die Oberfläche, wozu eine 190 m lange Unterfahrung der Fernbahngleise notwendig war. Direkt östlich des Bahnhofs Offenbach Ost verzweigen sich heute die beiden Äste nach Hanau bzw. Richtung Rodgau niveaugleich.

Die 11 km lange südmainische S-Bahn-Strecke von Offenbach nach Hanau ging am 28. Mai 1995, zum Start des Verkehrsverbunds RMV, gemeinsam mit dem Offenbacher City-Tunnel in Betrieb. Hier wurde aufgrund des starken Fernverkehrs eine eigene S-Bahn-Trasse angelegt, die bis Dietesheim südlich der Fernbahnstrecke liegt und dann auf die

**Frankfurt Süd** > **Lokalbahnhof** – S5 verlässt den City-Tunnel.
*– S5 train emerging from the city tunnel*

**OF-Marktplatz** – auch im Zentrum vom Offenbach verkehrt die S-Bahn im Tunnel.
*– the S-Bahn runs underground through the city centre of Offenbach, too.*

*the four northern tracks were dedicated to the S-Bahn. Between Südbahnhof and Stresemannallee, another tunnel was built to take the S-Bahn from the north to the south side of the mainline tracks; adjacent to this junction, several sidings were laid for the S-Bahn. In 1990, five S-Bahn lines terminated at Südbahnhof, while two continued to Stresemannallee.*

*In a first stage, the eastern leg was to run only as far as Mühlberg, but the location of this station was not clear for a long time, as neither was the alignment from there towards Offenbach. In the Oberrad area, the extensive housing schemes planned during the 1970s had to be coordinated with the S-Bahn project. Due to various reasons, though, these houses were not built, and the S-Bahn was eventually taken in a long curve to meet the mainline from Frankfurt to Hanau, which it follows on the surface for about 1.2 km. On this section, a station may be added at Oberrad in the future. From 1992 until 1995, Mühlberg became the terminus for lines S1 and S2. For the following section, an alignment parallel to the mainline route via Offenbach Hauptbahnhof, and an underground route through the Offenbach city centre were discussed. The latter alternative was chosen in 1983.*

*The construction of the 3.6 km Offenbach city tunnel started on 23 March 1988. The western ramp lies right at the boundary between Frankfurt and Offenbach. The underground station at Kaiserlei serves a business park in the west of Offenbach; it is located at the southern side of the huge Kaiserlei roundabout, which is spanned over by a viaduct for motorway A661. The existence of two supporting pillars determined the final location of the station. The Offenbach city tunnel first follows Berliner Straße and then Bieberer Straße, and despite its great depth of 20 m, it was built entirely by cut-and-cover. Along the narrow Bieberer Straße, some buildings had to be secured by means of bored piles, and close to Ostbahnhof, several houses had to be underpinned in order to excavate beneath them. The three underground stations are very spacious and certainly among the most appealing in the Rhine-Main area. The vaulted ceiling is a special feature rarely found in cut-and-cover stations. At Offenbach Ost, the S-Bahn gets aligned on the southern side, and a 190 m tunnel therefore had to be made beneath the mainline tracks. Just east of Offenbach Ost station, the S-Bahn diverges in a flat junction into a branch to Hanau and another to Rodgau.*

*The 11 km S-Bahn route between Offenbach and Hanau opened together with the Offenbach city tunnel on 28 May 1995, the same day the RMV came into force. Due to the heavy long-distance traffic on this section, a separate track*

Nordseite verschwenkt. Die gesamte Strecke ist bis auf den Begegnungsabschnitt Mühlheim – Dietesheim eingleisig, wobei auch die Station Steinheim nur eine Bahnsteigkante aufweist. An der Nordseite der bestehenden Mainbrücke unmittelbar östlich der Station Steinheim wurde eine eingleisige Brücke für die S-Bahn errichtet. Die Lage der S-Bahn-Gleise im Hanauer Hauptbahnhof wurde so gewählt, dass diese in Zukunft auch von der nordmainischen Strecke aus angefahren werden können.

Als die S-Bahn Hanau erreichte, waren auch die Bauarbeiten an der 25 km langen Strecke von Stresemannallee nach Darmstadt bereits in vollem Gang. Hier wurden ebenfalls entlang der bestehenden Fernbahngleise eigene S-Bahn-Gleise errichtet, wobei diese zwischen Neu-Isenburg und Langen an der Westseite, sonst an der Ostseite liegen. Zwischen Langen und Darmstadt verfügt die S-Bahn nur über ein Gleis, hat jedoch zwischen Egelsbach und Erzhausen einen Begegnungsabschnitt. Die S-Bahn nach Darmstadt wurde 1997 fertig gestellt, die Station Langen-Flugsicherung wurde jedoch erst 2002 eingerichtet.

Mit der zweiten Ausbaustufe war der S-Bahn-Bau in der Region Rhein-Main jedoch noch nicht abgeschlossen. Für das ursprünglich vorgesehene Netz fehlten noch die Rodgau-Strecken, die nordmainische S-Bahn nach Hanau sowie die Riedbahn nach Riedstadt-Goddelau. Der Ausbau der letzteren ist im Zusammenhang mit der geplanten ICE-Neubaustrecke zwischen Frankfurt und Mannheim zu sehen, die weiter östlich verlaufen und auch Darmstadt anbinden soll. Für die S7 wurden deshalb nur die Bahnsteige auf 76 cm erhöht sowie einige Bahnübergänge beseitigt.

Bei der Rodgaubahn mitsamt ihrem Dietzenbacher Ast handelte es sich um zwei Nebenbahnstrecken, so dass hier kein Fernverkehr zu berücksichtigen war. Allerdings mussten beide Strecken erst zweigleisig ausgebaut und elektrifiziert werden. Nur die letzten 1,2 km des Dietzenbacher Astes, auf dem seit 1982 kein Personenverkehr mehr stattgefunden hatte, blieben eingleisig. Zusätzliche Stationen wurden in Waldhof und in Dietzenbach Mitte errichtet, während die bestehenden 12 Bahnhöfe umgebaut und zahlreiche Bahnübergänge beseitigt wurden.

Es bleibt nun abzuwarten, ob die immer wieder verschobene Verwirklichung der nordmainischen S-Bahn in den nächsten Jahren konkrete Formen annimmt. Der optimistischste Fertigstellungstermin liegt derzeit im Jahr 2016. Dieser Ast könnte zusammen mit der heutigen S5 eine neue Durchmesserlinie bilden, die an der Konstablerwache vom bestehenden City-Tunnel ausfädelt.

Der viergleisige Ausbau der Strecke nach Bad Vilbel (S6) wird durch Anwohnerklagen gegen den Planfeststellungsbeschluss von 2004 weiter verzögert. Neben dem Umbau der bestehenden Stationen soll dabei in Ginnheim ein neuer S-Bahnhof eingerichtet werden, der eine Umsteigemöglichkeit zur Stadtbahn an der Haltestelle Niddapark bringen würde. An dieser Stelle gab es bereits vom 28. April 1989 bis zum 15. Oktober 1989 einen provisorischen Halt für die BUGA 89 (Bundesgartenschau). In einer zweiten Phase sollen die eigenen S-Bahn-Gleise bis Friedberg verlängert werden.

Mit der Regionaltangente West (RTW) ist seit über zehn Jahren in der Region Rhein-Main ein neuartiges Schnellbahnsystem geplant, das mit 2-System-Fahrzeugen betrieben werden soll und teilweise auf DB-Gleisen, auf Stadtbahngleisen und auf neuen Strecken verkehren soll. Die Regionaltangente West würde Neu-Isenburg, den Flughafen Frankfurt, Frankfurt-Höchst und Bad Homburg miteinander verbinden. Ein Abzweig könnte von Praunheim zum Nordwestzentrum gebaut werden.

*was laid for the S-Bahn, up to Dietesheim on the south side, and then on the north side. Only the Mühlheim – Dietesheim section is double-track; Steinheim station has just one platform edge. To the north of the existing Main bridge, a single-track bridge was added for the S-Bahn. At Hanau Hauptbahnhof, the present S-Bahn tracks may later also be connected to the planned S-Bahn route along the north side of the Main River.*

*When the S-Bahn reached Hanau, the construction of the 25 km route from Stresemannallee to Darmstadt was well underway. Separate S-Bahn tracks were laid parallel to the existing mainline tracks, mostly along the eastern side, but between Neu-Isenburg and Langen along the western side. Between Langen and Darmstadt the S-Bahn is only single-track, but between Egelsbach and Erzhausen there is a passing loop. While the S-Bahn was extended to Darmstadt in 1997, Langen-Flugsicherung station was added in 2002.*

*With phase 2 concluded, the S-Bahn Rhein-Main had not yet reached its full extension. The initial project also included the Rodgau routes, the route to Hanau along the north side of the Main River, and the 'Riedbahn' to Riedstadt-Goddelau. The latter is related to the project for a new high-speed line between Frankfurt and Mannheim, which will run further east via Darmstadt. Platforms just 76 cm high were therefore erected for line S7, and several level crossings were eliminated.*

*The 'Rodgaubahn' and its branch to Dietzenbach were secondary railway lines, so no long-distance traffic had to be taken into account. Both routes, however, had to be doubled and electrified. Only the southernmost 1.2 km of the Dietzenbach branch, which had not seen any passenger traffic since 1982, have remained single-track. At Waldhof and Dietzenbach Mitte, additional stations were built, while the existing 12 stations were upgraded and numerous level crossings were eliminated.*

*It is still unclear whether the long-planned S-Bahn route along the north side of the Main River will finally be built in the mid-term future. The most optimistic date for completion is now 2016. This branch could become a new cross-region line served by S5, which would diverge from the city tunnel at Konstablerwache.*

*The quadrupling of the route to Bad Vilbel (S6) has been delayed by legal action taken by neighbours against the planning permission granted in 2004. Besides the upgrading of the existing stations, a new S-Bahn station providing interchange with Stadtbahn line U1 at Niddapark will be built at Ginnheim, where a temporary station was in service from 28 April 1989 until 15 October 1989 during the BUGA 89 (German Garden Show). In a second stage, the dedicated S-Bahn tracks are planned to be extended all the way to Friedberg.*

*For more than ten years, the 'Regionaltangente West' (RTW) has been planned in the Rhine-Main region. This would become a new type of rail system, with dual-system vehicles operating on DB tracks, Stadtbahn tracks as well as newly-built tracks. The RTW would link Neu-Isenburg to Frankfurt Airport, Höchst and Bad Homburg; a branch would run from Praunheim to Nordwestzentrum.*

### Fahrzeugpark der S-Bahn Rhein-Main

1) 77 dreiteilige Einheiten der Baureihe **ET420**, die 67,4 m lang und 2,90 m breit sind. Mit Auslieferung der ersten ET423-Einheiten nach München, kam es zu einer Umverteilung der ET420-Wagen. Im Jahr 2008 waren von der 3. Bauserie (1976-78) im Rhein-Main-Gebiet 17 Einheiten im aktiven Einsatz, von der 4. Bauserie 49 (1978-79) und von der 5. Bauserie (1979-80) noch 11. Alle Fahrzeuge wurden ursprünglich in Orange/Kieselgrau ausgeliefert, doch bis 2004 bekamen alle den verkehrsroten Anstrich.

ET420 284 (Flughafen/Airport)

2) 100 Einheiten der seit 2002 auch nach Frankfurt gelieferten vierteiligen Baureihe ET423, welche zur 3. Bauserie (301-305, 325-334), sowie zur 4. bzw. 5. Bauserie (372-443) gehören. Diese sind ebenso 67,4 m lang, jedoch 3,02 m breit und durchgängig begehbar.

Beide Zugtypen können in Dreifachtraktion verkehren, da alle Bahnsteige eine Länge von 210 m haben, doch normalerweise werden Doppeltraktionen (= Vollzug) eingesetzt. Die S-Bahn-Züge sind seit März 2006 im Bahnbetriebswerk im ehemaligen Postbahnhof, an der Nordseite des Hauptbahnhofs, beheimatet. Die S-Bahn Rhein-Main fährt unter Oberleitung mit 15 kV Wechselstrom (16 2/3 Hz).

### *S-Bahn Rhein-Main Rolling Stock*

*1) 77 three-section units of class **ET420**, which are 67.40 m long and 2.90 m wide. When the first units of class ET423 were delivered to Munich's S-Bahn, the existing ET420s were redistributed among various other cities. In 2008, a total of 17 units of the third series (built in 1976-78) were still in service in the Rhine-Main area, 49 of the fourth series (1978-79), and 11 of the fifth series (1979-80). All trains originally carried an orange/pebble-grey livery, but by 2004, all had been repainted in red.*

*2) 100 four-section units of class ET423, delivered to Frankfurt since 2002; these belong to the third series (no. 301 to 305, and 325 to 334), as well as to the fourth and fifth series (no. 372 to 443). The ET423 trains are also 67.40 m long, but 3.02 m wide. All the cars are interconnected via gangways.*

*Both types of train can operate in triple units, which corresponds to a full platform length of 210 m, but they are mostly seen as double units. Since March 2006, the maintenance of the S-Bahn trains has been carried out at the Bahnbetriebswerk in the former Postbahnhof, on the northern side of the main railway station. Power (15 kV ac – 16 2/3 Hz) is supplied via a catenary.*

ET423 426 (Frankfurt Süd)

Ebener Einstieg nur bei 95 cm hohen Bahnsteigen auf exklusiven S-Bahn-Strecken
– *Level access into the vehicle only from 95 cm high platforms on dedicated S-Bahn routes*

Innenraum der Baureihe ET423
– *Class ET423 interior*

①

②

③

Der unterirdische Teil des **Frankfurter Hauptbahnhofs** ②-⑤ umfasst die Gleise 101-104, d.h. je zwei Gleise pro Richtung mit zwei Mittelbahnsteigen ③. Auf den äußeren Gleisen verkehren die S-Bahnen von/nach Galluswarte, während die inneren Gleisen den Linien Richtung Griesheim bzw. Niederrad dienen. Vor einiger Zeit wurde die Deckenverkleidung ⑤ (*Foto Olaf Wenke, 1993*) abgenommen, seither präsentiert sich die Station in einem unfertigen Zustand. Die orangefarbenen Kreise an den Außenwänden erinnern an die Londoner U-Bahn. Vom östlichen Ende der Bahnsteige ② gelangt man zur Station der U4/U5 (▶ S. 60), die eine Ebene höher halten. Mittige Aufgänge führen über ein Zwischengeschoss direkt in die Bahnhofshalle ①.

*The underground part of **Frankfurt Hauptbahnhof** [Central Station] ②-⑤ has four tracks, numbered 101-104, two for each direction, plus two island platforms ③. The outer tracks are used by trains to and from Galluswarte, while the inner two are shared by trains to and from Griesheim and Niederrad. Some time ago, the false ceiling ⑤ was removed, leaving the station in a somewhat unfinished state. The orange circles on the walls are reminiscent of the London Underground. From the eastern ends of the platforms ②, corridors connect with the U4/U5 station (▶ p. 60) one level above. The stairs located in the middle of the platforms lead, via a mezzanine, to the railway station concourse ①.*

④

⑤

Der S-Bahnhof **Taunusanlage** ①-③ erschließt das Frankfurter Bankenviertel. Die ursprünglich grün gefliesten Säulen ① (*Foto Olaf Wenke, 1989*) wurden leider im Jahr 2002 grau überstrichen. Als einziges Unterscheidungsmerkmal bleiben die stehenden Quadrate an den Wänden, aber auch diese haben ihre ursprünglich grüne Farbe zugunsten eines sehr dunklen Blautons verloren.

***Taunusanlage** station ①-③ serves Frankfurt's bank district. The supporting columns, initially clad in green tiles ①, were painted grey in 2002. The rotated squares on the walls are the only distinctive feature left; originally green, they were later repainted in a dark blue.*

Auch der S-Bahnhof **Hauptwache** ④⑤ ergraute im Jahr 2002 (die Stützen waren einst braun, ▶ S. 114), störender wirkt jedoch wie am Hauptbahnhof die offene Decke, da allerlei Leitungen und Kabel sichtbar sind. Der Rohbau des S-Bahnhofs wurde bereits in den sechziger Jahren zusammen mit der Station für die A-Strecke (▶ S. 27) errichtet. Hier hält die S-Bahn an einem Mittelbahnsteig, während die Stadtbahn parallel dazu über Seitenbahnsteige verfügt (▶ S. 87). Vom weitläufigen Zwischengeschoss ④ führen drei Treppenanlagen zur S-Bahn, ein weiterer, nur zur S-Bahn führender Zugang befindet sich am westlichen Ende im Bereich des Goetheplatzes.

*The previously brownish columns (▶ p. 114) in **Hauptwache** station ④⑤ also became grey in 2002. But what is more irritating in this station is the uncovered ceiling, which reveals all sorts of tubes and cables. The shell for this station had already been built back in the 1960s together with the station for route A (▶ p. 27). The S-Bahn's island platform is flanked by the side platforms used by the Stadtbahn (▶ p. 87). From the island platform, three flights of stairs lead to the large mezzanine ④; at the western side, near Goetheplatz, there is another entrance only for the S-Bahn.*

①

②

③

Im Jahr 1983 erreichten die S-Bahnen vom Westen her erstmals den Bahnhof **Konstablerwache** ①-③, wo man am selben Bahnsteig zu den Stadtbahnzügen der Linien U6 und U7 (▶ S. 88) im Richtungsbetrieb umsteigen kann. Da ein S-Bahn-Zug eine Maximallänge von 210 m erreichen kann, ein Stadtbahnzug aber nur knapp 100 m, setzt sich die Bahnsteigkante für die S-Bahn nach Westen fort ②, während die Stadtbahn bereits im Tunnel verschwindet. Beide Mittelbahnsteige sind vom zentralen Zwischengeschoss, aber auch über ein weiteres Zwischengeschoss ① am westlichen Ende der Station zugänglich. Hier befindet sich ein direkter Zugang in ein benachbartes Kaufhaus.
Als einziger S-Bahnhof in Frankfurt wurde die Station **Ostendstraße** im Schildvortrieb aufgefahren, woraus sich die Röhrenform ⑤ der Bahnsteigtunnel ergibt. Aus dem großen Anfahrschacht am Nordende des Bahnhofs wurde später ein großzügiger Zugangsbereich ④.

*In 1993, the first S-Bahn trains reached* ***Konstablerwache*** *①-③ from the western side. Cross-platform interchange is provided here between the S-Bahn and Stadtbahn lines U6 and U7 (▶ p. 88). As S-Bahn trains can be 210 m long, and Stadtbahn trains only 100 m, the platform edges served by the S-Bahn continue further west ② than those of the Stadtbahn, beyond the point where the Stadtbahn trains have already disappeared into the tunnel. Both island platforms are accessible via the main mezzanine, but also via a smaller vestibule at the western end of the station complex ①, which also accommodates a direct entrance into an adjacent department store.*
***Ostendstraße*** *is the only S-Bahn station in Frankfurt built using a tunnelling shield, which explains the tube-shaped platform area ⑤. The start shaft used for the excavation was later converted into a spacious entrance area at the northern end of the station ④.*

④

⑤

Südlich des Bahnhofs **Ostendstraße** ① unterquert die S-Bahn den Main und verzweigt sich in einen Ast Richtung Offenbach und einen zweiten Richtung Südbahnhof.
Bereits auf dem Ast Richtung Offenbach liegt der S-Bahnhof **Mühlberg** am östlichen Rand von Sachsenhausen. Der breite, stützenlose und gekrümmte Mittelbahnsteig ist nur am nördlichen Ende ② zugänglich und wird gegen Süden ④ hin enger. Zwischen 1992 und 1995 war hier Endstation für die Linien S1 und S2. Es ist gleichzeitig der letzte Bahnhof auf Frankfurter Gebiet auf der Strecke Richtung Südosten.

①

*South of **Ostendstraße** ①, the S-Bahn crosses beneath the Main River before splitting into two branches, one to Offenbach and the other to Südbahnhof.*
*Located in the eastern part of the district of Sachsenhausen, **Mühlberg** ②-④ is the first station on the Offenbach branch. The wide, curved island platform has no supporting pillars and is only accessible from the northern end ②; it becomes narrower towards the southern end ④. Mühlberg was the terminus for lines S1 and S2 between 1992 and 1995. It is the last station within the Frankfurt city boundaries on the southeastern lines.*

②

③

④

①

②

③

[S1/S2 West] Durch die Linien S1 und S2 werden die Stationen **Griesheim** ① und **Nied** ② mindestens alle 15 Minuten bedient.
Der wichtigste Knoten im Frankfurter Westen ist **Höchst** ③, wo die Nebenstrecken aus Königstein sowie aus Bad Soden einmünden. Das Bahnhofsgebäude stammt von 1914.
Die S1 befährt die Strecke der ältesten hessischen Eisenbahn, die 1840 von Frankfurt ausgehend **Wiesbaden** erreichte. Der weitgehend in seiner Ursprungsform erhaltene Bahnhof ④⑤ stammt aus dem Jahre 1906, als die drei ehemaligen Kopfbahnhöfe einige Hundert Meter nach Süden verschoben wurden. Hier enden auch die Linien S8 und S9.

*[S1/S2 west] **Griesheim** ① and **Nied** ② stations are served by lines S1 and S2 at least every 15 minutes.*
*The biggest interchange in the west of Frankfurt is **Höchst** ③, where the branch lines from Königstein and Bad Soden join the S-Bahn routes. The station building dates from 1914.*
*Line S1 continues along the oldest railway line in Hesse, which, starting from Frankfurt, reached **Wiesbaden** in 1840. The well-restored station there ④⑤ was opened in 1906, when the three former terminal stations were moved a few hundred metres south. Wiesbaden is also the terminus for lines S8 and S9.*

④

⑤

[S1/S2 West] An der Station Farbwerke trennt sich die S2 von der S1. Vor Verlassen des Frankfurter Stadtgebiets hält sie an der Station **Zeilsheim** ①, die erst 2007 eingerichtet wurde. Entlang des Schwarzbachs und des Daisbachs erreicht sie im Mischverkehr mit den Regionalbahnen nach Limburg über **Hofheim** ② und **Eppstein** ③ ihren Endpunkt Niedernhausen.

*[S1/S2 west] At Farbwerke station, line S2 diverges from the S1 route. A new station was added at **Zeilsheim** ① in 2007, which is still on Frankfurt territory. The S-Bahn runs through the valley of the Schwarzbach and Daisbach Rivers on tracks shared by regional trains to Limburg. Passing through **Hofheim** ② and **Eppstein** ③, line S2 reaches its current terminus at Niedernhausen.*

Seit 1955 ist Wiesbaden eine ‚straßenbahnfreie' Stadt (übrigens mit 275.000 Einwohnern neben Münster die größte Stadt in Deutschland ohne städtischen Schienenverkehr!). Doch mit der **Nerobergbahn** hat auch Wiesbaden dem Bahnfreund mehr zu bieten als nur die S-Bahn. Diese 438 m lange, mit Wasserballast betriebene Standseilbahn wurde 1888 eröffnet und 2004/05 generalsaniert. In der Bergstation wird der nach unten fahrende Wagen mit Wasser gefüllt und so der andere Wagen, von dem an der Talstation das Wasser abgelassen wurde, hinaufgezogen. Auf dem Weg zum 245 m hohen Neroberg überwindet die Bahn einen Höhenunterschied von 83 m.

*Wiesbaden has been a 'tram-free' city since 1955 – together with Münster, both with a population of 275,000, it is the largest city in Germany without any form of rail-based urban rail system. For the railway enthusiast, however, the city offers not only the S-Bahn, but also the **Nerobergbahn**, a funicular powered by the weight of water. The tank of the downbound car is filled with water at the top, and the other car, emptied at the bottom station, is thus pulled up the hill. The line opened in 1888 is 438 m long, and on its way to the 245 m high Neroberg it has to negotiate a change in altitude of 83 m. The peculiar funicular was modernised in 2004/05.*

①

②

③

[S3/S4 West] Die Linien S3 und S4 verkehren weitgehend auf derselben Strecke und bilden zusammen einen 15-Minuten-Takt. Die beiden eingleisigen Äste ab Niederhöchstadt werden somit nur alle 30 Minuten bedient. Vom Stadtzentrum verkehrt bis **Rödelheim** ①, dem letzten Bahnhof auf Frankfurter Stadtgebiet, auch die S5 auf denselben Gleisen. Direkt hinter der Stadtgrenze liegt der kürzlich umgebaute Halt **Eschborn Süd** ②.
Von **Niederhöchstadt** ③ fährt die S4 in nordwestlicher Richtung weiter nach Kronberg. Der Halt Kronberg Süd wird seit 1999 auf den Netzplänen angezeigt, auch wenn es bereits vorher einen provisorischen Halt ‚Werk Braun' für die Arbeiter einer Fabrik gab.
Die S4 endet in **Kronberg** ④, einer der wohlhabendsten Gemeinden in Hessen.

④

*[S3/S4 west] Lines S3 and S4 provide a 15-minute headway on their shared route; the two northern branches are single-track and only served every 30 minutes. The section from the city centre to* ***Rödelheim*** *①, the last station in Frankfurt, is also shared by line S5.* ***Eschborn Süd*** *station ②, which has recently been rebuilt, is found right after leaving the city of Frankfurt.*
*From* ***Niederhöchstadt*** *③, line S4 continues northwest to Kronberg. The station at Kronberg Süd has only been shown on network maps since 1999, although some trains had previously stopped for factory workers at a stop called 'Werk Braun'.*
*Line S4 terminates at* ***Kronberg*** *④, one of Hesse's wealthiest communities.*

①

②

[S3/S4 West] Während die Strecke nach Kronberg bereits seit 1874 existiert, wurde die Spange von Niederhöchstadt bis Bad Soden im Vorgriff auf den S-Bahn-Betrieb erst 1970-72 fertig gestellt. Derzeit ist zwischen Niederhöchstadt und Schwalbach (Limes) der einfache Halt Schwalbach Nord im Bau. Er soll vor Ende 2008 in Betrieb genommen werden.
Auf der sog. Limesbahn wurde zwischen dem alten Ortskern und der neuen Wohnstadt Limes die quasi unterirdische und kürzlich renovierte Station **Schwalbach am Taunus (Limes)** ①-③ errichtet. Der gesamte Bahnhofsbereich wurde abgedeckt und teilweise überbaut, beiderseits schließt eine Strecke im Einschnitt an. Die Station selbst ist auch eingleisig und verfügt über nur eine Bahnsteigkante.
Die S3 endet heute in **Bad Soden** ④ auf dem östlichen Stumpfgleis. In den Anfangsjahren des S-Bahn-Betriebs machten manche Züge hier Kopf und fuhren weiter bis Höchst. Derzeit verkehren auf dieser Spange trotz elektrifizierter Strecke die Dieseltriebwagen ⑤ der Hessischen Landesbahn als RMV-Linie 13 im Halbstunden- bzw. Stundentakt.

③

*[S3/S4 west] Whereas the line to Kronberg dates back to 1874, the link between Niederhöchstadt and Bad Soden was only opened between 1970 and 1972. Between Niederhöchstadt and Schwalbach (Limes) a simple station is under construction: Schwalbach Nord is scheduled for completion in late 2008.*
*The so-called 'Limesbahn' includes a quasi-underground station at* ***Schwalbach am Taunus (Limes)*** *①-③, which has recently been renovated; the entire single-track station is covered by a square and some buildings.*
*In* ***Bad Soden*** *④, line S3 terminates on the eastern track. During the first years of S-Bahn operation, some trains used to reverse here to continue their journey to Höchst. At present, this section is served by diesel trains ⑤, operated every hour or half-hour by the Hessische Landesbahn as RMV line 13.*

④

⑤

[S5 West] Der oberirdische S-Bahnhof **Galluswarte** ① entstand 1978 gemeinsam mit dem ersten Abschnitt des Innenstadttunnels. Mit mindestens acht Zügen pro Stunde Richtung Innenstadt bietet er einen U-Bahn-mäßigen Anschluss des Gallusviertels, das außerdem noch von den Straßenbahnlinien 11 und 21 erschlossen wird.
Die Station **Frankfurt-Messe** ② wurde erst 1999 auf der bestehenden Strecke eingerichtet, sie liegt in Hochlage mitten im Messegelände, während der U-Bahnhof Festhalle/Messe (U4) nur die östlichen Messehallen erschließt.
Bis zum Bahnhof **Frankfurt West** verkehren die vier Linien S3-S6 gemeinsam. Stadteinwärts hält hier die S6 auf der unteren Ebene ③ quasi an einem Hausbahnsteig, während die S3-S5 in beiden Richtungen, die S6 aber nur stadtauswärts auf der oberen Ebenen verkehrt (▶ S. 110). Durch diese Anordnung konnte die S6 direkt nördlich des Bahnhofs kreuzungsfrei ausgefädelt werden.
Nördlich von Rödelheim (▶ S. 124) zweigt die S5 von den Linien S3 und S4 ab und bedient die Nachbarstädte **Oberursel** ④ (mit einem an die Berliner S-Bahn erinnernden Bahnsteigdach) und **Bad Homburg**, wo das Empfangsgebäude von 1907 ⑤ erhalten ist.

*[S5 west] The surface station **Galluswarte** ① was opened together with the cross-city tunnel in 1978. The minimum of 8 trains per hour makes the S-Bahn service in the Gallusviertel seem almost metro-like, and it is complemented by tram lines 11 and 21.*
*The elevated **Frankfurt-Messe** ② [fairgrounds] station was only added in 1999. It is located in the centre of the trade fair terrain, whereas the Stadtbahn station Festhalle/Messe (U4) lies at its eastern edge.*
*Lines S3 to S6 share the same tracks up to **Frankfurt West** station. Inbound S6 trains stop on the lower level ③, while the rest of the inbound and all the outbound trains use an elevated platform (▶ p. 110). This arrangement was made to allow for a grade-separated junction north of the station.*
*North of Rödelheim (▶ p. 124), line S5 diverges from lines S3 and S4 to continue towards **Oberursel** ④ (with a platform roof reminiscent of the Berlin S-Bahn) and **Bad Homburg**, where the station building ⑤ from 1907 has been preserved.*

[S6 West] Im Zuge des lang geplanten Ausbaus der Bahnstrecke nach Friedberg sollen eigene S-Bahn-Gleise verlegt und am Schnittpunkt mit der U1 an der Station Niddapark ein S-Bahnhof errichtet werden. Derzeit ist der einzige Umsteigepunkt zwischen Stadtbahn und S-Bahn im Norden der S-Bahnhof **Eschersheim** ①, der etwa 200 m vom Stadtbahnhalt Weißer Stein (▶ S. 35) entfernt liegt.
Seit langem ist geplant, die U5 zum S-Bahnhof **Frankfurter Berg** ②, der bis 1986 Bonames hieß und bereits seit den frühen Jahren der Main-Weser-Bahn besteht, zu verlängern, um einen weiteren Umsteigeknoten zu schaffen.
**Bad Vilbel Süd** ③ ist der erste Haltepunkt außerhalb Frankfurts. Er erschließt das Stadtzentrum von Bad Vilbel besser als der am nördlichen Rand gelegene S-Bahnhof **Bad Vilbel** ④.
Die Linie S5 endet seit Beginn des S-Bahn-Zeitalters in **Friedberg** ⑤, wo man zu verschiedenen Regionalbahnen und zum IC Richtung Kassel umsteigen kann.

*[S6 west] Together with the long-planned upgrading of the railway line to Friedberg separate S-Bahn tracks will be laid and a new station added where the route intersects with line U1 at Niddapark. Currently, the only interchange station between Stadtbahn and S-Bahn in the northern part of Frankfurt is at* ***Eschersheim*** *①, an S-Bahn station some 200 m from the Stadtbahn stop Weißer Stein (▶ S. 35).*
*A planned extension of Stadtbahn line U5 to* ***Frankfurter Berg*** *②, which was called Bonames until 1986 and is one of the older stations on the Main-Weser-Bahn, would create yet another interchange between the Stadtbahn and S-Bahn networks.*
***Bad Vilbel Süd*** *③ is the first stop outside Frankfurt; it is located closer to the Bad Vilbel town centre than the following station called* ***Bad Vilbel*** *④.*
*Since the start of S-Bahn operation, line S5 has terminated at* ***Friedberg*** *⑤, where transfer is provided to several regional rail lines as well as to IC trains towards Kassel.*

①

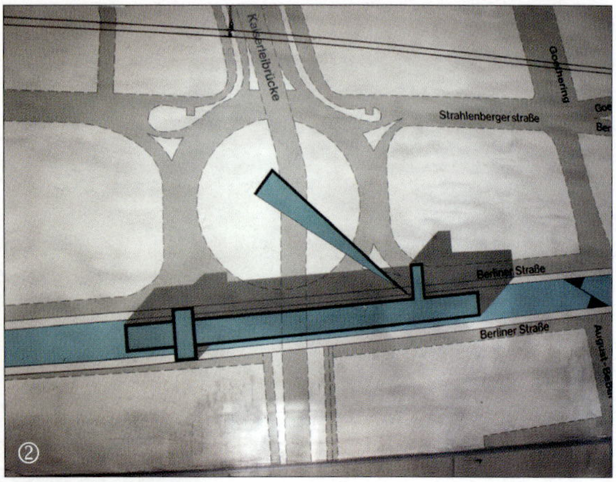

②

③

[S1/S2, S8/S9 Ost] Der 1995 in Betrieb genommene Offenbacher City-Tunnel umfasst drei unterirdische Stationen, die weitgehend baugleich sind, sich jedoch durch kleine Farbakzente voneinander unterscheiden. Der westlichste ist der S-Bahnhof **Kaiserlei** ①-③. Er liegt direkt an der Stadtgrenze unter dem Kaiserlei-Kreisel (großflächige Umgebungspläne ② wurden in die Wandgestaltung aufgenommen) und erschließt eine Bürostadt am westlichen Stadtrand Offenbachs. Seine Kennfarbe ist ein Türkis, das an die heutige Hausfarbe der VGF erinnert. Durch eine Glaspyramide, in der auch ein Aufzug untergebracht ist, wird ein Teil des Bahnsteigs mit Tageslicht versorgt.
Der Tunnel führt unter der Berliner Straße weiter, und erreicht den S-Bahnhof **Ledermuseum** ④, bei dem die gewölbte Decke durch gelbe Streifen gegliedert wird.

④

*[S1/S2, S8/S9 east] The Offenbach city tunnel, completed in 1995, comprises three underground stations with a common design, but with subtle colour additions to distinguish them. The westernmost is **Kaiserlei** station ①-③, located right on the border between Frankfurt and Offenbach and below the huge Kaiserlei roundabout (large area maps ② were integrated into the station design); it serves a business park on the western edge of Offenbach. The station is enhanced with a turquoise tone reminiscent of the VGF's corporate colour. A glass pyramid accommodating a lift allows daylight to fall into the station.*
*The S-Bahn tunnel continues along Berliner Straße on its way to the next station **Ledermuseum**; in this station, the vaulted ceiling is given structure by yellow stripes ④.*

[S1/S2, S8/S9 Ost] An den jeweiligen Bahnsteigenden befindet sich gegenüber des Lageplans eine geometrische Zeichnung, wie hier im S-Bahnhof **Ledermuseum** ①②.
Die zentralen Einkaufsstraßen im Zentrum von Offenbach erschließt der S-Bahnhof **Marktplatz** ③④, der als Kennfarbe Rot erhielt. Verglichen mit anderen S-Bahnhöfen, die im Laufe der letzten Jahrzehnte in Deutschland gebaut wurden, gehören die unterirdischen Offenbacher Stationen wegen ihrer großzügigen Form sicherlich zu den beeindruckendsten.

*[S1/S2, S8/S9 east] In all three stations, the wall opposite the large area map is decorated with a geometrical pattern, like here at* ***Ledermuseum*** *station ①②.*

*The central shopping streets in Offenbach are within walking distance from* ***Marktplatz*** *station ③④, which features red as its distinctive colour. Compared to the other S-Bahn stations built around Germany in recent decades, those in Offenbach are without doubt among the most appealing.*

①

②

③

[S8/S9 Ost] Der Bahnhof **Offenbach Ost** ①② wurde für den S-Bahn-Betrieb nach Hanau, der 1995 begann, völlig umgebaut, da direkt westlich davon der Offenbacher City-Tunnel angeschlossen werden musste. Seit 2003 zweigen östlich der Station die Linien S1 und S2 nach Süden ab, und seither halten in Offenbach Ost nur noch S-Bahn-Züge.

Die S-Bahn-Strecke zwischen Offenbach Ost und Hanau ist größtenteils nur eingleisig, für Zugbegegnungen wurde zwischen Mühlheim und **Mühlheim-Dietesheim** ③ ein zweigleisiger Abschnitt eingerichtet.

In **Hanau Hauptbahnhof** ④ enden die Linien S8 und S9 auf den östlichsten Gleisen. Eines Tages soll hier auch die sog. Nordmainische S-Bahn ankommen.

④

*[S8/S9 east] In 1995, **Offenbach Ost** station ①② was totally rebuilt for S-Bahn service, as the Offenbach city tunnel had to be connected immediately west of the station. Since 2003, lines S1 and S2 have diverged from the route to Hanau towards the south, the station now being served exclusively by S-Bahn trains.*

*The S-Bahn route between Offenbach Ost and Hanau is mostly single-track, with a passing loop between Mühlheim and **Mühlheim-Dietesheim** ③.*

*At **Hanau Hauptbahnhof** ④, lines S8 and S9 terminate on the easternmost tracks; in the future, the so-called 'Nordmainische S-Bahn', i.e. the line along the north bank of the Main River, will end here, too.*

[S1/S2 Ost] Die S-Bahn-Strecken von Offenbach über Rodgau nach Rödermark–Ober-Roden und nach Dietzenbach wurden erst 2003 in Betrieb genommen. An vielen Stationen, wie in **Obertshausen** ①, ist das alte Bahnhofsgebäude noch erhalten, es bleibt allerdings oft ungenutzt.
An der Endstation **Rödermark–Ober-Roden** ② trifft die S1 auf die Regionalbahnstrecke von Dreieich-Buchschlag nach Dieburg.
In **Heusenstamm** ③ wurde das alte Bahnhofsgebäude vorbildlich renoviert und in eine Gaststätte umfunktioniert.
Als Mittelpunkt eines neuen Stadtteils wurde der S-Bahnhof **Dietzenbach Mitte** ④ 2003 auf der bestehenden Strecke neu eingerichtet, während die Endstation **Dietzenbach Bahnhof** ⑤ auf einen eingleisigen Halt ohne Abstellanlage reduziert wurde.

*[S1/S2 east] The S-Bahn routes from Offenbach to Rödermark–Ober-Roden via Rodgau and to Dietzenbach were only completed in 2003. At many stations, like at* ***Obertshausen*** *①, the old station building has been preserved, but is no longer used for this purpose.*
*At the terminus* ***Rödermark–Ober-Roden*** *②, line S1 meets the regional rail line from Dreieich-Buchschlag to Dieburg.*
*At* ***Heusenstamm*** *③, the old station building was perfectly renovated and is now used as a restaurant.*
*Planned as the centre of a new neighbourhood,* ***Dietzenbach Mitte*** *station ④ was added in 2003 along the existing railway line, while the terminus* ***Dietzenbach Bahnhof*** *⑤ was reduced to a simple single-track stop without any sidings.*

①

②

③

[S3-S6 Süd] Der Name der heutigen unterirdischen Station **Lokalbahnhof** ①-③ erinnert an den Ausgangspunkt der ehemaligen *Frankfurt-Offenbacher Lokalbahn* (1848-1955), die erste Eisenbahnverbindung zwischen den beiden Nachbarstädten. Der alte Kopfbahnhof lag etwas weiter nördlich, wo sich bis heute eine Straßenbahnhaltestelle befindet. Der S-Bahnhof hingegen liegt direkt neben den zum Südbahnhof laufenden Fernbahngleisen.
Die Gestaltung des 1990 eröffneten S-Bahnhofs entspricht seiner Zeit, mit bräunlichen Platten an den Wänden ②. Einen kleinen Akzent setzt ein Wandmosaik ① am westlichen Ausgang. Das Motiv bezieht sich auf den *Ebbelwei* (Apfelwein), da viele Gaststätten in dieser Gegend das traditionelle Getränk ausschenken.
Die S-Bahn-Züge verlassen den Innenstadttunnel zwischen Lokalbahnhof und Südbahnhof (bzw. **Frankfurt Süd**). Hier steht bereits seit 1873 ein Bahnhof, das heutige Empfangsgebäude ④⑤ stammt aus dem Jahr 1914. Es musste für den Bau der U-Bahn Anfang der achtziger Jahre teilweise abgetragen und anschließend wieder aufgebaut werden. Die S-Bahn-Züge halten an den beiden nördlichen Mittelbahnsteigen.

*[S3-S6 south] The name of the present **Lokalbahnhof** station ①-③ refers to the terminus of the former 'Frankfurt-Offenbacher Lokalbahn' (1848-1955), the first railway line to link the two neighbouring cities. The old station was located further north at the site of the present tram stop of that name, whereas the S-Bahn station lies next to the mainline tracks. The design of Lokalbahnhof station, opened in 1990, is typical of that era, with brownish panels cladding the walls ②. The western entrance is decorated with a mosaic ① depicting the traditional apple wine (rather like cider), which is served in many pubs in the area.*
*The S-Bahn trains emerge from the city tunnel between Lokalbahnhof and Südbahnhof (in this case actually **Frankfurt Süd**). At the latter, the station building ④⑤ dates from 1914, although parts of it were demolished and later rebuilt for the construction of the U-Bahn. The S-Bahn trains use the two island platforms on the northern side.*

④

⑤

①

②

[S3/S4 Süd] Die S-Bahn erreichte im Jahr 1990 den Bahnhof **Stresemannallee** ①, der zur Weiterführung Richtung Darmstadt an der Südseite der bestehenden Bahnanlagen eingerichtet wurde, weshalb die S-Bahnen vom Südbahnhof kommend in einem Tunnel die Fernbahngleise unterqueren müssen.
Die Verlängerung der S-Bahn bis Darmstadt konnte 1997 in Betrieb genommen werden, der Halt Langen-Flugsicherung wurde jedoch erst 2002 eingefügt. Der letzte Halt in Frankfurt ist **Louisa** ②, wo man zur Straßenbahnlinie 14 umsteigen kann. Der Bahnhof **Neu-Isenburg** ③, dessen Empfangsgebäude noch teilweise als solches genutzt wird, liegt am westlichen Rand der Stadt.
In **Dreieich-Buchschlag** ④, wo man ein modernes Bahnsteigdach, das auf traditionellen Stützen ruht, sehen kann, besteht Anschluss an die Regionalbahn nach Dieburg.
An Wochentagen endet die S4 in **Langen** ⑤, nur an Wochenenden werden einzelne Fahrten wie die S3 bis Darmstadt durchgebunden.

③

*[S3/S4 south] In 1990, the S-Bahn reached **Stresemannallee** station ①, which, for a future extension towards Darmstadt, was placed on the southern side of the mainline tracks; S-Bahn trains therefore have to burrow under the mainline tracks in a short tunnel.*
*The extension to Darmstadt was completed in 1997, but the Langen-Flugsicherung station was only added in 2002.*
*The last stop in Frankfurt is **Louisa** ②, where transfer to tram line 14 is provided. The station building at **Neu-Isenburg** ③ is still partly used as such; the station is located at the western edge of the town.*
***Dreieich-Buchschlag** station ④ features a modern platform roof resting on traditional iron supports; this is the interchange station for regional trains to Dieburg.*
*On weekdays, S4 trains terminate at **Langen** ⑤, whereas on weekends, some S4 trains continue to Darmstadt like line S3 always does.*

④

⑤

①

[S8/S9 West] Der S-Bahnhof **Stadion** ①-③ wurde für die Fußball-WM 2006 ausgebaut und umbenannt, denn er hieß früher ‚Sportfeld'. Zwei Mittel- und ein Seitenbahnsteig sind durch zwei Fußgängertunnel miteinander verbunden. Der östliche Tunnel ist mit Motiven aus der Sportwelt geschmückt ③. Das Frankfurter Waldstadion (derzeit offiziell ‚Commerzbank-Arena') liegt etwa 1 km entfernt, zwischen dem S-Bahnhof und der Endstelle der Straßenbahnlinie 21. Das Bahnhofsgebäude wird heute als Wohnhaus genutzt.

Der Bahnhof **Rüsselsheim** ④ entstand 1863 an der Mainbahn der *Hessischen Ludwigsbahn*. Seit 1980 fährt die S-Bahn über Mainz nach Wiesbaden (S8). Die kürzere Strecke der S9 über die Mainbrücke bei Bischofsheim wurde erst im Jahr 2000 eingerichtet.

②

③

④

*[S8/S9 west] The S-Bahn station* ***Stadion*** *①-③ was rebuilt and renamed for the FIFA World Cup 2006; it used to be called 'Sportfeld'. One side and two island platforms are connected via two pedestrian tunnels, the eastern being decorated with sports themes ③. The Frankfurt Waldstadion ( the 'forest stadium', although its current official name is the 'Commerzbank-Arena') is about 1 km away, about half way to the tram terminus of line 21. The station building now accommodates apartments.*

***Rüsselsheim*** *station ④ was opened by the 'Hessische Ludwigsbahn' on its Mainbahn route in 1863. Since 1980, the S-Bahn has been running to Wiesbaden via Mainz (S8). The shorter S9, which operates across a bridge near Bischofsheim, was only introduced in 2000.*

[S8 West] Bis Dezember 2006 hieß der heutige Bahnhof **Mainz Römisches Theater** ② einfach ‚Mainz Süd'. Direkt südlich der Bahnanlagen ① wurden in den letzten Jahren die Überreste des Theaters der einstigen römischen Siedlung Mogontiacum freigelegt. 2006 wurde das Empfangsgebäude abgerissen und die Bahnsteigdächer abgetragen, seither stehen die gusseisernen Säulen wie ein Skelett da.
Der **Mainzer Hauptbahnhof** ③④ wurde 1884 nach einem Entwurf des Architekten Philipp Johann Berdellé eröffnet. Er liegt auf der Westseite der Innenstadt und ist mit allen Mainzer Straßenbahnlinien erreichbar.

①

②

③

*[S8 west] Until December 2006, the station today known as* ***Mainz Römisches Theater*** *② was simply called Mainz Süd. Just south of the railway station ①, the remains of a Roman theatre were uncovered in recent years; they belong to a Roman settlement called Mogontiacum. In 2006, the station building was demolished and the platform roofs were removed, leaving a skeleton of cast iron supports.*
***Mainz Hauptbahnhof*** *[Central Station] ③④ was designed by Philipp Johann Berdellé and opened in 1884. It is located on the western side of the city centre and is served by all of Mainz' tram lines.*

④

①

②

③

④

[S8/S9 West] Die unterirdische Station **Frankfurt am Main Flughafen Regionalbahnhof** ①-④ wurde bereits am 14. März 1972 in Betrieb genommen, also einige Jahre vor Beginn des S-Bahn-Betriebs. Anfangs wurde er nur von Pendelzügen bedient, ab 28. Mai 1972 dann mit durchgehenden Zügen. Da dieser Bahnhof von Anfang an auch von Regional- und Fernzügen benutzt wurde, erhielt er einen 400 m langen Mittelbahnsteig ④, sowie einen 210 m langen Seitenbahnsteig ③. An beiden Enden der Station schließt ein insgesamt 2,2 km langer Tunnel an. 1980 begann dann mit der Linie S15 auf der Flughafenstrecke der eigentliche S-Bahn-Betrieb, wobei die Züge bis 1983 im oberen Teil des Hauptbahnhofs endeten. Der Namenszusatz ‚Regionalbahnhof' kam 1999 mit Inbetriebnahme des Fernbahnhofs (siehe nächste Seite) hinzu. Heute halten in diesem Bahnhof neben den S-Bahn-Linien S8 und S9 auch einige Regionalzüge, darunter die Dieseltriebwagen von und nach Saarbrücken, was sich negativ auf die Luftqualität in der Station auswirkt. Wie an anderen S-Bahn-Stationen hinterlassen die unverkleideten Decken einen schlechten Eindruck. In renovierter Form präsentiert sich nur der östliche Zugang ②.

*[S8/S9 west] The underground airport station **Frankfurt am Main Flughafen Regionalbahnhof** ①-④ was opened on 14 March 1972, some years before S-Bahn operation started. Initially served by shuttle trains, through service began on 28 May 1972. The station used to be shared by long-distance and regional trains, and therefore has a 400 m island platform ④, plus a 210 m side platform ③. From both ends of the station, the S-Bahn continues in a tunnel with a total length of 2.2 km. Proper S-Bahn service started in 1980 with line S15, which until 1983 terminated on the surface tracks at Hauptbahnhof.*

*The appendage 'Regionalbahnhof' was added in 1999, when a new station was opened for long-distance trains (see next page) – both Airport stations also display English signs. The regional station is still used by some diesel trains to and from Saarbrücken, which has a negative impact on the air quality within the underground station. Like at some other S-Bahn stations, the uncovered ceiling leaves a bad impression. Refurbishment has only been completed at the eastern platform access ②.*

①

②

Am 30. Mai 1999 wurde im Zuge der Neubaustrecke Frankfurt – Köln die neue Station **Frankfurt am Main Flughafen Fernbahnhof** ①-③ eröffnet. Diese liegt parallel zum älteren Regionalbahnhof, mit dem sie über eine ca. 200 m lange eingehauste Brücke ① verbunden ist. Vom Frankfurter Flughafen, dem größten in Deutschland, erreicht man mit der Bahn somit direkte Ziele wie Amsterdam, Brüssel, Wien oder Interlaken in der Schweiz.

*On 30 May 1999, a new station for long-distance trains, called **Frankfurt am Main Flughafen Fernbahnhof** ①-③, was opened on the new high-speed line between Frankfurt and Cologne. It lies parallel to the older regional station, the two being linked via a 200 m encased bridge ①. Germany's busiest airport is thus linked by rail to cities like Amsterdam, Brussels, Vienna, or Interlaken in Switzerland.*

③

Innerhalb des Frankfurter Flughafens verkehrt die **Sky Line** als Verbindung ⑤ zwischen den einzelnen Terminals. Da die fahrerlose, gummibereifte Hochbahn zwischen den Terminals 1 und 2 ④ auch ohne Sicherheitskontrolle zugänglich ist, ist der jeweils westliche Wagen auch für Flughafenbesucher benutzbar, während der östliche nur Fluggästen nach Durchschreiten der Kontrollen vorbehalten ist.

*Within the airport, the **Sky Line** provides a link ⑤ between the various terminals. The driverless rubber-tyred elevated rail system can be accessed without passing through security check to travel from Terminal 1 to Terminal 2 ④; while the western car is reserved for visitors, the eastern car is only for passengers within the security area, which is separated from visitors by a sophisticated platform arrangement.*

④

⑤

Station – Linien | *Lines* - Seite | *Page*

Station – Linien | *Lines* - Seite | *Page*



Station – Linien | *Lines* - Seite | *Page*



U unterirdischer Bahnhof der Stadtbahn
- *underground Stadtbahn station*
U* oberirdische Haltestelle ohne Bahnübergänge
- *surface station without level crossings*
S S-Bahnhof | *S-Bahn station*

(F) Station in Frankfurt
(OF) Station in Offenbach

* derzeit im Bau | *currently under construction*

Die Seitenzahlen beziehen sich auf die Bilder der einzelnen Stationen. Bei S-Bahn-Stationen, von denen kein Bild vorhanden ist, verweist die Seitenzahl in Klammern auf das S-Bahn-Kapitel.

*The page numbers refer to the photos available for individual stations; for S-Bahn stations which are not illustrated in this book the page number in brackets indicates the S-Bahn chapter.*

**Liniennetzplan Frankfurt am Main**

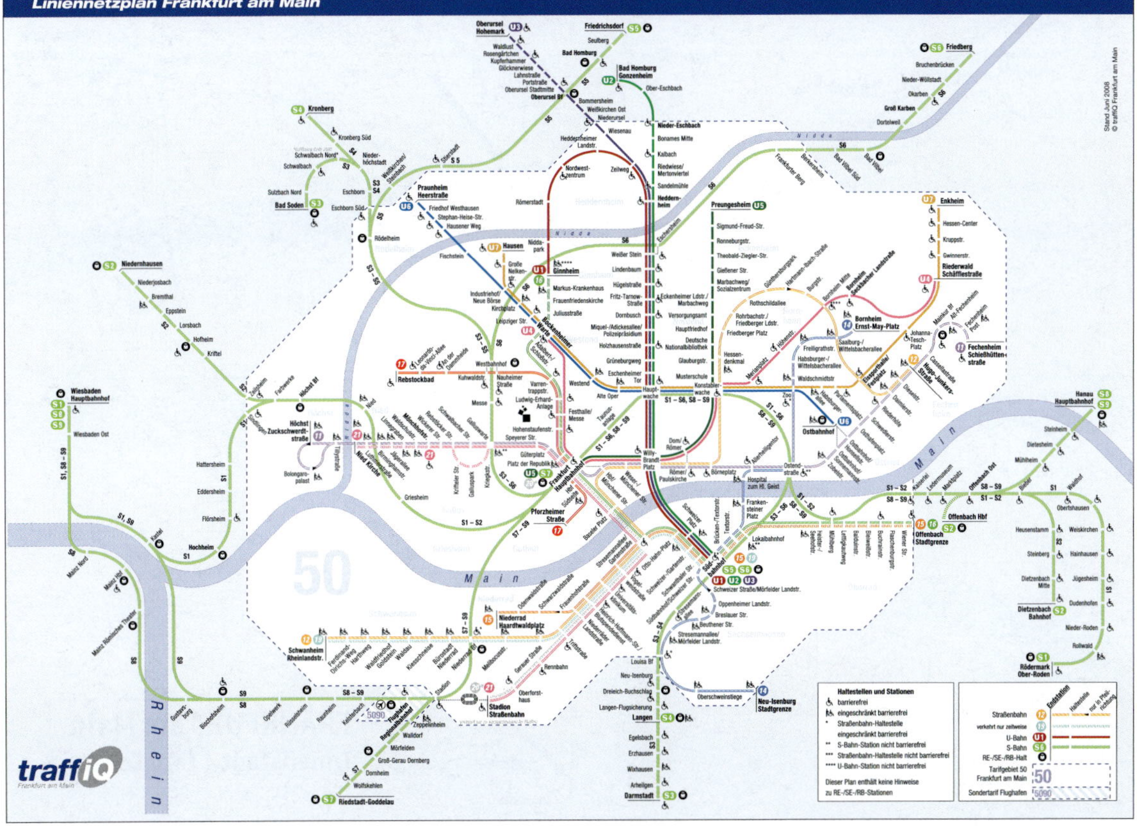

- Walter Söhnlein & Jürgen Leindecker: **Die Frankfurter Lokalbahn** und ihre Elektrischen Taunusbahnen. - 2000, GeraMond, München, ISBN 3932785045
- Anton Wiedenbauer & Hans-Jürgen Hoyer: **Fahrt in die Zukunft** – Die Geschichte der Frankfurter Straßenbahn. - 1968, Verlag Waldemar Kramer, Frankfurt/Main
- Dieter Höltge & Günter H. Köhler: **Straßen- und Stadtbahnen in Deutschland** – Hessen. - 1984, EK-Verlag, Freiburg, ISBN 3882553308
- Jens Krakies & Frank Nagel: **Stadtbahn Frankfurt am Main** – Eine Dokumentation. - 1988, Stadt Frankfurt/Main, ISBN 3923907036
- RMV (Hrsg.): **Eisenbahnen in der Region Frankfurt RheinMain**. - 2002, Hestra-Verlag, Darmstadt, ISBN 3777103047

**WEBSITES**
- Verkehrsgesellschaft Frankfurt am Main mbH – www.**vgf-ffm**.de
- traffiQ – Lokale Nahverkehrsgesellschaft Frankfurt am Main mbH – www.**traffiq**.de
- RMV (Rhein-Main-Verkehrsverbund) – www.**rmv**.de
- Trampage Frankfurt am Main (von Stephan Kyrieleis) – www.**trampage**.de

- U-Bahnen & Stadtbahnen weltweit | *worldwide* – www.**urbanrail.net** – with links to other websites
- U-Bahnen & Stadtbahnen in Deutschland – www.**u-bahnen-in-deutschland**.de – mit Links zu anderen Websites

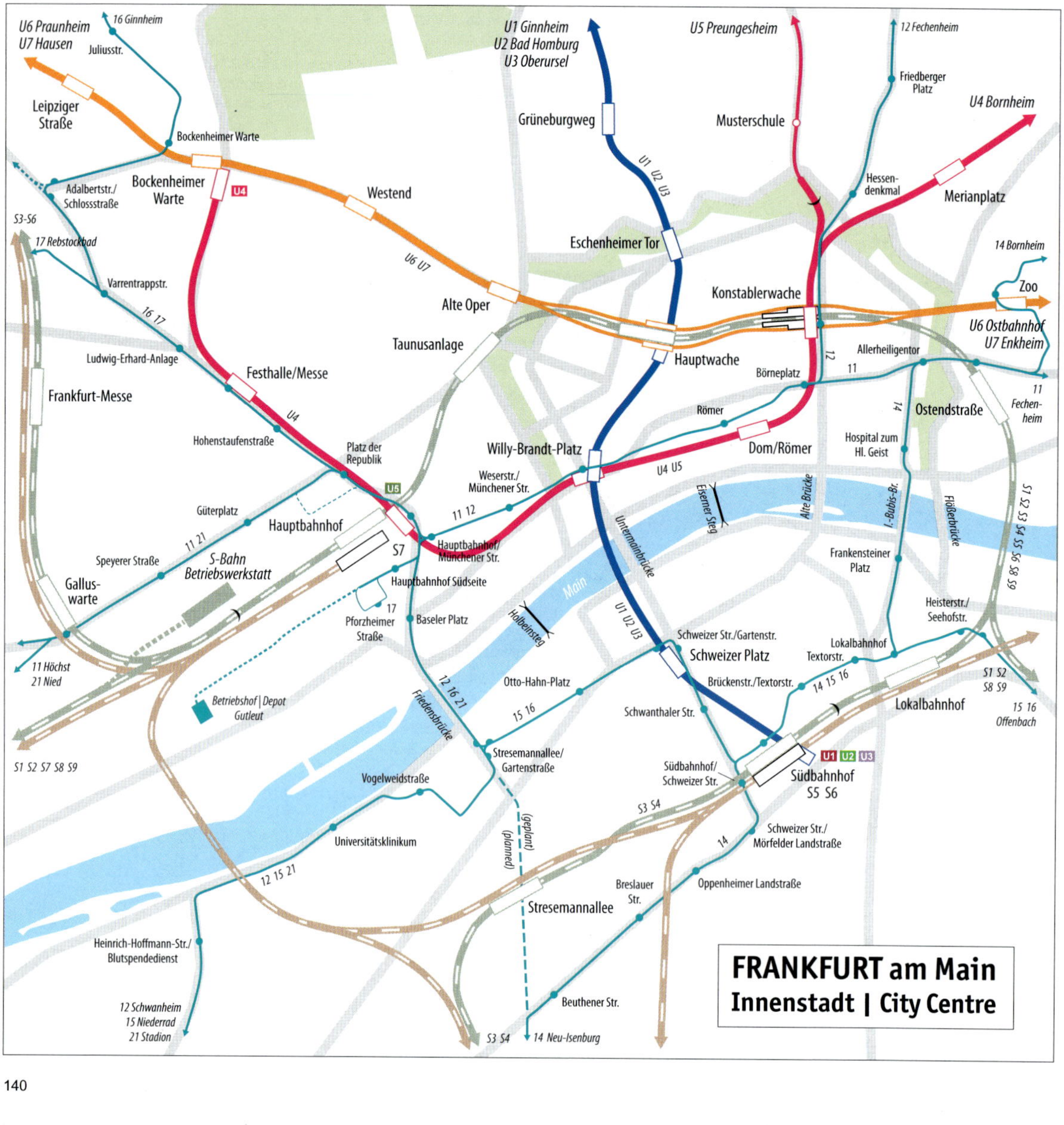

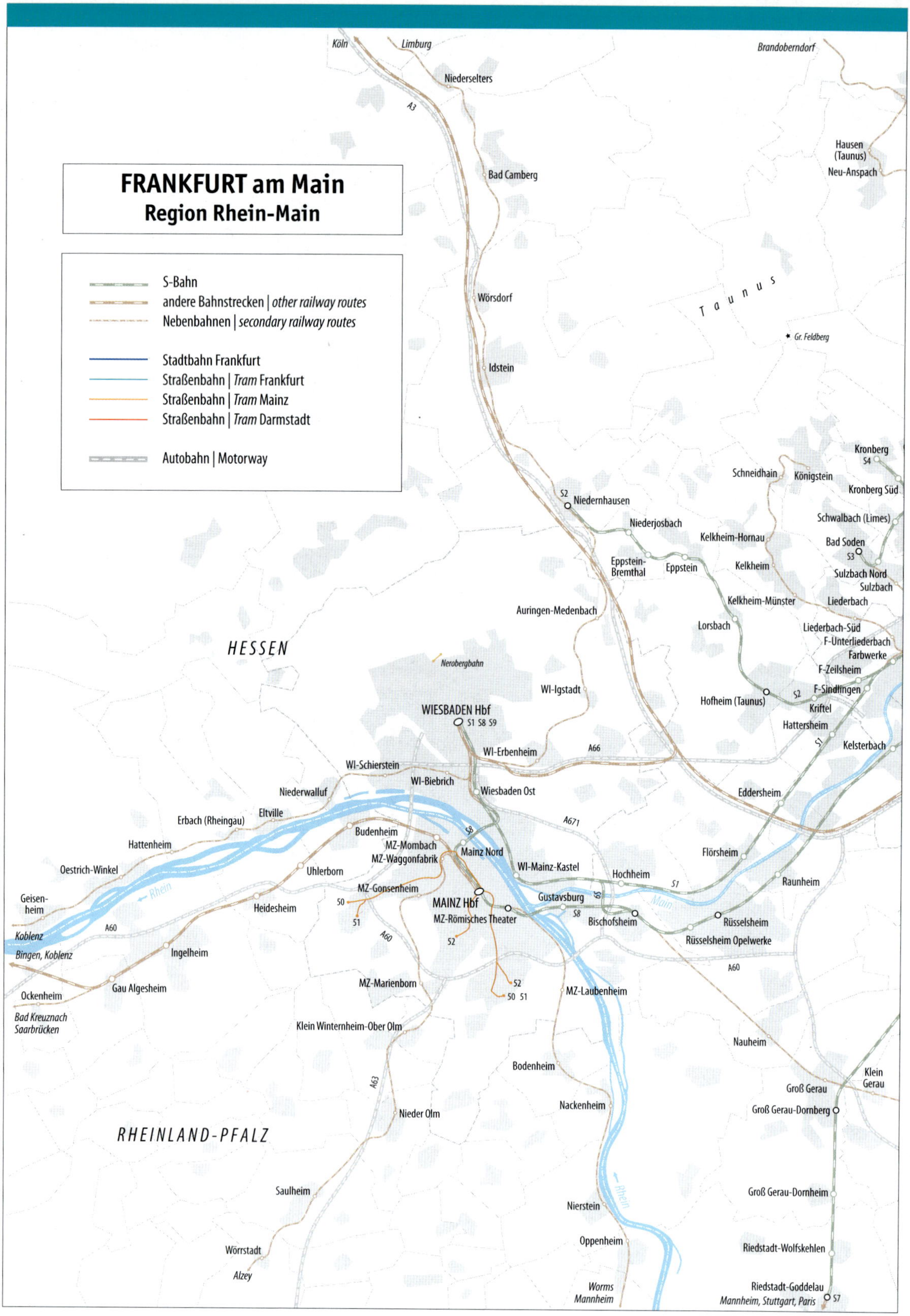

FRANKFURT am Main
Region Rhein-Main
S-Bahn
andere Bahnstrecken | other railway routes
Nebenbahnen | secondary railway routes
Stadtbahn Frankfurt
Straßenbahn | Tram Frankfurt
Straßenbahn | Tram Mainz
Straßenbahn | Tram Darmstadt
Autobahn | Motorway
Köln
Limburg
Brandoberndorf
Niederselters
A3
Bad Camberg
Hausen (Taunus)
Neu-Anspach
Wörsdorf
Taunus
Gr. Feldberg
Idstein
Kronberg
S4
Schneidhain
Königstein
Kronberg Süd
S2
Niedernhausen
Schwalbach (Limes)
Niederjosbach
Kelkheim-Hornau
Bad Soden
S3
Eppstein-Bremthal
Eppstein
Kelkheim
Sulzbach Nord
Sulzbach
Kelkheim-Münster
Liederbach
Auringen-Medenbach
Lorsbach
Liederbach-Süd
F-Unterliederbach
Farbwerke
HESSEN
Nerobergbahn
F-Zeilsheim
WI-Igstadt
F-Sindlingen
Hofheim (Taunus)
Kriftel
WIESBADEN Hbf
S1 S8 S9
Hattersheim
WI-Erbenheim
A66
Kelsterbach
WI-Schierstein
WI-Biebrich
Niederwalluf
Wiesbaden Ost
Eddersheim
Eltville
Erbach (Rheingau)
A671
Budenheim
Hattenheim
MZ-Mombach
Mainz Nord
Flörsheim
MZ-Waggonfabrik
Oestrich-Winkel
Uhlerborn
WI-Mainz-Kastel
Hochheim
Raunheim
Geisen-heim
Rhein
MZ-Gonsenheim
Heidesheim
MAINZ Hbf
Gustavsburg
Main
MZ-Römisches Theater
Bischofsheim
Rüsselsheim
A60
Koblenz
Bingen, Koblenz
Ingelheim
Rüsselsheim Opelwerke
Ockenheim
Gau Algesheim
MZ-Marienborn
MZ-Laubenheim
Bad Kreuznach
Saarbrücken
Klein Winternheim-Ober Olm
Nauheim
Bodenheim
A63
Klein Gerau
Groß Gerau
Nackenheim
Groß Gerau-Dornberg
Nieder Olm
RHEINLAND-PFALZ
Groß Gerau-Dornheim
Saulheim
Nierstein
Oppenheim
Riedstadt-Wolfskehlen
Wörrstadt
Alzey
Worms
Mannheim
Riedstadt-Goddelau
Mannheim, Stuttgart, Paris
S7

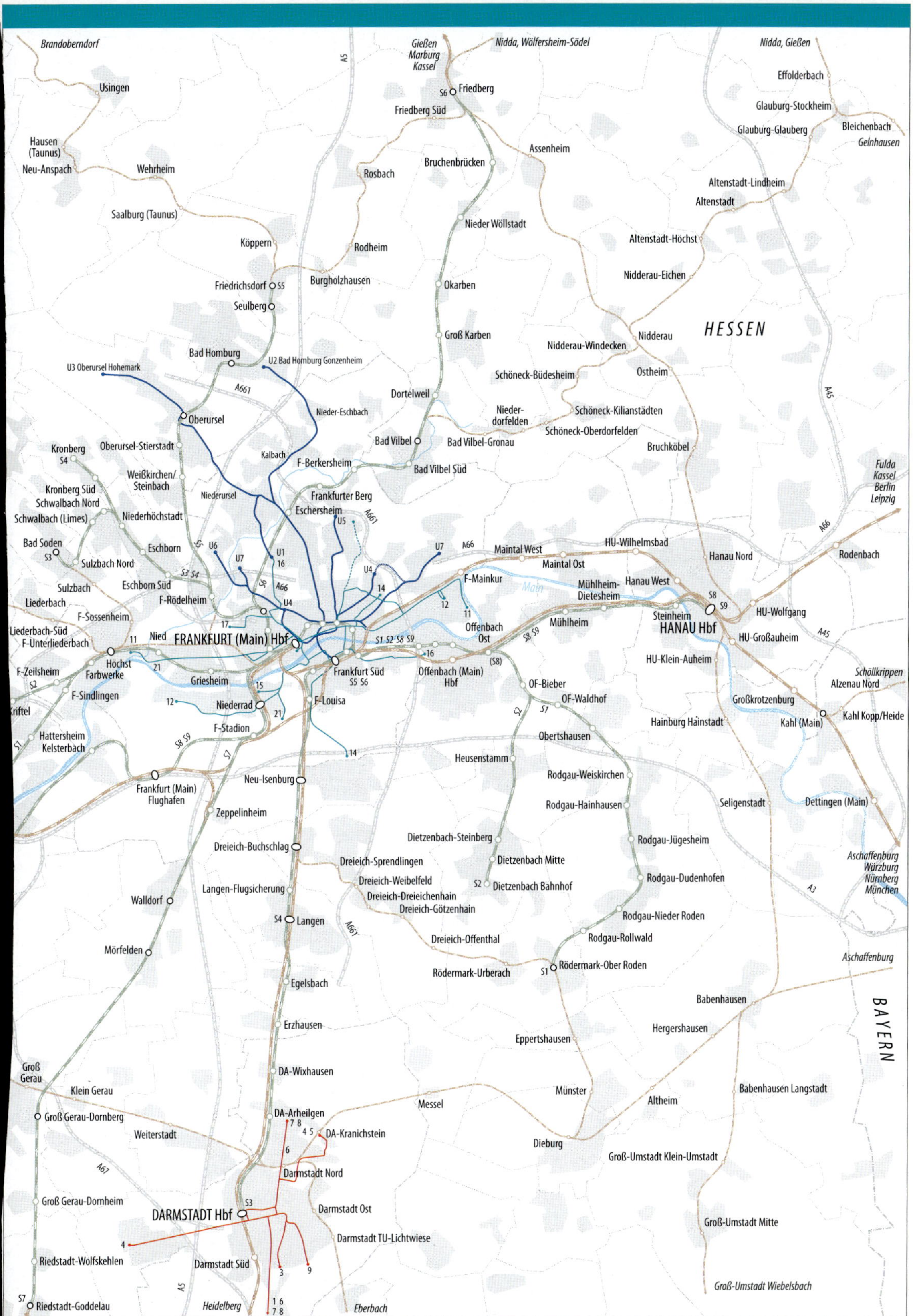

Brandoberndorf
Usingen
Hausen (Taunus)
Neu-Anspach
Wehrheim
Saalburg (Taunus)
Köppern
Friedrichsdorf S5
Seulberg
Bad Homburg
U3 Oberursel Hohemark
U2 Bad Homburg Gonzenheim
Oberursel
Oberursel-Stierstadt
Kronberg S4
Kronberg Süd
Weißkirchen/ Steinbach
Schwalbach Nord
Schwalbach (Limes)
Niederhöchstadt
Bad Soden S3
Sulzbach Nord
Eschborn
Sulzbach
Eschborn Süd
Liederbach
F-Rödelheim
F-Sossenheim
Liederbach-Süd
F-Unterliederbach
Nied
Höchst
Farbwerke
F-Zeilsheim S2
F-Sindlingen
Kriftel
Hattersheim
Kelsterbach
Griesheim
Niederrad
F-Stadion
Frankfurt (Main) Flughafen
Zeppelinheim
Neu-Isenburg
Dreieich-Buchschlag
Langen-Flugsicherung
S4 Langen
Walldorf
Mörfelden
Egelsbach
Erzhausen
DA-Wixhausen
DA-Arheilgen
DA-Kranichstein
Darmstadt Nord
Darmstadt Ost
DARMSTADT Hbf
Darmstadt TU-Lichtwiese
Darmstadt Süd
Heidelberg
Eberbach
Groß Gerau
Klein Gerau
Groß Gerau-Dornberg
Weiterstadt
Groß Gerau-Dornheim
Riedstadt-Wolfskehlen
S7 Riedstadt-Goddelau
Messel
Gießen Marburg Kassel
Nidda, Wölfersheim-Södel
S6 Friedberg
Friedberg Süd
Rosbach
Rodheim
Burgholzhausen
Bruchenbrücken
Nieder Wöllstadt
Okarben
Groß Karben
Dortelweil
Bad Vilbel
Bad Vilbel-Gronau
Bad Vilbel Süd
Nieder-Eschbach
Kalbach
F-Berkersheim
Frankfurter Berg
Niederursel
Eschersheim
FRANKFURT (Main) Hbf
Frankfurt Süd
F-Louisa
F-Mainkur
Offenbach Ost
Offenbach (Main) Hbf
OF-Bieber
OF-Waldhof
Obertshausen
Heusenstamm
Rodgau-Weiskirchen
Rodgau-Hainhausen
Rodgau-Jügesheim
Rodgau-Dudenhofen
Rodgau-Nieder Roden
Rodgau-Rollwald
S1 Rödermark-Ober Roden
Rödermark-Urberach
Dietzenbach-Steinberg
Dietzenbach Mitte
S2 Dietzenbach Bahnhof
Dreieich-Sprendlingen
Dreieich-Weibelfeld
Dreieich-Dreieichenhain
Dreieich-Götzenhain
Dreieich-Offenthal
Eppertshausen
Münster
Dieburg
Altheim
Babenhausen
Hergershausen
Babenhausen Langstadt
Groß-Umstadt Klein-Umstadt
Groß-Umstadt Mitte
Groß-Umstadt Wiebelsbach
Assenheim
Nidda, Gießen
Effolderbach
Glauburg-Stockheim
Glauburg-Glauberg
Bleichenbach
Gelnhausen
Altenstadt-Lindheim
Altenstadt
Altenstadt-Höchst
Nidderau-Eichen
Nidderau
HESSEN
Nidderau-Windecken
Ostheim
Schöneck-Büdesheim
Nieder-dorfelden
Schöneck-Kilianstädten
Schöneck-Oberdorfelden
Bruchköbel
Maintal West
Maintal Ost
HU-Wilhelmsbad
Hanau Nord
Mühlheim-Dietesheim
Hanau West
Mühlheim
Steinheim
HANAU Hbf
S8 S9
HU-Wolfgang
HU-Großauheim
HU-Klein-Auheim
Rodenbach
Fulda Kassel Berlin Leipzig
Schöllkrippen
Alzenau Nord
Großkrotzenburg
Kahl (Main)
Kahl Kopp/Heide
Hainburg Hainstadt
Seligenstadt
Dettingen (Main)
Aschaffenburg Würzburg Nürnberg München
Aschaffenburg
BAYERN
Main
A5
A661
A66
A45
A3
A67

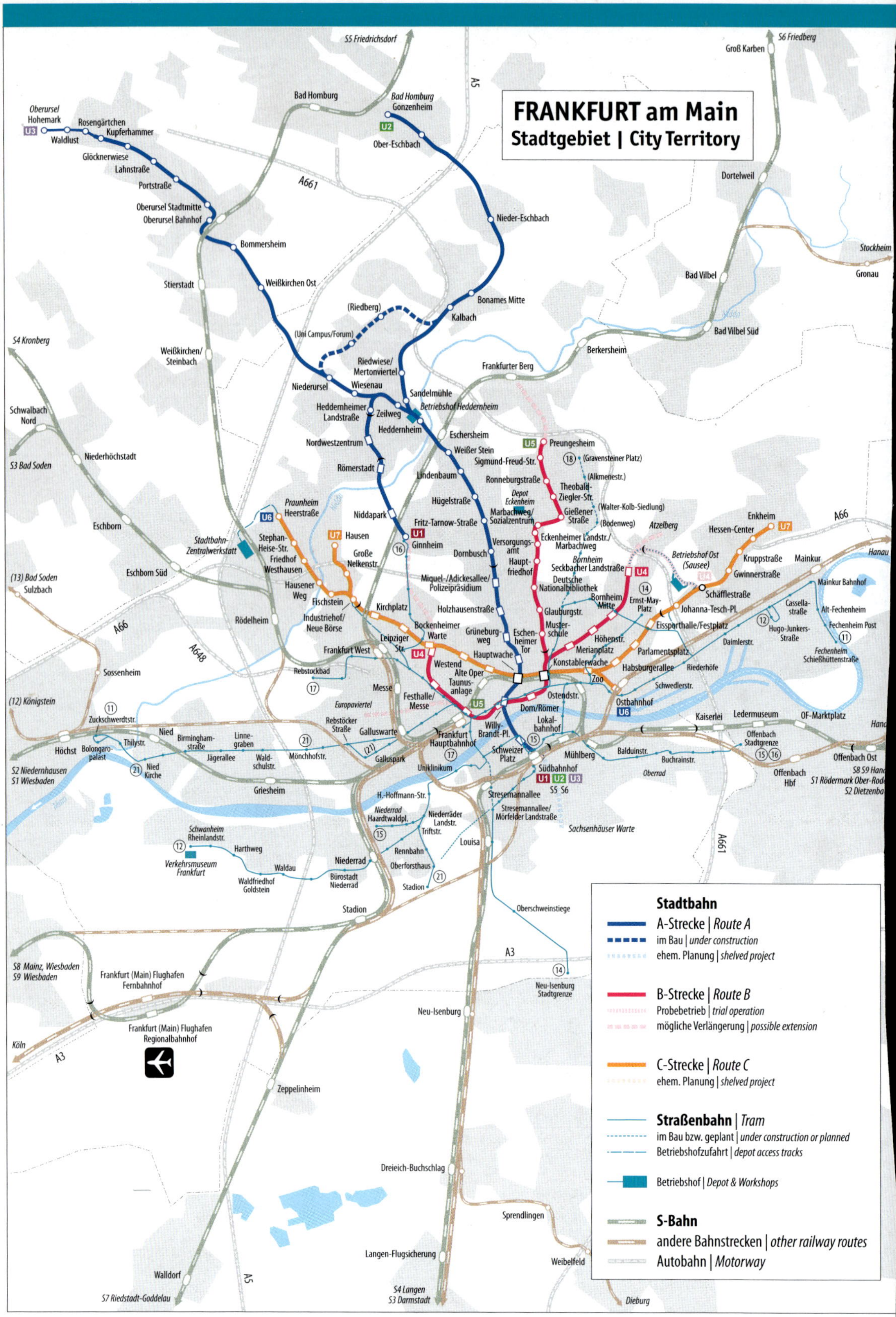
FRANKFURT am Main
Stadtgebiet | City Territory
Stadtbahn
A-Strecke | Route A
im Bau | under construction
ehem. Planung | shelved project
B-Strecke | Route B
Probebetrieb | trial operation
mögliche Verlängerung | possible extension
C-Strecke | Route C
ehem. Planung | shelved project
Straßenbahn | Tram
im Bau bzw. geplant | under construction or planned
Betriebshofzufahrt | depot access tracks
Betriebshof | Depot & Workshops
S-Bahn
andere Bahnstrecken | other railway routes
Autobahn | Motorway
S5 Friedrichsdorf
S6 Friedberg
Groß Karben
Bad Homburg
Bad Homburg Gonzenheim
U2
Ober-Eschbach
A5
A661
Oberursel Hohemark
U3
Waldlust
Rosengärtchen
Kupferhammer
Glöcknerwiese
Lahnstraße
Portstraße
Oberursel Stadtmitte
Oberursel Bahnhof
Bommersheim
Weißkirchen Ost
Stierstadt
Nieder-Eschbach
Dortelweil
Stockheim
Gronau
Bad Vilbel
Bad Vilbel Süd
Nidda
Berkersheim
Bonames Mitte
Kalbach
(Riedberg)
(Uni Campus/Forum)
S4 Kronberg
Weißkirchen/ Steinbach
Frankfurter Berg
Riedwiese/ Mertonviertel
Niederursel
Wiesenau
Sandelmühle
Betriebshof Heddernheim
Heddernheimer Landstraße
Zeilweg
Heddernheim
Eschersheim
Schwalbach Nord
Nordwestzentrum
Weißer Stein
U5
Preungesheim
(18)
(Gravensteiner Platz)
(Alkmenestr.)
S3 Bad Soden
Niederhöchstadt
Römerstadt
Lindenbaum
Sigmund-Freud-Str.
Ronneburgstraße
Theobald-Ziegler-Str.
(Walter-Kolb-Siedlung)
Hügelstraße
Depot Eckenheim
Gießener Straße
Marbachweg/ Sozialzentrum
(Bodenweg)
Niddapark
Fritz-Tarnow-Straße
Eschborn
U6
Praunheim Heerstraße
U7
Hausen
U1
Ginnheim
(16)
Dornbusch
Versorgungsamt
Eckenheimer Landstr./ Marbachweg
Atzelberg
Enkheim
U7
A66
Hessen-Center
Stephan-Heise-Str.
Stadtbahn-Zentralwerkstatt
Große Nelkenstr.
Friedhof Westhausen
Haupt-friedhof
Seckbacher Landstraße
U4
Betriebshof Ost (Sausee)
Kruppstraße
Mainkur
Hanau
Eschborn Süd
Hausener Weg
Miquel-/Adickesallee/ Polizeipräsidium
Deutsche Nationalbibliothek
(14)
Ernst-May-Platz
U4
Gwinnerstraße
Mainkur Bahnhof
(13) Bad Soden
Sulzbach
Fischstein
Kirchplatz
Holzhausenstraße
Glauburgstr.
Bornheim Mitte
Schäfflestraße
Johanna-Tesch-Pl.
Cassellastraße
Alt-Fechenheim
Rödelheim
Industriehof/ Neue Börse
A66
A648
Bockenheimer Warte
Grüneburgweg
Eschenheimer Tor
Musterschule
Höhenstr.
Eissporthalle/Festplatz
(12)
Hugo-Junkers-Straße
Fechenheim Post
(11)
Daimlerstr.
Leipziger Str.
Frankfurt West
U4
Westend
Hauptwache
Merianplatz
Parlamentsplatz
Fechenheim Schießhüttenstraße
Rebstockbad
(17)
Alte Oper
Konstablerwache
Habsburgerallee
Riederhöfe
Sossenheim
Messe
Taunusanlage
Zoo
Schwedlerstr.
(12) Königstein
Festhalle/ Messe
Ostendstr.
Ostbahnhof
U6
(11)
Europaviertel
U5
Dom/Römer
Kaiserlei
Ledermuseum
OF-Marktplatz
Zuckschwerdtstr.
Rebstöcker Straße
Galluswarte
Willy-Brandt-Pl.
Lokalbahnhof
Offenbach Stadtgrenze
Nied
Birmingham-straße
Linne-graben
(21)
Frankfurt Hauptbahnhof
(15)
Höchst
Bolongaro-palast
Thilystr.
Jägerallee
Wald-schulstr.
Mönchhofstr.
Galluspark
(17)
Schweizer Platz
Mühlberg
Balduinstr.
Buchrainstr.
(15) (16)
Offenbach Ost
S2 Niedernhausen
S1 Wiesbaden
(21)
Nied Kirche
Griesheim
Uniklinikum
Südbahnhof
U1 U2 U3
S5 S6
Oberrad
Offenbach Hbf
S8 S9 Hanau
S1 Rödermark Ober-Roden
S2 Dietzenbach
H.-Hoffmann-Str.
Stresemannallee
Niederrad Haardtwaldpl.
Niederräder Landstr.
Stresemannallee/ Mörfelder Landstraße
(15)
Triftstr.
Sachsenhäuser Warte
Schwanheim Rheinlandstr.
(12)
Harthweg
Rennbahn
Louisa
A661
Verkehrsmuseum Frankfurt
Waldau
Niederrad
Oberforsthaus
Waldfriedhof Goldstein
Bürostadt Niederrad
(21)
Stadion
Stadion
Oberschweinstiege
A3
(14)
Neu-Isenburg Stadtgrenze
S8 Mainz, Wiesbaden
S9 Wiesbaden
Frankfurt (Main) Flughafen Fernbahnhof
Neu-Isenburg
Frankfurt (Main) Flughafen Regionalbahnhof
Köln
A3
Zeppelinheim
Dreieich-Buchschlag
Sprendlingen
Langen-Flugsicherung
Weibelfeld
Walldorf
A5
S4 Langen
S3 Darmstadt
Dieburg
S7 Riedstadt-Goddelau